Michaelina Wautier

Illuminating Women Artists: Renaissance and Baroque

The series *Illuminating Women Artists* launches at a critical moment in contemporary culture. It marks a significant intervention within the broader movement underway among scholars, museums, collectors and the wider world of cultural heritage to make evident and contextualise historically the contributions of women artists. As such, the books, each written by a leading specialist in the field of art history, will appeal to audiences from the academic sphere to the general public. Beautifully illustrated, the volumes collectively offer an unprecedented visual contextualisation of the lives and works of their subjects, to whom in some cases a monograph has yet to be dedicated. Books in the sub-series *Illuminating Women Artists: Renaissance and Baroque* critically reappraise the lives and works of female artists in Europe from the fifteenth to the early eighteenth centuries. Many of the women represented by the volumes were celebrated professional artists in their own eras, yet their names and works have not been passed down continually in the history of art. As the first series dedicated to correcting this omission, the books interweave established conclusions with new discoveries to reframe how women's artistic production is approached and understood.

Michaelina Wautier

KATLIJNE VAN DER STIGHELEN

TRANSLATED FROM THE DUTCH BY HAN VAN DER VEGT

GETTY PUBLICATIONS

LOS ANGELES

To my granddaughters Ada, Jutta, and Leela

Published in the United States of America by Getty Publications, Los Angeles
1200 Getty Center Drive, Suite 500
Los Angeles, California 90049-1682
getty.edu/publications

Distributed in the United States and Canada by the University of Chicago Press

Printed in Bosnia and Herzegovina

A catalogue record for this book is available from the Library of Congress
ISBN 979-8-88712-017-1

Published simultaneously in the United Kingdom by Lund Humphries
Originated by Lund Humphries
Second Home Spitalfields
60-80 Hanbury Street
London E1 5JH
UK
lundhumphries.com

Copy edited by Julie Gunz
Project managed and designed by Crow Books
Set in Adobe Caslon Pro

Front cover: Michaelina Wautier, *Boy with a White Cravat* (detail), ca. 1650–55, oil on canvas, 41.7 × 33.6 cm (16⅜ × 13¼ in.), The Kremer Collection

Back cover: Michaelina Wautier, *Self-Portrait*, ca. 1650, oil on canvas, 120 × 102 cm (47¼ × 40⅛ in.), Private Collection, Boston, MA

With generous support from the Tavolozza Foundation

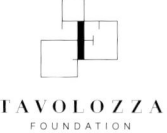

TAVOLOZZA
FOUNDATION

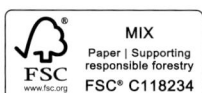

MIX
Paper | Supporting responsible forestry
FSC
www.fsc.org
FSC® C118234

Contents

Series Foreword

Illuminating Women Artists: Renaissance and Baroque was conceptualized at a moment of reinvigorated interest in contemporary culture about women artmakers and their contributions to the visual arts. A burgeoning awareness of the implications of structural bias as it relates to gender, race and sexual identity simultaneously infused new perspectives into academic research, museum exhibitions and acquisitions of art, both public and private. Books in *Illuminating Women Artists* engage with insights of these related cultural initiatives to advance a feminist enterprise through the study of their subjects. The volumes investigate the lives and contributions of women of the fifteenth through the seventeenth centuries, embedding them into their specific social and historical contexts. Accounting for diverse identities and experiences, they make evident various ways that early modern women negotiated, and sometimes resisted, structural constraints in the sphere of the visual arts.

Illuminating Women Artists is indebted to feminist art-historical studies that were first produced in the 1970s in response to the broader women's rights movements of that time. This foundational scholarship aimed to disrupt the traditional academic focus on early modern male artists by writing their female counterparts into the discipline of art history. Since then, feminist scholarship has investigated gender norms that created different conditions for women and men who sought to practice art as professionals or amateurs. It is now understood that women were ambitious, successful and fully embedded in artistic practice on a variety of levels, and were not merely marginal to the story of masculine creation and triumph that has yet to be seriously decentered in art history. This work also began to make clear the challenges of the category of the 'woman' artist, pointing toward a certain fluidity in gender and sexual identities with which some current scholarship is concerned. Certainly, the term 'artist' is also fraught in gendered terms, given for example that early modern women sometimes worked in media that were undervalued in later centuries and thus were obscured in the scholarship.

This series considers early modern women artists within their social, cultural, temporal and geographic contexts, with analyses that remain sensitive to their individual cultural moments. Broadly conceptualized, this was a period of transformation – in politics, religion, science, exploration and travel – that opened opportunities for women artmakers. Furthermore, a literary defense of women's merits began to challenge the patriarchal misogynist ideas that sought to suppress women and their potential. Some women artists may have been aware of this incipient feminism or have visually voiced related issues in their art. But the female artists represented by the series also identified with the social structures of their place and time. These structures, prominent among them gender, class and race, contributed to shaping their identities and to forming their conceptions about others. While women challenged normative structures in important ways (some more overtly than others), they also were acculturated into dominant cultural attitudes and thus complicit in supporting social hierarchies of class and race that underpinned colonialist and other ambitions rooted in bias. Renaissance and Baroque women artists themselves derived from a spectrum of social classes – artisan, merchant, professional or patrician – but, so far, none has come to light that can be identified as anything other than racially white. Membership in these classes made it possible for some women artists to have servants or even to enslave persons who contributed to their households. This practice reduced their own domestic obligations and freed time for artmaking, but in turn contributed to reinforcing existing systems of social stratification regarded as the norm.

Societal limitations disadvantaged most early modern women who aspired to a life in the visual arts. For example, girls were excluded from the formal apprenticeship system through which most male artists were trained, and therefore they sought informal instruction, often from male relatives. Women practitioners who married and became mothers generally experienced a lapse in artistic production while they attended to the responsibilities that came with these roles. On the other hand, fathers sometimes supportively promoted their daughters as artists, which also aggrandized the family and improved its financial standing through patronage and sales.

Some gendered conditions with which female artists contended did not necessarily impede their success, but, even when women's artistic production was critically acclaimed, it was often evaluated according to gender stereotypes. Certain women nonetheless independently challenged, and circumvented or ruptured, restrictive gender protocols to enable prolific art production. In the process, they revised those protocols and influenced the history of art. Some established their own professional studios and trained pupils, both female and male, who in turn established themselves as professionals in workshops of their own. Others produced large bodies of work as amateurs, and some rendered porous the boundaries between these two statuses by bridging them. Still others produced works for members of communities to which they belonged, such as professed nuns in enclosed convents, or for personal reasons, such as to have in their possession a portrait of a family member. Some worked under contract for patrons, producing images for prestigious European courts and churches, where their art came under the eyes of the public. Others were involved with scientific enquiry, producing illustrations for research and publications in the fields of natural history and entomology. These women in the aggregate produced works that varied widely in subject, including both sacred and secular themes, and in the artistic media in which they worked. Represented in the latter category were the familiar forms of sculpture, painting and printmaking, and also other ways of artmaking that were valued more highly in the past than they are in the present, including papercutting, embroidery and weaving.

Five decades of sustained research have transformed our understanding of early modern women artists. *Illuminating Women Artists: Renaissance and Baroque* takes stock of this work through books that offer state-of-the-question analyses of their subjects. These peer-reviewed volumes variously interweave established conclusions with new discoveries investigated through emerging modes of analysis to reframe our understanding of the lives, artistic production and works of art by European women. The books make a substantive case for women's presence in aesthetic culture, and trace the complex circumstances that conditioned their making of art, their careers and their lives. Together they reveal the varied ways in which women of the fifteenth through the seventeenth centuries skillfully and often successfully navigated restricting gender norms to stake out productive lives as artmakers and develop innovative approaches to the works they produced. The volumes offer an unprecedented contextualization of their subjects, to whom in some cases a monograph has not previously been dedicated.

Marilyn Dunn, Loyola University Chicago
Andrea Pearson, American University, Washington, DC
September 2025

Acknowledgements

It seems a challenge doomed in advance to put a completely unknown seventeenth-century artist on the map, especially if this artist is a woman. The recognition of Michaelina Wautier's achievements can be attributed to a number of thinkers and actors who, against all odds, believed in this recovery project. In 1994, Marijke Seresia founded the non-profit institution Gynaika to highlight discrimination against women in the art world.[1] In 1996, this institution published a book about 'forgotten women in the arts', containing the first monographic article about Michaelina Wautier.[2] Gynaika, together with Paul Huvenne, the director of the Koninklijk Museum voor Schone Kunsten Antwerpen, and Liesbeth Brandt Corstius, the director of the Museum voor Moderne Kunst Arnhem, facilitated the first exhibition about female artists in the Netherlands. The 1999 catalogue, which I co-edited with Mirjam Westen and which was entitled *Elck Zijn Waerom*, included three of Wautier's paintings.[3] Six years later, a scholarly article offered the first survey of her oeuvre.[4] An important step towards her modern-day fame was made in 2018, when an exhibition in the Antwerp MAS showed her oeuvre in all its splendour: *Michaelina Wautier 1604–1689: Glorifying a Forgotten Talent*. Peter De Wilde, CEO of VisitFlanders and of the Flanders Heritage Agency, had initiated the idea to include an exhibition of Wautier's work in the *Cultural City Festival Antwerp Baroque 2018: Rubens Inspires*. Without this proposal, there would not have been an exhibition. Ben Van Beneden, then the director of the Rubenshuis, advocated for the first

scholarly catalogue, for which Katrijn Van Bragt and Hannelore Magnus made an enormous effort as well. Marieke van Bommel, the director of the MAS, opened the doors of her museum widely for this purpose. I thank everybody, including those I do not name here, who, through their contributions, made it possible for Wautier to be born again in 2018. Without them she would 'still be a footnote in art history at best'.[5] My sincere thanks also go to Toerisme Vlaanderen for funding the translation of this book. Without their support, the publication of a monograph about Michaelina Wautier in Lund Humphries' landmark series *Illuminating Women Artists* would not have been possible.

I also owe a debt of gratitude to friends and colleagues who have steadfastly believed in Wautier and in me. In the first place, Hans Vlieghe and Lieke van Deinsen, who with their critical comments and valuable suggestions have given this book a veritable facelift. Credit is also due to Bert Schepers, Marjan Sterckx, Bert Timmermans and Bert Watteeuw, who, through their enthusiasm and friendship, have kept the flame alive. I was inspired and challenged by the scholarly team collaborating on the exhibition *Michaelina Wautier: Malerin* in the Kunsthistorisches Museum in Vienna (2025–6), especially Gerlinde Gruber, who made every effort to give this ravishing exhibition and the accompanying catalogue its international appeal. Peter Kerber, Jean Bastiaensen, Charlotte Roosen, Anne Delvingt, Pierre-Yves Kairis, Sabine van Sprang, Lara de Merode, Kirsten Derks and Alice Limb: all of them have guided, corrected and broadened my vision of Wautier and have brought new source material to light. I was also fortunate to have Han van der Vegt as a critical first reader who translated the Dutch text into English with insight and creativity. A special word of thanks to Diego de Wautier, who allowed me to consult the rich family archive. I would like to express my gratitude to the series editors, Andrea Pearson and Marilyn Dunn, for their insightful feedback and inspiring suggestions. Rebeccah Williams took care of the illustrations in an exemplary manner. Special thanks to Lucie Ewin who has tirelessly accompanied the book's production and assisted me with great care and precision in the last phase of the editing process. Acquisitions editor Erika Gaffney has been my empathetic guide from the start of the book project, providing both practical and substantive advice, and I cannot thank her enough. And finally, for daily discussions and soundboard therapy, boundless gratitude to my husband Jan de Meere and my children Govert and Nive, Cecilia and Carl-Philip and Laetitia. They always keep my feet on the ground and make me realise what an unimaginable luxury it is to be able to do art historical research in the margin of real life.

Introduction

Michaelina Wautier (*c*.1614–89) was an unparalleled artist active in the mid-seventeenth century in the Southern Netherlands. Her talent, technical expertise and versatility were exceptional. She painted at least 35 works, of which about half are fully signed, ranging from huge altarpieces to charming genre scenes and extraordinary flower garlands. Until 2018, her name was virtually unknown. A first exhibition at the Antwerp MAS definitively put her on the map. From then on, her fame has only grown. In 2022, the Museum of Fine Arts in Boston held an exhibition focused on Wautier's five-painting series *The Five Senses*, in which the artist illustrates sight, hearing, smell, taste and touch. In 2025–6, the Kunsthistorisches Museum in Vienna organised a monographic exhibition devoted to the painter, which subsequently travelled to the Royal Academy in London. Global interest in Wautier is so vibrant because she has been freshly plucked from oblivion and because her paintings are so original and impressive. This book offers a chance to meet an artist forgotten by art history. Recently discovered biographical information is gathered to sketch her family background. Unlike most early modern female painters, she was not the daughter of a painter. It is even possible that, as a child, she never visited a painter's studio, but her upbringing in elite circles doubtless triggered her interest in art and culture. Then there is her brother Charles, some five years older, who was also a painter and may well have been her role model as an artist.[1]

The Wautier family originated from Mons, but Charles and Michaelina's artistic careers developed in Brussels, near the archducal court. During the first half of the seventeenth century, not Brussels but rather Antwerp was the artistic centre of Northern Europe. Peter Paul Rubens (1577–1640) and Anthony van Dyck (1599–1641) were the preeminent examples of the Flemish Baroque. When Wautier moved to Brussels in the 1640s, these two were no longer alive, but their fame travelled even to South America.[2]

Since 2018, much more has been revealed about her life, but it remains the case that several hypotheses weigh heavily on the analysis of her career and personality. She is not the type of female artist who restricted her artistic ambitions and struggled to do what she wanted. She belonged to a small group of privileged seventeenth-century women who, due to their background, their talent and their perseverance, could develop a professional career to leave a unique oeuvre. In this study, Wautier is called 'Michaelina' when her childhood is discussed and for clarity when distinguishing her from her brother Charles and her other siblings. Elsewhere, she is simply called 'Wautier'. To reference her, the term 'artist' is used without the addition of 'woman' or 'female', just as her brother is not mentioned as a 'male artist'. She was an artist first and foremost, and only secondly a woman.

In 1929, Virginia Woolf wrote *A Room of One's Own*, a revolutionary book in which the author posits that two components are necessary to liberate women: 'independent incomes and rooms of their own', or access to 'their own private space'. While Woolf considers this, her gaze sweeps the room: 'Be that as it may, I could not help thinking, as I looked at the works of Shakespeare on the shelf . . . it would have been impossible, completely and entirely, for any woman to have written the plays of Shakespeare in the age of Shakespeare'. She feels compelled to demonstrate this idea: 'Let me imagine, since facts are so hard to come by, what would have happened had Shakespeare had a wonderfully gifted sister, called Judith, let us say. Shakespeare himself went, very probably – his mother was an heiress – to the grammar school, where he may have learnt Latin – Ovid, Virgil and Horace – and the elements of grammar and logic.' Not everything would have gone right, but he still found his way to London, where he became a celebrated actor 'and lived at the hub of the universe'. 'Meanwhile his extraordinarily gifted sister, let us suppose, remained at home' and, although she was as talented as her brother, she did not go to school and was married to a local wool trader. She did not want to get married, she was not even seventeen, and ran away from home, to London: 'the force of her own gift drove her to it', but 'she could get no training in her craft', was made pregnant by an 'actor-manager', 'and so – who shall measure the heat and violence of the poet's heart when caught and tangled in a woman's body? – killed herself one winter's night and lies buried at some cross-roads where the omnibuses now stop outside the Elephant and Castle'.[3]

In Woolf's telling, brother William and sister Judith are equally talented, but the brother is given an intellectual education, moves in the proper circles and can realise his gifts. His sister, by contrast, has to run away to London, where there is no place for her, leading ultimately to her suicide. This narrative is centuries old, but nobody has ever expressed the harshness of the inequality better than Virginia Woolf. By now, we know that Woolf created this image also out of self-interest and that much is to be said against her one-dimensional image of Judith, but the story of brother and sister still holds true.

However, in the case of brother and sister Charles and Michaelina Wautier, both moved from Mons to Brussels and both succeeded in becoming artists. It is unknown where Charles received his artistic training but it is natural to assume that he trained his younger sister and that they both were familiar with classical tradition. It cannot even be ruled out

that they travelled together to Italy. In Brussels, they bought a house together and probably also shared a studio. Charles's network of aristocratic clients was probably larger than Michaelina's, but it opened many doors for her as well. Moreover, she became a more original and technically more proficient artist than her brother, as will become evident from an analysis of their works. Although many women artists had brothers who were active as painters, it was rare for a sister to receive an equally high level of education and surpass her sibling(s) in technical expertise and artistic quality. Gesina ter Borch (1631–90) is a prime example of a woman surrounded by artistic family members who succeeded in creating unparalleled renderings of domestic life in Zwolle, showcasing a distinct artistic style that set her apart from her brothers. Remarkably, she achieved this without any formal training.[4]

This volume is the first book to explore Michaelina Wautier and her oeuvre as a whole, offering a comprehensive and in-depth look at her life and work. The first chapter focuses on her biography, enriched by recent archival research. Additional sources have helped to reconstruct her social context, which was populated by military commanders, intellectuals and aristocrats. In the second chapter, her main patron, Archduke Leopold Wilhelm of Austria (1614–62), is introduced alongside two owners of her works who could not be more different: an Italian general and a French dance master. The third chapter argues that Michaelina's brother Charles was instrumental in advancing her career. Unusually, recent investigations of her work have inspired a new interest in his. In the fourth chapter Michaelina is compared to some sixteenth- and seventeenth-century women artists by whom she may have been inspired and challenged. The last chapter provides an overview of her paintings, focusing on the various genres she worked in with flair, including portraits, religious paintings, flower still lifes, genre paintings, head studies and mythological scenes. Their original iconography, daring style and melancholic lyricism reveal the work of a highly distinctive and unforgettable Baroque artist.

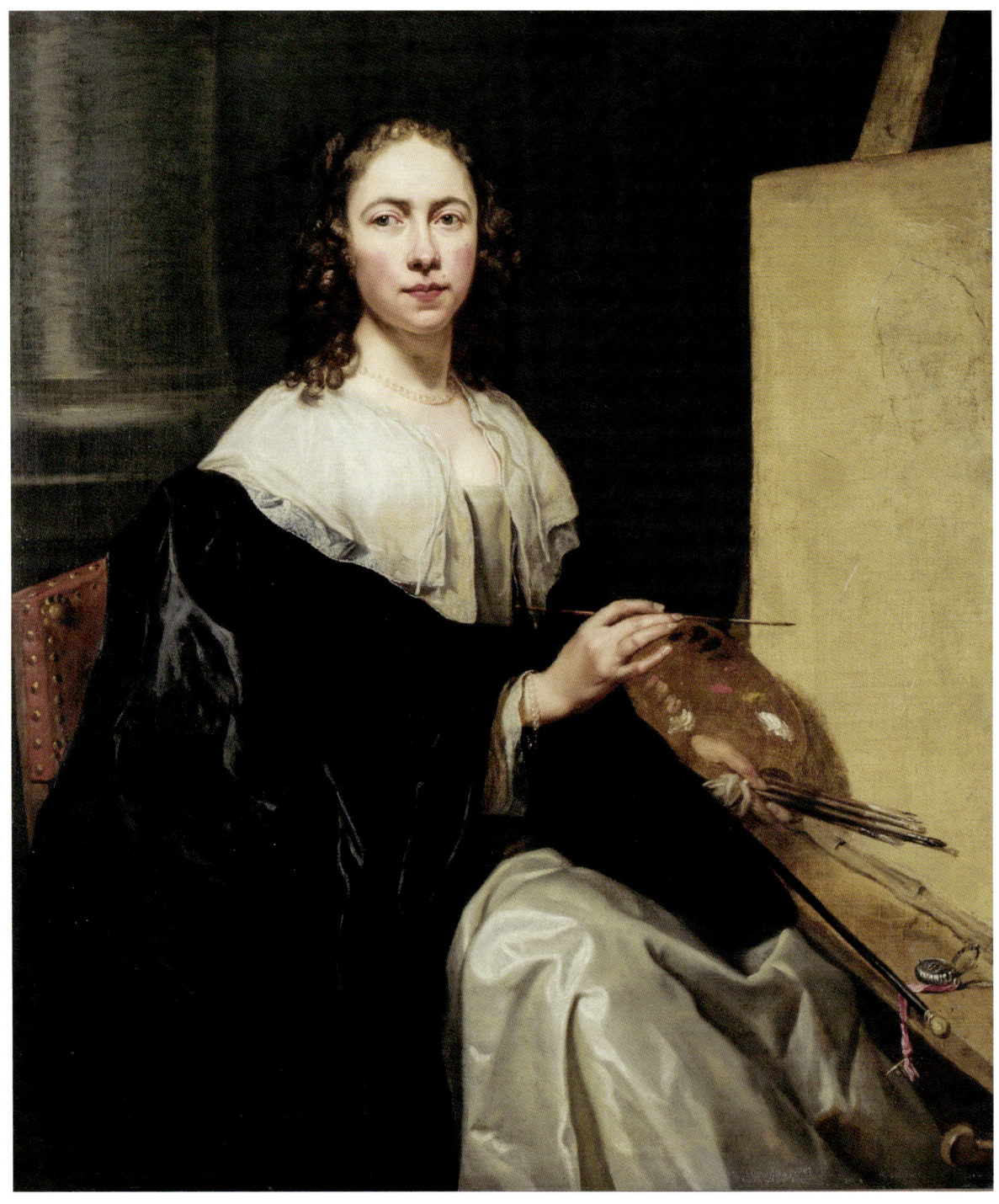

1　Michaelina Wautier, *Self-Portrait*, c.1650, oil on canvas, 120 × 102 cm (47 ¼ × 40 ⅛ in), private collection, Boston, MA

The True Story behind the Artist

Who was Michaelina Wautier? As is so often the case with artistic or literary women from the past, we lack the means to definitively reconstruct their lives and oeuvres. Therefore, we need to use our historical imaginations to yield plausible hypotheses about what may have been, to be rigorously tested against historical evidence.[1]

For Wautier, there is very little of an intimate nature in the archives: we have no personal papers, her only known will was lost, and her name is not mentioned in contemporary correspondence.[2] The only extant self-referential statements are in visual form: her paintings and one drawing. Her signature appears on approximately half of her works and is somewhat unusual, as she wrote out her full name in cursive rather than block letters. Moreover, she and others did not use in her daily life the first name she signed with. Official notary deeds refer to her as 'Michèle' or 'Michiel[l]e'. The Latin version, 'Michaelina', was reserved for her artistic oeuvre and can be seen as an 'artist's name'.[3] Most clearly, her first name can be read on the print an Antwerp engraver made of her portrait of Andrea Cantelmo (fig.2), which is analysed below. The engraving of the portrait was done by the Antwerp craftsman Paulus Pontius, from a painting of the Italian artillery general who was well connected in Antwerp. Interestingly, this engraving uses the spelling of 'Michaelina Woutiers'.

'Woutiers' is a Dutch variant of 'Wautier', the French version of the name she herself used for her paintings and her drawing. On the back of the drawing of an antique bust (fig.3), she calligraphed 'Michaelina Wautier fecit': 'Michaelina Wautier made this'. By adding 'fecit' or occasionally 'invenit et fecit', Wautier emphasised her activity as a painter and 'inventor'.

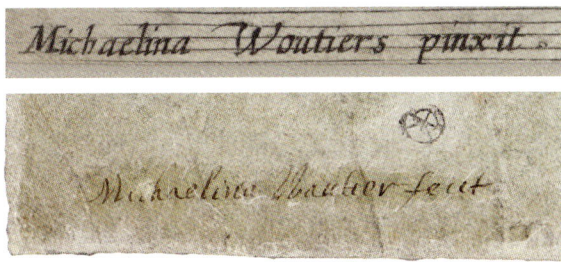

2   Paulus Pontius after Michaelina Woutiers [Wautier], *Portrait of Commander Andrea Cantelmo*, 1643, engraving on paper, 40.3 × 29.8 cm (15 ⅞ × 11 ¾ in), private collection, detail of her name in the inscription: '*Michaelina Woutiers pinxit, Paull[us] / Pontius fecit exc[udit]. Et Excell[entissi]me suae / Lub[ens] Mer[ito] Dedicavit. 1643*'

3   Michaelina Wautier, *Study after an Antique Head of Ganymede*, c.1640–50, black and white chalk on paper, 41.3 × 46 cm (16 ¼ × 18 ⅛ in), private collection, detail of her signature on the back of the drawing

Not only did she make the painting, she also 'invented' it or rather, 'conceived' it. It is telling of her intention that her earliest known history piece carries the signature 'Michaelina Wautier fecit et invenit 1649'. By adopting this approach, she positioned herself within the tradition of male Southern Netherlandish painters who distinguished between the conception and execution of an artwork. It was doubtless a conscious choice for Wautier, as must have been the use of Latin for the inscriptions. These determinations on her part typify an astute woman with great intellectual and artistic ambitions.

Wautier painted two known self-portraits, the origins, designs and executions of which are completely different. The first fits with the centuries-old tradition in which both women and men have endeavoured to immortalise themselves as painters (fig.1). On the basis of an estimate of her age at thirty to forty, the date for this self-portrait may be around 1650. Her second self-portrait, from *c*.1655–9, is atypical and completely original among known examples of women's self-representations from this period. This is a *portrait historié* in which she depicted herself as a bacchante, a follower of the god of wine, Bacchus (see fig.63).[4] These two images present strikingly different aspects of her personality: the self-confident, determined and formidable painter and the playful, escapist bacchante, lost in a boisterous procession. Yet, both share a detachedness, a self-contained aloofness. Commanding in the self-portrait, and more open and innocent in the Bacchus painting, she is the observer, even observing those who are observing her.

THE ART OF SHOWING WHO YOU ARE

Gina Strumwasser has drawn attention to the extraordinary achievement of women 'who met the challenge of being female professionals and succeeded as artists at a time when such accomplishments were not expected or encouraged'.[5] Wautier is one of them, and nowhere did she express this better than in her monumental self-portrait, in which she presents herself as a painter. Examples of female artists' self-portraits at the easel are rare in the seventeenth-century Low Countries.[6] An exception is one by Judith Leyster (1609–60), dated to *c*.1630–33, who shows herself turning in her chair away from her canvas to smile pleasantly at the viewer. Typologically, several elements correspond to Wautier's portrait, such as the presence of an easel and brushes in the artists' hands, but the atmosphere is completely different. The two artists also operated under different conditions; unlike Wautier, Leyster was registered with a painters' guild, in Haarlem, and she trained apprentices.[7] Women artists elsewhere in Europe produced self-portraits as well. In Italy, Artemisia Gentileschi (1593–after 1654) dominated the scene. Her self-portrait from *c*.1638–9 was registered with the Trustees of the Sales of Charles I in October 1649, at Hampton Court, as 'A Pintura A painteinge: by Arthemisia', for which reason it is regarded as an allegory of painting (fig.4). Although Gentileschi's physiognomy would have been recognised by her contemporaries, the rhetorical pose and the interaction with the canvas indicate the allegorical nature of the image. Thus, it seems that some female artists found it more advantageous to depict themselves as the allegory of 'Pictura' than to make direct assertions about their skills.[8] Gentileschi included her own image in many of her paintings, however, as if she were using her portrait as a signature, thereby making assertions that paralleled textual signatures.[9]

The approach exemplified by Wautier's self-portrait differs from those of certain other female artists. Compared to Gentileschi's diagonally arranged composition, Wautier's is more static. Her expression is serious, but there is a shade of a smile around her mouth that suggests not submissive charm but rather a sense of triumph. Portraits of other women from this era reveal a similar self-awareness and poise. One such work is the anonymous portrait in similar dimensions of

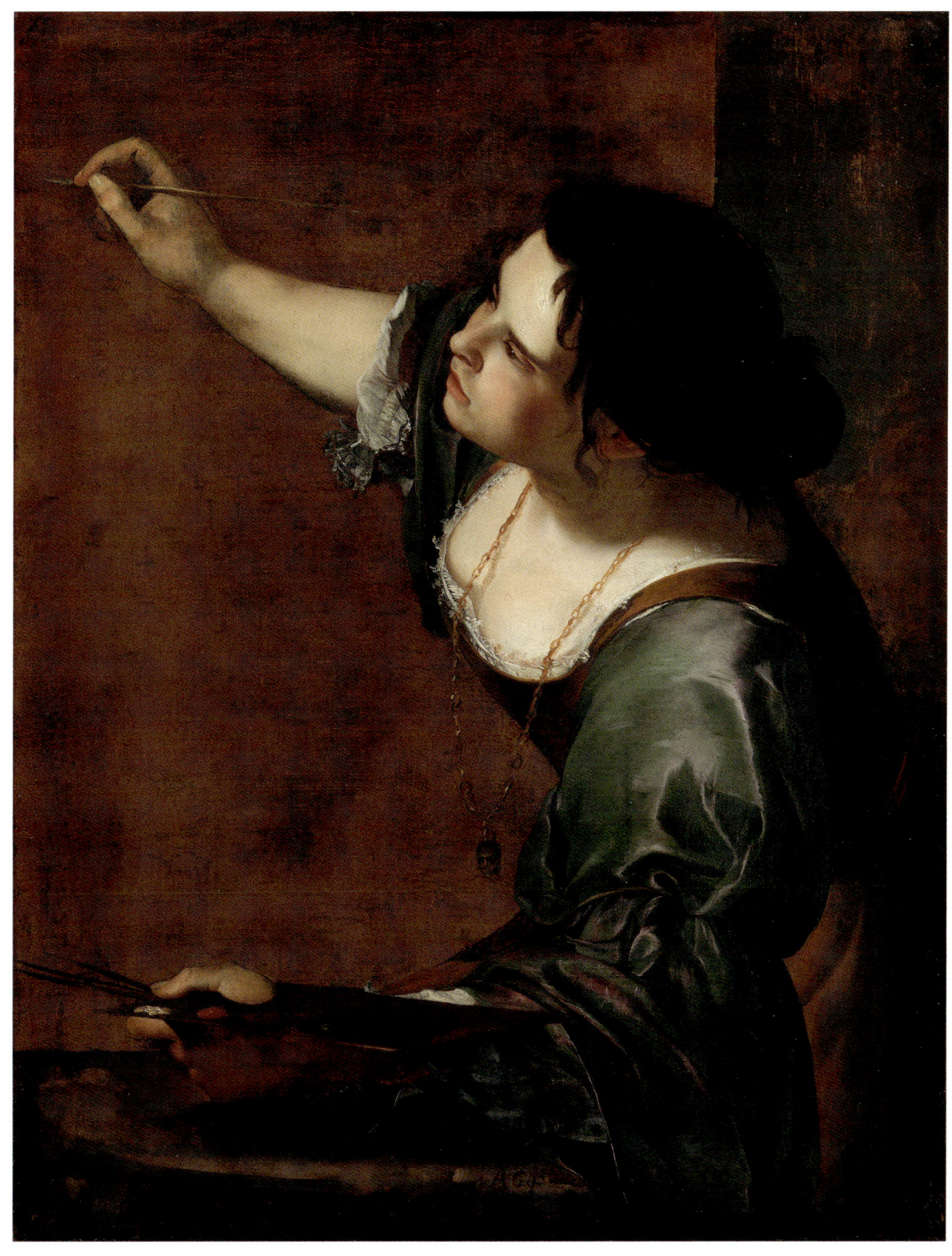

4 Artemisia Gentileschi, *Self-Portrait as the Allegory of Painting* (*La Pittura*), *c.*1638–9, oil on canvas, 98.6 × 75.2 cm (38 ⅞ × 29 ⅝ in), Royal Collection Trust

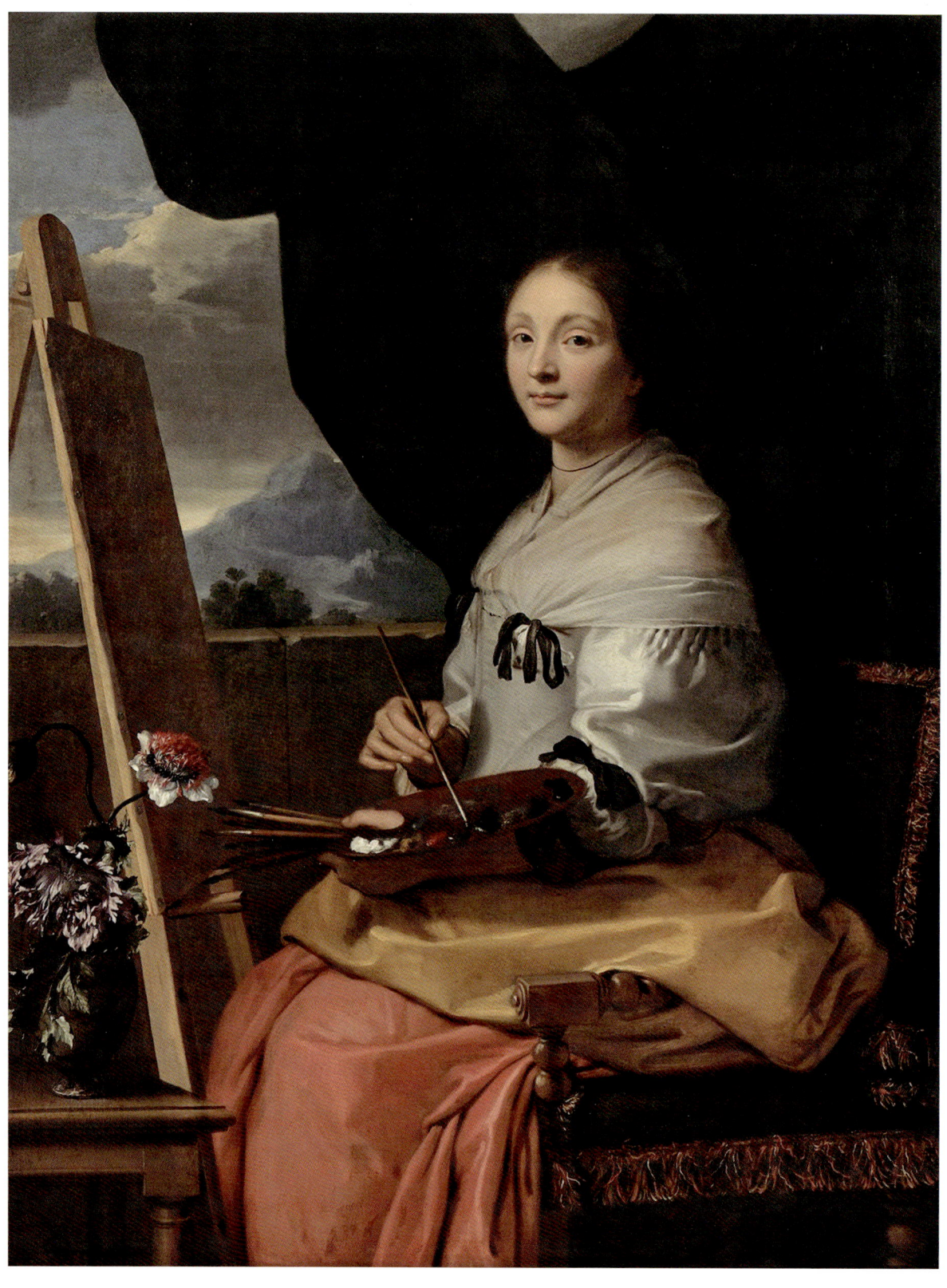

5   Anonymous French artist, *Portrait of Cathérine Duchemin*, *c.*1660–70, oil on canvas, 130 × 96 cm (51 ⅛ × 37 ¾ in),
Chateau de Versailles

the flower painter Cathérine Duchemin (1630–98) (fig.5).[10] The portrayal of Duchemin is more polished and flattering than Wautier's, however, for some moles are apparent on Wautier's face, which adds to the realistic impression of her physiognomy.[11] In this case, recognisability eclipses aesthetics. Wautier has made her silhouette as voluminous as possible by draping a broad cape around her shoulders, a figural monumentality matched by the relatively large size of the canvas.[12] The garment is difficult to categorise; it appears to be a tabard, but it does not feature sleeves and we can see neither lapels nor buttonholes, which suggest that it is a fantasised cape. Her white silk garment is topped by a trapezoid double collar. Possibly, this is a 'kamdoeck', a casual scarf or veil, which would add to the informality of her appearance. The ribbons of the collar are loosely tied, partly revealing her cleavage, giving the painting a certain intimacy.[13] As opposed to most female artists who appear in images made in this period, she does not wear a head covering or an apron that would guard against possible paint stains.[14] The combination of recognisable and imaginary items of clothing affords the portrait a certain timelessness, enhanced by the majestic manner in which the painter is enthroned: Wautier sits on a low Spanish-style chair, and to the left behind her rises a pillar suggesting spaciousness and which possibly, as in Peter Paul Rubens's final self-portrait (Kunsthistorisches Museum, Vienna), conveys the idea of 'Constantia' as a philosophical statement.[15]

Objects represented in the painting convey the self-conception Wautier wished to communicate to viewers of the portrait. The brush she holds in her right hand lends the painting a certain immediacy, for it is ready in her hand to start work. The palette and other brushes in her left hand are typical painter's tools, as is the mahl stick, featured in nearly all sixteenth- and seventeenth-century painters' self-portraits (but in this case added only very late in the composition).[16] Resting on the ledge of the easel, the mahl stick seems placed to prevent the precious

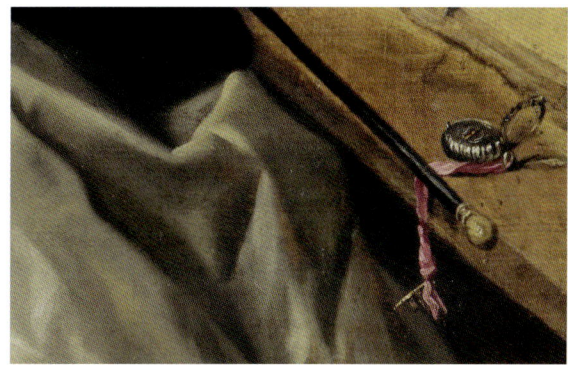

6 Michaelina Wautier, *Self-Portrait*, *c.*1650, oil on canvas, 120 × 102 cm (47 ¼ × 40 ⅛ in), private collection, Boston, MA, detail showing watch from fig.1

watch lying near it from falling. Pocket watches were rare and valuable in the seventeenth century, and Wautier has given it a ribbon to which its key is attached (fig.6). The ticking of the 'horologie' (watch) gave a contemporary sense of time and thus ushered in the early modern era. This detail may be a reference to transience, although it is unclear if she intended it to indicate the vanity of art expressed through appearances, or a sign of eternal fame: 'Ars longa, vita brevis', 'art is long, life is short'.[17] Did she think that life is fleeting but that she could survive through her art? This is not the only work in which Wautier flirted with the passing of time. In her painting *Two Boys Blowing Bubbles*, the bubbles may float now but will soon burst (see fig.51), and she suspends her flower garlands from *bucrania*, ox skulls that in antiquity were used as an explicit symbol for impermanence (see figs 48–9). At the same time, it is striking that the versatile and erudite Wautier did not include books or antique objects in her portrait that might indicate sources of inspiration as, for instance, Lavinia Fontana did when she portrayed herself in a *studiolo*.

The question remains for whom Wautier intended this exceptional self-portrait. Several options are possible: that she exhibited the painting in her own house, that she presented it to an admirer, or that an unidentified patron commissioned it.[18] More information about the work is available from later centuries. Archival sources indicate that the portrait was much admired starting at least in the eighteenth century. From 1727 on it was preserved in Althorp House, the residence of the prestigious Spencer family. The catalogue from 1851 describes it as a self-portrait, of 'Artemisia Gentileschi. Herself.'[19] In 1989, it was auctioned off at Sotheby's as a portrait of Anna Maria van Schurman, attributed to Abraham van den Tempel.[20] It is meaningful that three artistic women of the early modern period were confused with one another. Famous in her own day, in 1989 Wautier was unknown. This once again illustrates that research into 'forgotten' female artists leads to new identifications and interpretations. In this way, one woman opens the door to another.

HER PARENTS AND (HALF) SIBLINGS

The formal self-portrait reveals how Wautier wished to be seen and known, if ideally, but it also tells us very little about its subject. For this, we can turn to recent archival research that has yielded new information about her biography, family history and the environment that provided opportunities for her to become the artist she grew to be.[21]

Wautier's parents, Charles Wautier and Jenne George, and Michaelina herself, were born in Mons, a city around 50 km to the south-west of Brussels with approximately 12,000 inhabitants.[22] Mons was important enough to be included in the *Orbis Terrarum* by Georg Braun and Frans Hogenberg from 1590 (fig.7). Wautier's birthplace had flourished intellectually from the second half of the sixteenth century onward. Relevant to the interests of Michaelina, artists such as the sculptor Jacques du Broeucq (*c.*1505–84), the composer Orlandus Lassus (*c.*1531–94), the organist-calligrapher Maximilien de la Haize (1593–1653), and the astronomer Charles

Malapert (1581–1630) were born and had worked there. The chronicles of the sexton of the Church of Saint-Germain in Mons are important sources about everyday events in the city, providing a useful impression of a provincial yet thriving town perpetually impacted by war. The writer describes Spanish victories and defeats, political events such as the inauguration of the Archduke Leopold Wilhelm, the beheading of 'le roi d'Angleterre Charles premier du nom' (Charles I of England), and also displays of fireworks and the price of cheese.[23]

The Wautier family had established important social and political networks in and beyond Mons. They were advantageously located in the city, even if their home was relatively modest, for they resided on the Rue d'Havré, one of the most important streets, leading straight to the marketplace.[24] This was a densely built urban area with terraced houses, according to illustrations of the period. Charles was well connected even at an early age, for he had been a page to Pedro Enríquez de Acevedo (*c.*1536–1610), the Duke of Fuentes. The Duke became commander-in-chief of the Spanish troops in the Netherlands in 1592 and was briefly Governor of the Spanish Netherlands in 1595. Pages like Charles received an education in weaponry and were familiarised with the rules of etiquette applicable to the circles of their lord.[25] He may have had a military career, but if so, nothing is known of it. His title was lord *in* Ham-sur-Heure, indicating that he had estates or grounds in the village. This title should be distinguished from that carried by the eminent De Merode family, who were lords *of* Ham-sur-Heure, and thus had legal power in the municipality.[26] The lords De Merode and members of the Wautier family certainly knew each other, and this relation doubtless had positive consequences for the social position of the Wautier family. Furthermore, Michaelina's father was not only at home in a military environment with aristocratic connections, but there were also prominent intellectuals in his own family. Most important was the De Houst family from Ath; the

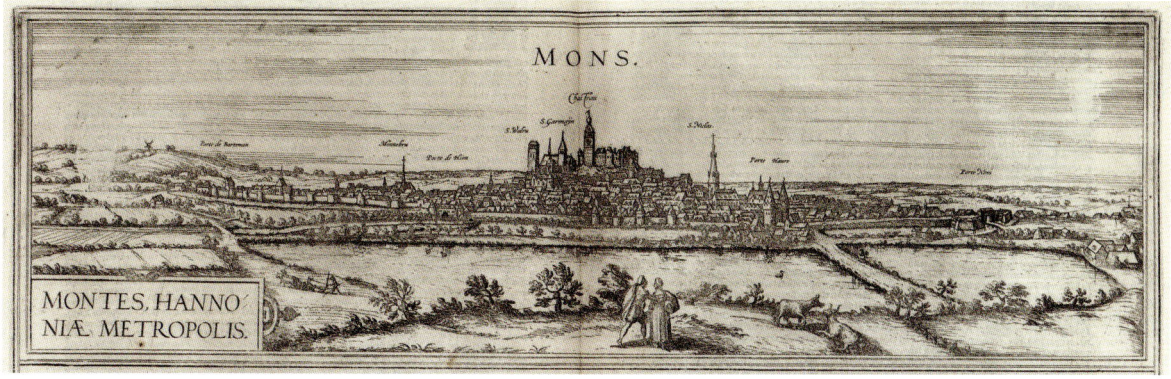

7 Georg Braun and Frans Hogenberg, 'Mons – Montes Hannoniae Metropolis [View of Mons]', in *Civitates Orbis Terrarum*, vol.II, Cologne, 1590

good relations with this family are apparent from the fact that three of its members were godfather or godmother to his children.[27] Jacobus Ustius (d.1638), a famous humanist from this family, had studied with the Leuven professor Justus Lipsius, the founder of Neostoicism in the Low Countries.[28]

The families of Michaelina's parents presumably knew each other in Mons, where in 1594 Charles had married Barbe Hallet (1565–1601), with whom he had five children (we may assume she died in childbirth).[29] Within a year after her death, Charles married Jenne, in the Church of Saint-Germain. They had five sons and two daughters, the youngest being Michaelina, before Charles died in 1617; Jenne died much later, in 1638, when Michaelina was around 24 years old. The baptismal certificates for all five sons have been discovered: Jacques (b.1602), Nicolas (b.1607), Charles (b.1609), Pierre (b.1611) and Léon (b.1616). With regard to the two daughters, only 'Marie Magdelaine' is registered, born on 2 September 1604. The absence of any baptismal record for Michaelina has led to great confusion, which will be discussed later. Where or whether the Wautier children went to school is unknown. In Mons, there were no schools for the education of girls. To solve this problem, Jean Malapert, brother of the famous astronomer Charles, and his wife, Marie de Guise, founded a monastery and school for the education of noble girls in Mons in 1633, although the school was not active until 1648.[30] It is possible that Michaelina was educated at home, as girls in higher circles often were. An example in this respect is the scholar Anna Maria van Schurman (1607–78), who related in her autobiography how she, in the company of her brothers, was taught Latin and Greek by a private tutor and achieved the best results of the three.[31] Neither do we know anything about the education of Michaelina's brothers. Possibly, they were taught by a private tutor or schooled at the Jesuit college established in Mons in 1598. Evidence of contact between members of the Wautier family and the Jesuits in Brussels during the early 1640s could imply that they were acquainted with the religious order while still residing in their native city.[32] It is also important to remember that Michaelina painted the portrait of the Italian Jesuit Martino Martini in 1654 (see fig.58).

Since women were generally much less visible than men of the period, it should not be surprising that no seventeenth-century archival source mentions a 'Michaelina Wautier'.[33] Because so few traces about women remain, reconstructing their biographies can be difficult. A particular challenge in Wautier's case is that her family name was spelled in many ways. Variations in the spelling of first and family names are quite common in seventeenth-century sources but, based on the notary deeds to which she was a party and which were drawn up both in French and in Dutch, it appears that the painter herself consistently used the spelling 'Wautier'. Furthermore, the artist of whom several paintings are itemised in the 1659 inventory of Archduke Leopold Wilhelm's art collection, to be discussed extensively later on, is referred to by the name of 'Magdalena Woutiers'.[34] This, combined with the absence of a baptismal certificate in the name of Michaelina, was why, in 2018, it was assumed that the names 'Marie Magdelaine' and 'Michaelina' referred to the same woman.[35] Additional archival research has now indisputably proved that there were two sisters in the Wautier family, of whom Marie Magdelaine was born in 1604. By the end of their lives, they were dwelling together in the same house in Brussels, where Marie Magdelaine died in 1687 and 'Michèle' in 1689.[36] Newly found documents have shown that Marie Magdelaine was a 'devotaire', which is to say a 'devout daughter' or 'spiritual daughter'. These were mostly prosperous ladies comparable to Beguines, though not living in a religious community. The 'invisibility' of Michaelina's sister may be explained by her choice to spend her life as a 'filia devota'.[37]

The baptism records for the family of Charles Wautier and Jenne George suggest that a child was born into the family every two years. Only between the fifth and the sixth child is there a break, an interval of five years, which suggests that the birth of a second daughter fell in this period, between 1613 and 1618.[38] The father of this large, blended family died on 24 November 1617. Since Léon Wautier was born on 11 July 1616, it is probable that Michaelina was born around 1614 or after the death of her father. She certainly could not have been born in 1604 as previously believed, for that is the birth year of Magdelaine. Most likely, *c.*1614 is the best approximation of Michaelina's birth.

JENNE GEORGE, HER IMMEDIATE AND DISTANT FAMILY

Insight into the family of Wautier's mother Jenne George is provided in a *Mémorial de famille* (*Livre de raison*), a leather-bound manuscript preserved in the National Archive in Mons.[39] The primary author of the *Mémorial* was Michaelina's great-uncle Jean George, while other members of the George and Hallet families supplemented his account with descriptions of miscellaneous events. The record is rather unstructured and the narrative is incoherent. It reads like a private diary, an effect enhanced by Jean George's anecdotal style. It abounds with spelling errors, and he regularly employs dialect expressions. For that reason, the remarks sound true to life. Included in the narrative is a description of Jean's marriage to Jeanne Hallet and the postponement of the corresponding banquet because the wedding was on a Sunday. Especially moving is the passage about his son Jean, who was 'born with a caul' and who died shortly thereafter. He also discusses his son Albert's first day at school, excursions with his wife to Boussu Castle (a Renaissance castle 10 km from Mons), and the accident in which a nephew was hit by a carriage on the way from Mons to Merbes-Sainte-Marie and died of the consequences. Jean George also reported on important historical events, such as the plague that arrived at Mons in 1615 and claimed 7000 or 8000 victims; but he also supplies the reader with a cure for toothache. In a disarming way, this manuscript reports on daily reality in Mons over a period of more than a century, providing important insights into the intimate life of a Mons bourgeois family. This city and this family also constituted Wautier's world.

Although the birth date of Jenne George is not known, from the *Mémorial de famille* it can be deduced that she was widowed at a young age and was left alone to raise at least five sons, two daughters and a stepson. She never remarried. Apparently, there was no financial reason for another marriage, as she could manage very well on the income she had from numerous debentures and interests from her own and the Wautier families.[40] These families were not only connected through Charles Wautier's first wife Barbe Hallet, for her sister Jeanne Hallet later married Jenne George's brother Jean George. This approach to marriage was not exceptional. The familial cluster in which Michaelina grew up is an example of the endogamy that pervaded both aristocratic and bourgeois social strategies. The last will of Jeanne Hallet also affords us a look into the Wautiers' world.[41] Drawn up on 12 September 1628, the will describes her aunt as a 'bourgeoise et marchande' (bourgeois and merchant). She bequeathed her personal belongings to her four unmarried daughters. They acquired some small valuables, but no paintings or other works of art are mentioned. Each daughter also received part of the house and the furnishings and, on top of that, an ample dowry to the value of 3500 Hainaut pounds (more than 20,000 guilders). The family of Michaelina Wautier's mother certainly knew the value of money.

It appears that Marie Bocquet, Jean George's stepdaughter, was also important to the social fabric of Michaelina's family. In 1597, Bocquet became the godmother of Marie Wautier, a daughter of Michaelina's father Charles by his first marriage. In the Rue d'Havré, where the Wautier family and members of the George family lived, Bocquet

and her husband Jacques van der Beken ran the Hostellerie du Pot d'Estai (The Pewter Kettle). Notwithstanding these commercial activities, Marie Bocquet was a member of an intellectually and literarily active family.[42] Jehan Bocquet and his son Charles wrote a chronicle of Mons and in 1618 published a collection of *Ballades*.[43] The clichéd and misogynous character of verses such as 'La vertu des femmes, Plorer, Filler et maldire' may have been intended playfully, but the reduction of 'female virtue' to 'weeping, fantasising and cursing' is pejorative and perpetuates gender bias of a kind with which Michaelina may have been familiar. As another point of contact, Marie Bocquet had sons who studied at the University of Leuven, and Léon Wautier, Michaelina's brother, also enrolled there.[44] Moreover, Jenne George, Michaelina's mother, was, together with her daughter, a member of the Confrérie de Nostre Dame, a Catholic society in the parish of Saint-Nicolas-en-Havré in Mons. All Jenne's children except Michaelina were baptised at this church.[45] The social context, network and economic stability of both the paternal and maternal sides of Michaelina's family may have created opportunities for their children, including Michaelina.

FROM THE RUE D'HAVRÉ TO THE COURT CITY OF BRUSSELS

After her husband's death, Michaelina's mother continued to live on the Rue d'Havré until she died in 1638. At that time, Michaelina was around 24 years old and probably had not yet left her mother's house. Of note in this context is the earliest known painting by Wautier, a portrait of the artillery general Andrea Cantelmo (1598–1645), of which only an engraving has been preserved, dated 1643 (fig.8). It is possible that Wautier produced the painting in Mons, since Cantelmo may have stayed there in July of 1642, providing a reasonable point of contact for

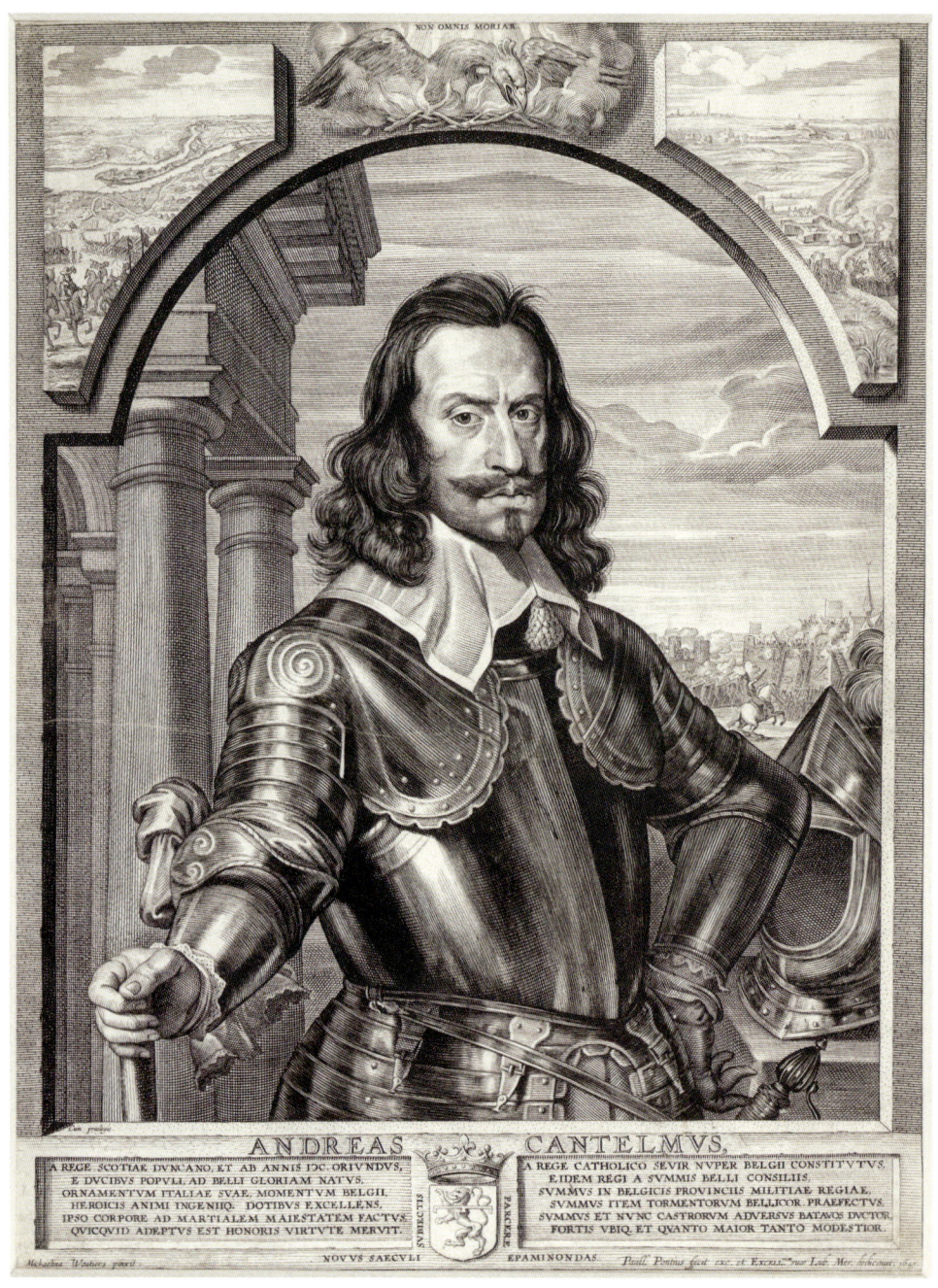

8   Paulus Pontius after Michaelina Woutiers [Wautier], *Portrait of Commander Andrea Cantelmo*, 1643, engraving on paper, 40.3 × 29.8 cm (15 ⅞ × 11 ¾ in), private collection

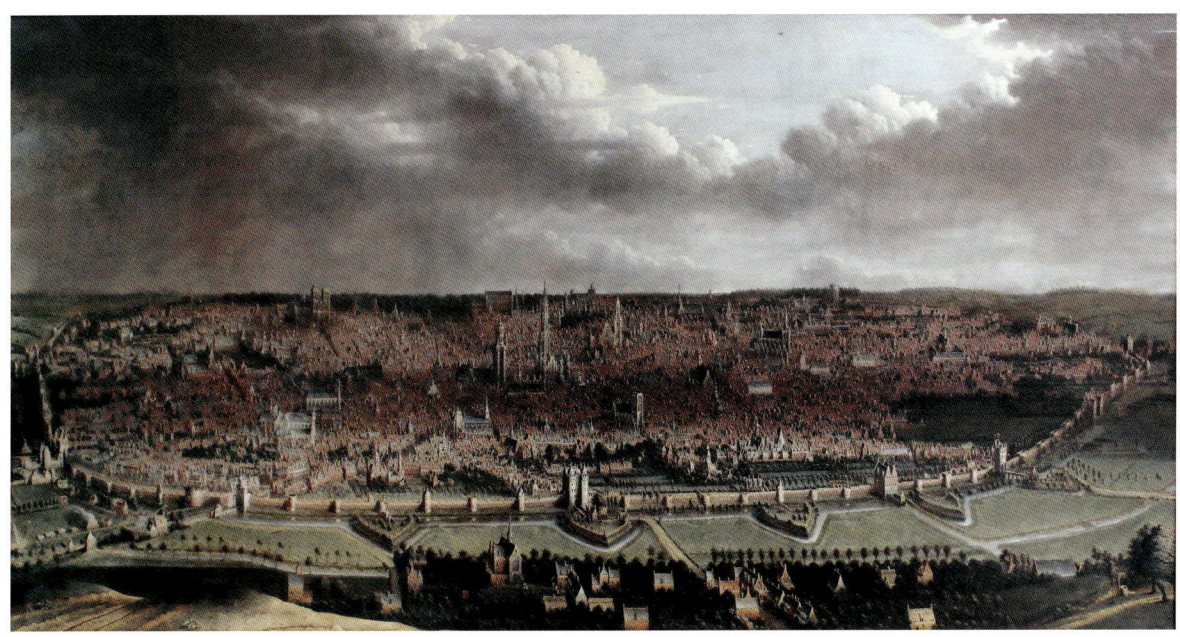

9 Jan Baptist Bonnecroy, *View of Brussels*, *c.*1665, oil on canvas, 169 × 301.5 cm (66 ½ × 118 ¾ in), Royal Museums of Fine Arts of Belgium, Brussels, permanent loan of the King Baudouin Foundation

artist and subject.[46] However, it is equally likely that the portrait was executed in Brussels, where Wautier relocated from Mons and where she established her professional life. Her brothers Pierre and Léon were living there before her, which likely provided emotional and practical incentives, but that Charles was able to make a living there as a painter certainly made the city much more attractive. The success of artists like Charles and Michaelina can be attributed to the arrival of the Archduke Leopold Wilhelm, Governor of the Spanish Netherlands, in 1647. This occurrence marked the beginning of a golden decade in which the Brussels court would put art and music at the centre of attention. From the middle of the seventeenth century at the latest, both Charles and Michaelina were in contact with Leopold Wilhelm or with his entourage.

In September 1642, Charles Wautier for the last time paid his 'bourgeoisie', a kind of tax, in Mons,[47] and on 15 December 1642, he is reported to be working, already a painter, in Brussels.[48] At that time, Brussels was a spaciously laid-out court city, as appears from the impressive cityscape (*c.*1665) by Jan Baptist Bonnecroy (fig.9). This is the very first trace of Charles's activities as a painter; he was 33 years old. As Wautier's older brother, Charles would play a crucial role in her life and career and was probably the one who taught her the craft. Without Charles, who acted as her teacher and provided a studio, it is unlikely that Wautier would have developed the artistic expertise she did.

Pierre, an elder brother, is the only family member of whom we are certain Michaelina painted a portrait. This is one of the most impressive

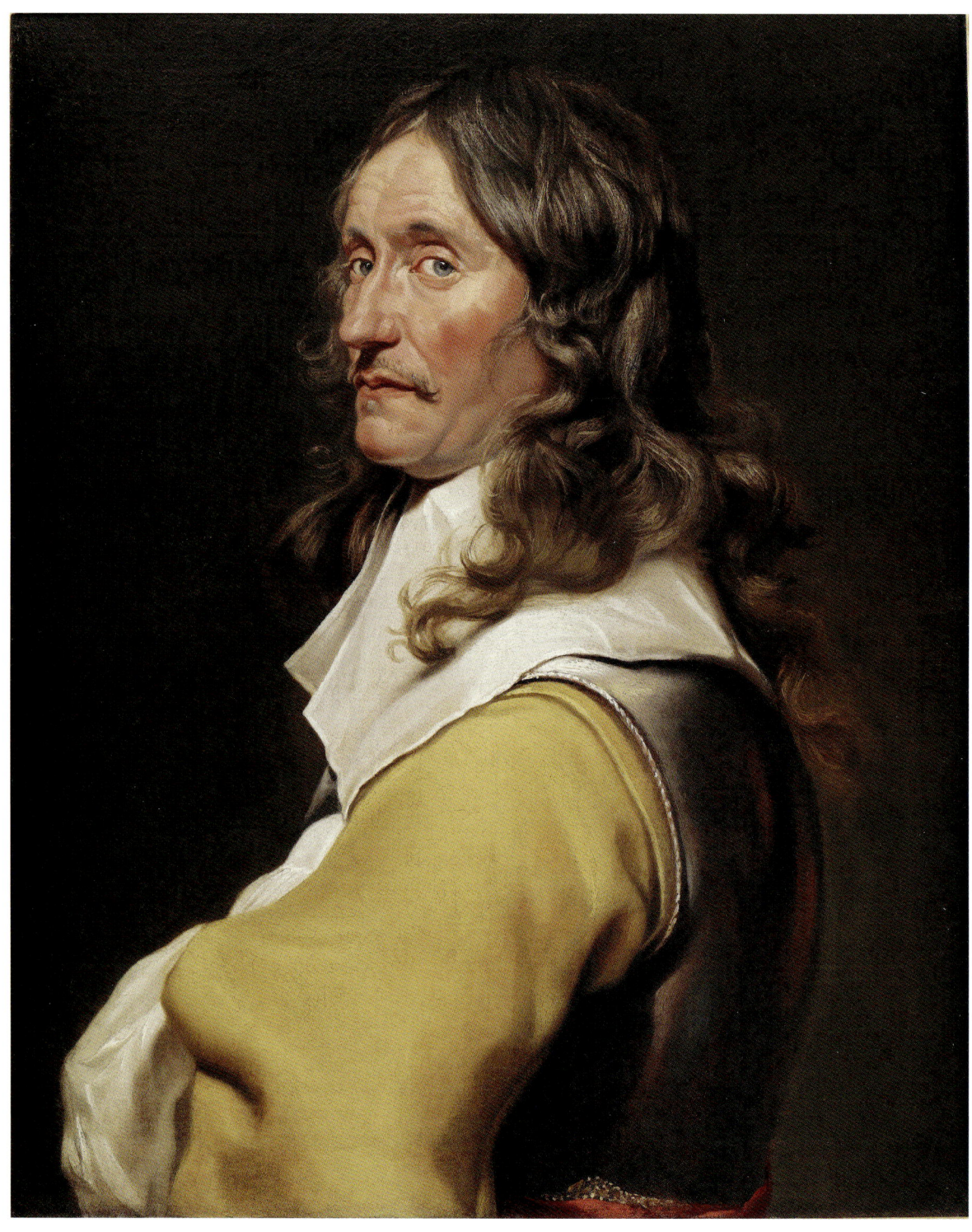

10 Michaelina Wautier, *Portrait of Pierre Wautier, Brother of Michaelina, as a Military Commander in the Spanish Army*, *c.*1654–64, oil on canvas, 73 × 58.5 cm (28 ¾ × 23 in), private collection, London

portraits she ever painted, rendering his strong personality in bold brushstrokes. On 23 September 1654, Pierre joined the army, becoming captain of a cavalry unit of 200 Walloon soldiers (fig.10).[49] By choosing a military career, he followed in the footsteps of his father, who had died 37 years earlier. Members of the De Merode family may have inspired him, and they may have helped him realise his ambitions through their contacts at court in Brussels.[50] Precisely when he settled in Brussels is unknown.[51] In 1662, he married Catharine de Witte, and they both died in 1664, the year their son Augustin-Charles was born. Augustin-Charles was to play an important role in the life of his uncle Charles – and possibly also in that of his aunt. In the same month of December 1642 when Charles can with certainty be situated in Brussels, the Brussels Jesuits drew up a contract for the lease of a house to Léon Wautier, for the following three years, later to be extended to 1648. Léon Wautier's house was on the Keizerstraat, while Charles moved into a house in the adjacent Gasthuisstraat.[52] In 1647, Wautier's youngest brother Léon enrolled at the Leuven University, and in 1653, he is mentioned as a priest in Mons.

On 27 June 1660, Léon Wautier died, barely 44 years old. A notarial deed was made, of which only a partial copy survives. This newly discovered deed, drawn up by a Brussels notary on 20 August 1660, is nonetheless of great value because it names all the living members of the Wautier family as the heirs to Léon Wautier. These are Charles, Pierre, 'damoiselle Michelle' and, finally, 'damoiselle Marie Magdelaine'. This is, at last, a sign of life of Michaelina's doppelganger, proof that there actually were two sisters in the Wautier family. Curiously, the approximately ten years younger 'Michelle' is listed before 'Marie Magdelaine', diverging from the order based on age.[53] The reason for this is unclear. Although the part of the copy that has been preserved tells us nothing about the nature of the possessions, we may assume that all four siblings inherited from

their childless brother, the priest of the Church of Saint Elizabeth in Mons.[54]

'JOUFFROUWE MICHIELLE WAUTIER SYNE SUSTERE'

On 17 March 1662, only two years later, Wautier visited the Brussels notary Jean Baptist Reps to have a will notarised. It is indeed a great loss that this document has not been preserved, for otherwise, we would have had a better picture not only of her possessions, but also of her affection for the people mentioned therein. That she had a will made can be determined from two later sources, in which her brother Charles confirms that he is her universal heir – according to the will – and refers to a house and various plots of land he had bought together with 'Miss Michiele Wautier his sister (whose universal heir he is)'.[55] Occasionally, Michaelina and her brother bought plots of land and invested in rent-charges. It appears from several notarial deeds that they acquired these new possessions together; they each signed these agreements before a notary. A year and a half later, on 7 August 1669, brother and sister acted as moneylenders and bought an interest, as revealed in the *Wijkboek* (parish book). Initially in the *Wijkboek* the buyers were described as 'Mr Charles Wautier and Miss Michielle Wautier, his wife'. Subsequently, 'his wife' was struck and replaced with 'syne sustere' (his sister). The Brussels clerk assumed he was dealing with a married couple and only afterwards realised they were brother and sister. The initial error tells us much about Charles and Michaelina's relationship. They seemed 'married' insofar as they shared financial interests and lived together in the same house from at least 1668 onwards (see Chapter 3). This evidence demonstrates that they were experienced in money matters and approached their investments as a common project.

On 7 February 1668, Michaelina and Charles bought a house near the Brussels Church of Our Lady of the Chapel, presumably the house in the

Heilige Geeststraat, and on 31 December 1669 they acquired another spacious house with a garden and several annexes on the other side of the church.[56] In the house in the Heilige Geeststraat, 'Mistress Maria Madalena Wautier' died on 7 October 1687. She must have been living there for at least a few years. This is evident from various wills that Charles had notarised between 1689 and his death in 1703, in which he refers to a field bed ('un lit de chant') that he left to his maid Jeanne le Doux and that stood 'dans le chambre de Damoiselle Magdelaine' ('in the room of Miss Magdelaine').[57] It is once again clear that he had two sisters and that the second, who was at least ten years older than Michaelina, also lived in his house. She was buried on 9 October 1687 in the Church of Our Lady of the Chapel and was identified as 'Mistress Maria Madalena Wautier in the church, [living] opposite the church in Heilige Geeststraate'.[58] Apart from her status as a 'devout daughter',[59] this older sister remains a mystery. No further traces of her can be found, either in Mons or in Brussels. As far as we know, she never married. She was never involved in Charles and Michaelina's financial transactions and apparently did not leave any possessions, which is unusual, to say the least. From the family capital, she must have had the means to determine her own life.

Two years later, on 30 October 1689, Michaelina Wautier died at the age of approximately 75 years. She was buried in the same church as her older sister, behind the presbytery, as noted in the parish registers: 'Miss Michael Wautier in the church behind the presbytery in the geest straet near the church'.[60] Upon her death, she was referred to as 'Miss Michael Wautier' for the first and only time. This was the name she used when signing her paintings, albeit in the feminine form.[61] Her older brother Charles would survive her by 14 years. By the end of their lives, the three surviving siblings lived in a beautiful house in Brussels. Shortly before his death, Charles moved in with his nephew and godchild, Augustin-Charles Wautier. According to

a contemporary notarial source, Charles's house was cleared after his death, but five years earlier, on 19 July 1698, a public sale of the paintings in Charles's possession, presumably works by both Charles and Michaelina, had been organised. Surprisingly, no further information or auction catalogue has been found.[62]

The scarcity of archival sources about 'Michaelina Wautier' has cast an aura of mystery around her life and career. However, by supplementing the available information with recently discovered sources, the contours of her early biography become clearer and, as we will see, her artistry is made more understandable. Michaelina and Charles were two artists born into a family of soldiers, magistrates, intellectuals and merchants from the lower nobility. The connections of their father to one of the most important noble families in the Low Countries must have created opportunities for them. Of importance as well were the ample financial resources that the Wautier family had at its disposal, which remained available after the death of the *pater familias* in 1617.

The origins of Charles's and Michaelina's artistic talents remain a mystery, however. In early modern times, it was unusual for boys who were not the sons of artists to be trained as artists, and it was extremely rare for a young woman without an artistic background to choose a career as a painter (see Chapter 4). Michaelina found a way to learn the craft via her brother, as he, in turn, would later learn from his sister. Based on their oeuvres, we can assume that they inspired each other and critiqued each other's paintings, and we can ask ourselves how they comparatively viewed their profession and their work. It is possible that they considered their paintings to be of equal quality, even though Michaelina may have secretly thought that she was a better and more versatile artist than Charles. Were they convinced that their paintings would stand the test of time? Charles would certainly not have imagined that he would be rediscovered 375 years after his death through the sister he had taught.

Their mother Jenne George must have supported Michaelina's ambitions and given her the freedom to make her own choices, which certainly would have been very different from what she herself had envisioned for her. Michaelina's fate turned out far better than Virginia Woolf's poor Judith, who committed suicide in despair.

2

Patrons, Patronage and Art Connoisseurs

An artist's career is always a *Gesamtkunstwerk*; no one can make it alone. From Wautier's biography, we have learned that her background supplied her with some advantages in pursuing a career as an artist. Her mother had the opportunity to help her financially and, even more importantly, she could rely on the artistic expertise of her brother Charles (Chapter 3). But her ambition to become an artist was unconventional, especially for a young woman from a family without an artistic tradition. She also lacked the direct support of a father who otherwise might have had the power and connections to launch her career. For how could she attract the attention of a potential clientele and convince them of her specific talents, so that they would invest in her? This chapter contextualises Wautier's early professional life in Brussels to better understand the opportunities available to women like her, and it situates her within networks of patronage and connoisseurship in the visual arts.

Formal positions for female artists of this period were more common than one might think. Several sixteenth-century princes invited female artists from Ghent, Bruges and Antwerp to their courts. Female painters from the Low Countries enjoyed special fame, doubtlessly connected to the excellent reputations that their male relatives enjoyed. Henry VIII of England, for instance, invited Susanna Horenbout (active *c.*1520–40), who was a lady-in-waiting to his third, fourth and sixth wives: Jane Seymour, Anne of Cleves and Catherine Parr. From various sources, it appears that she was more in demand as a companion than as an artist, but her talent will nonetheless have opened some doors. The same can be said of Levina Bening (*c.*1520–76), the wife of Joris Teerlinck, also in the service of Henry VIII and subsequently of Edward VII, Mary I and Elizabeth I.[1] No works have been preserved that can be attributed to either artist with any certainty. An interesting recent attribution to Horenbout is the design of the funeral tomb of her mother, Margaret Saunders, who may also have been a painter of miniatures, at All Saints' Church in Fulham (fig.11).[2] As for the Habsburgs, Mary of Hungary, Charles V's younger sister, appreciated the painter Catharina van Hemessen (1528–after 1581), whom she invited in 1556, together with her husband, to her court in Valladolid.[3] All three of these artists were artists' daughters (see Chapter 4). Archduchess Isabella, Governor of the Spanish Netherlands, was also impressed by artistic women. Around 1625, she ordered 15 small paintings by Anna Francisca de Bruyns (1604/5–56) with the *Mysteries of the Rosary*, which she then sent to

Pope Paul V as a gift.[4] Isabella's interest in the arts will doubtless have been influenced by Sofonisba Anguissola (1532/5–1625), who stayed at the court of Isabella's father Philip II of Spain, and who almost certainly educated Isabella Clara Eugenia and her sister Catalina in drawing and painting. Around 1573 she painted portraits of the then seven- or eight-year-old Infanta and her sister (Galleria Sabauda, Turin; private collection).[5]

As far as we know from the limited available information, few patrons in the mid-seventeenth-century Spanish Netherlands awarded commissions to female artists. The same applies to collectors acquiring paintings by women. The supply was small and we may ask what their reasons could be for such a choice. Were they attracted to the quality of the work per se, or were they fascinated by the extraordinary phenomenon of a contemporary female painter capable of producing high-quality work? Shedding light on the reception of these artists is the case of still-life painter Clara Peeters (probably 1587–after 1636). With sufficient certainty, we can identify her as Clara Lamberts, who was born into a Mechelen artistic family and who married Henrick II Peeters in 1605.[6] She is assumed to have lived in Antwerp during her active period. She is thus an artist born into an artistic environment, who in the period c.1610–20 introduced the new genre of 'banquet pieces' or 'breakfast pieces' with great success (fig.12). How she sold her work is not demonstrated in known documents, but we can assume that she did so via the Antwerp art dealers. Already in 1627, in Rotterdam, a 'fish, from Clara Peeters' is mentioned (a painting of a fish, a copy from a Clara Peeters painting) in the inventory of a painter's wife, and in 1636, one of her paintings is listed in an Amsterdam collection. This indicates that some of Peeters's works circulated in the Dutch Republic during her lifetime. The copies made of her paintings show that her work had become quite popular. Even more importantly, two of her paintings were found in the

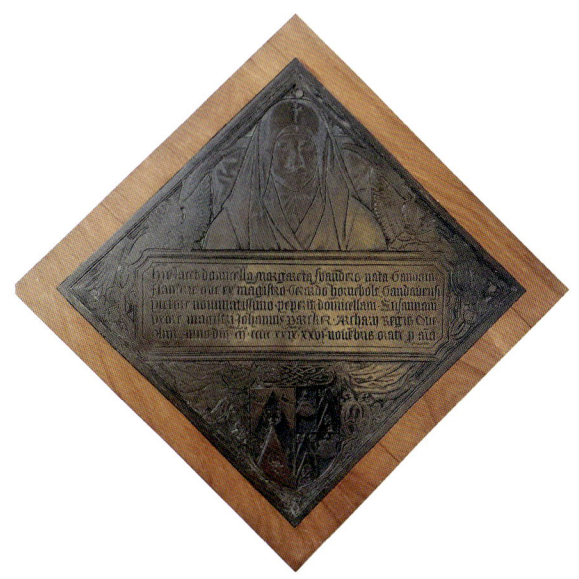

11   Susanna Horenbout (attributed), Brass commemorating Margaret Saunders, Susanna Horenbout's mother, 1529, All Saints' Church, Fulham

Madrid collection of Diego Messia, the Marquis of Leganés, one of the most prominent collectors of his time.[7] Antwerp was famous for its trade contacts with Spain, but the presence of these works in Madrid demonstrates that her still lifes were highly valued and that an aristocratic collector appreciated them enough to buy them. These still lifes were examples of a new and very decorative genre, which may have motivated their acquisition.

On all Peeters's signed still lifes, her first name 'CLARA' is spelled out in full, followed by either the initial P or the full surname Peeters, which may indicate that she was conscious of how being a woman distinguished her and she even used this as an additional sales argument, as some art dealers may also have done.[8] In the example shown in fig.13, she has signed her name on a knife in the foreground of the composition. The presence of the knife, which was

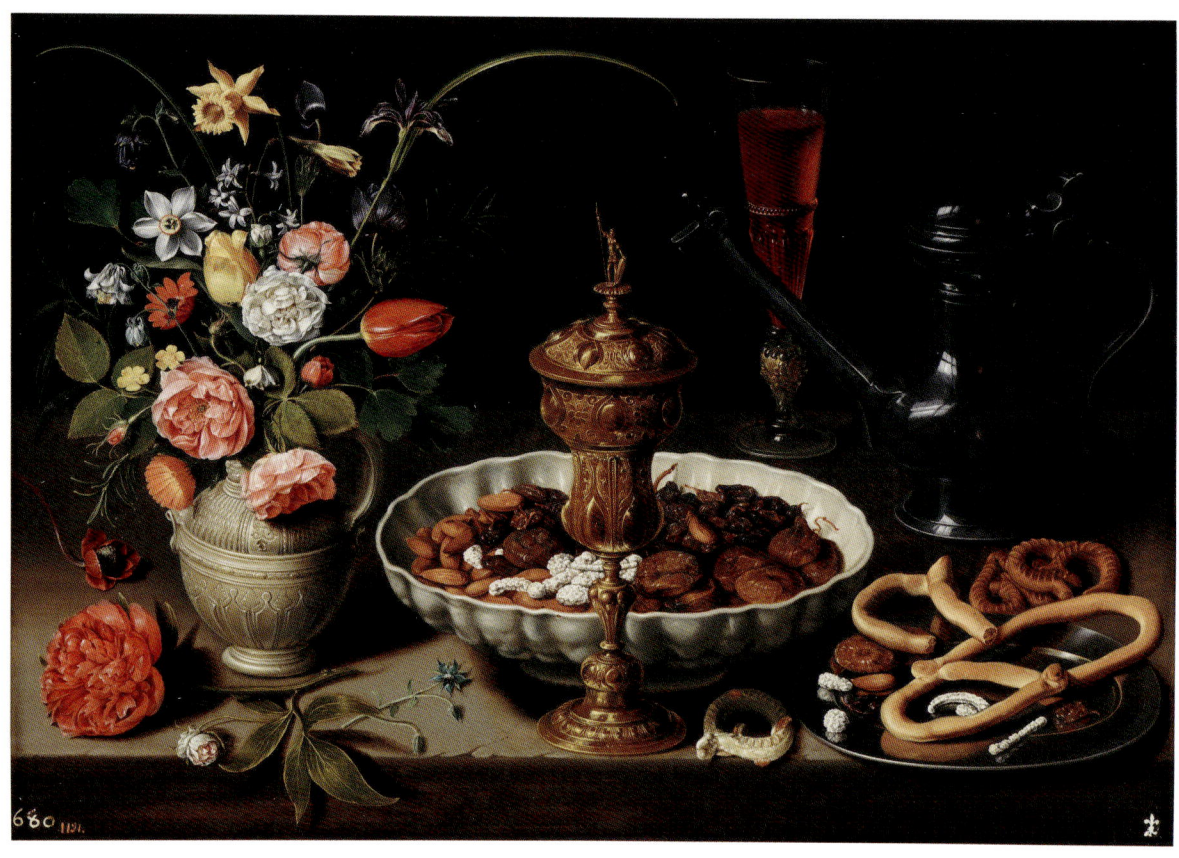

12 Clara Peeters, *Still Life with Flowers, Gilt Goblet, Eatables and a Pewter Flagon*, 1611, oil on panel, 52 × 73 cm (20 ½ × 28 ¾ in), Museo Nacional del Prado, Madrid

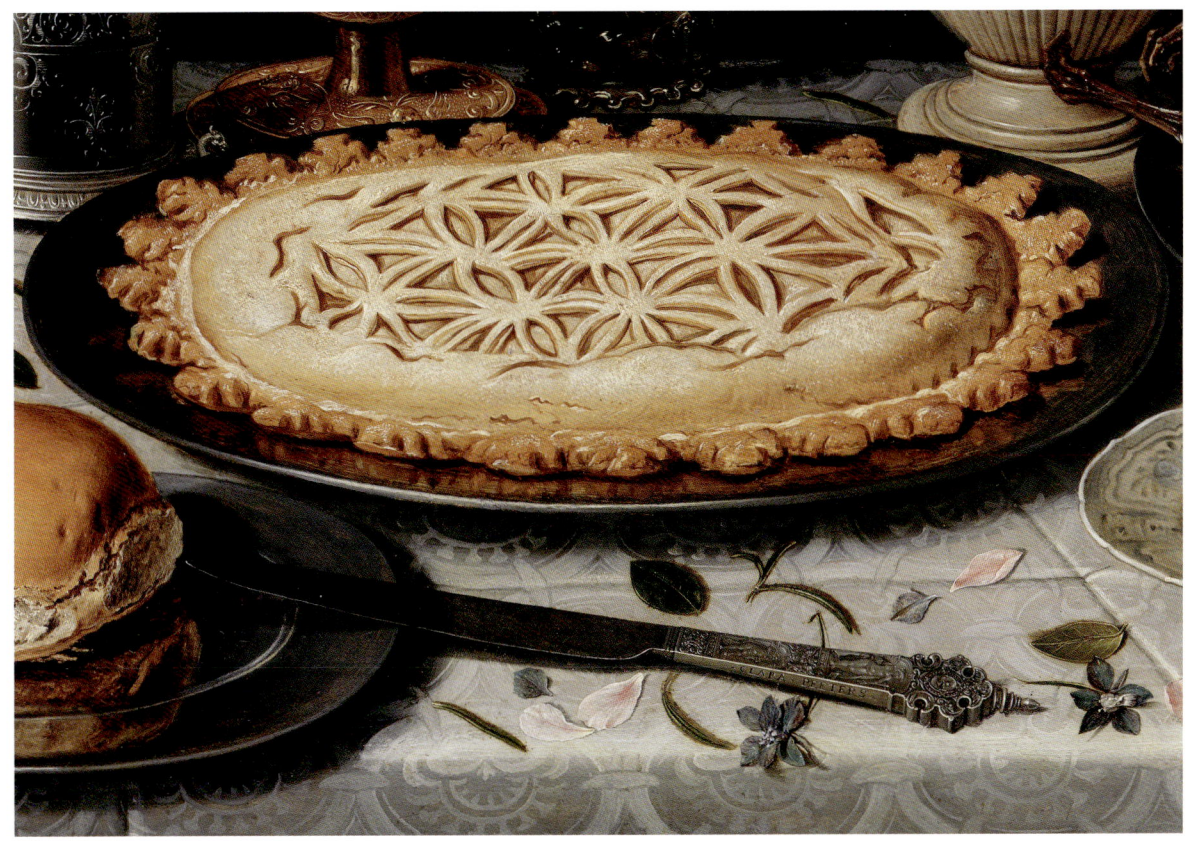

13 Clara Peeters, *Table with Cloth, Foodstuffs and Other Objects*, *c.*1611, oil on panel, 55 × 73 cm (21 ⅝ × 28 ¾ in), Museo Nacional del Prado, Madrid, detail with signature

frequently given as a wedding gift, made particularly clear that the author of the painting was a woman.[9] These pieces were exquisite and highly sought-after items for prominent collectors, thanks to the exclusivity of the genre and the fact that they were executed by a female artist. Somewhat surprising is the fact that Peeters used the name of her husband as a signature on all of her paintings, especially because both her own family and her husband's included several artists about whom nearly nothing is known. However, she seemed to have been only 17 when she married, which might have convinced her to prefer Henrick Peeters's name above that of her own father, Nicasius Lamberts.[10] The fact that a father's reputation could influence the decision-making process is evident in the cases of the aforementioned two women artists at the London court. For example, Susanna Horenbout was always referred to as a member of her own artistic family in contemporary sources, rather than as the wife of one of her two husbands, John Parker or John Gilman, neither of whom was an artist. However, Levina Teerlinck was never described as the daughter of the famous Bruges-based miniaturist painter Simon Bening, who was probably not well known at the Tudor court, but as the wife of Joris or George Teerlinck, who later became Keeper of the Palace of Westminster and Yeoman of the King's Crossbows. Hailing originally from the provincial city of Blankenberge, he had arrived in London with his wife around 1545.

THE BRUSSELS COURT AS THE PLACE TO BE

Wautier's travel itinerary and her reasons for relocating from Mons to Brussels cannot be easily reconstructed. When did she make this move? Did she have reasons to stay in Mons during the early 1640s, when it was a relatively small town with only approximately 12,000 inhabitants?[11] By contrast, Brussels, thanks to the Archdukes Albert and Isabella, who had succeeded in creating an auspicious economic climate, had become a prosperous court

city which, at the time of the Infanta Isabella's death in 1633, had a population of approximately 70,000.[12] Several witnesses from the beginning of the seventeenth century report on the luxury of the Brussels court and the high expenditure on its accommodations, dinners and fashionable clothing. With his keen interest in the visual arts and music, the Archduke succeeded in giving the Brussels court an international allure. This was one of the reasons why Queen Christina of Sweden came to stay there for a while from the end of 1654 to September 1655.[13] Moreover, the court and its entourage played a large part in the urban dynamics of the city and influenced its morphology. While the courtiers, the nobility and citizens of independent means, the higher public servants and the higher clergy had settled in 'Upper Brussels' near the royal Coudenberg Palace, the lower part of Brussels had a much more common and poorer population.[14] The better situated citizens enjoyed their luxury, and paintings were much desired objects.[15] It seems that the metropole of Brussels would have attracted Wautier, and she would have had easy access to the advantages of urban life: the dwellings of the Wautiers that we know of were in the central part of the city, within walking distance of the Coudenberg.[16]

ANDREA CANTELMO: A GENERAL AS AN ARTISTIC SUBJECT

In August 1642, the Dutch artist and poet Anna Roemer Visscher (1583–1651) went to Leuven to visit Erycius Puteanus (1574–1646), the successor of Justus Lipsius (1547–1606), a professor of Latin rhetoric. There, she happened to meet the artillery general Andrea Cantelmo, and wrote a poem about him in which she expressed her mixed feelings regarding this 'Spanish ghost': 'I cannot tell whether 't was truth or dream . . . And was it Mars I met? Not rough nor grim, irate / But excellently gentle, courteous, nearly staid? / Was it Cantelmo, he who never yields, / A friend of science, fearsome in the field?'[17] This talented woman was clearly impressed by the strong personality of this contemporary personification of the war god Mars, but simultaneously surprised by the courteous manner of the artillery general, who apparently was not only a famous adversary on the battlefield, but just as much 'a friend of science'.[18]

Wautier met Cantelmo in the same period and was possibly just as impressed by the general as Visscher. He was, in fact, the subject of the earliest known painting by Wautier, of which we only have an engraving made later by Paulus Pontius (see fig.8). Cantelmo was a formidable figure, the son of the Duke of Popoli, a Neapolitan artillery general in the service of the Spanish King. In 1632, he arrived in the Low Countries in charge of an Italian regiment, to defend the city of Maastricht. Afterwards, as general of the artillery (1637–9/1641–3) and the cavalry, he would achieve a number of military successes that led to his promotion to *maître de camp général* in 1643. He is thought to have been the first general to use exploding barrels or 'mines' on the battlefield. During the relief of Kallo on the night of 20 to 21 June 1638, one of the bloodiest battles of the Eighty and Thirty Years' Wars, he, in his capacity of artillery general, led the largest force.

Andrea Cantelmo was an active patron of the arts. To commemorate his victory in the Battle of Kallo, he commissioned a monumental work from the battle painter Peter Snayers (1592–1667), which depicts him as a commander in action.[19] The painting dates from the early 1640s, the period when Wautier painted the portrait on which Paulus Pontius based his engraving. In exactly the same period, Cantelmo was the client for a series of tapestries depicting *The Seven Liberal Arts*, the cartoons for which were ordered from the workshop of Cornelis Schut (1597–1655). Some of the cartoons for this series referred to war and strategy. In the representation of *Astrologia*, Cantelmo is pictured kneeling in armour.[20] In this period he therefore presented himself as an erudite art connoisseur looking for authoritative artists in both Brussels and Antwerp. But Brussels may well have been the focus of his endeavours. It is no coincidence that he placed the commission for the design of the tapestry cartoons with Cornelis Schut, the brother of Anna Schut, who was married to Peter Snayers and, as an intelligent, enterprising woman, kept Snayers's international network alive.[21]

Cantelmo and Wautier's portrait of him must have played a considerable part in launching her career. It also seems likely that the art-loving Italian commander took a considerable risk by commissioning his portrait from her, given that she was not yet well established as a painter. He may have seen earlier portraits by Wautier, which have not been preserved but which, if they existed, may have convinced him. The *portrait historié* of a family, in which the parents have been depicted as Isaac and Rebecca, possibly gives an idea of these early works (see fig.35).

As for a first meeting of Wautier and Cantelmo, since Wautier's brother Pierre (see fig.10) was promoted to cavalry captain in 1654, it is logical to suppose that he earlier occupied an officer's rank, that he met Cantelmo in that capacity, and that he introduced him to Michaelina. The engraving from the portrait bears the date of 1643, but the original may have been made before that. In July 1642, Cantelmo bivouacked with his army in Givet, where he was wounded in the leg and had to recuperate for a few days. On 28 July, he left Givet in the direction of Mons. Whether he visited the city itself is unknown. It is hardly likely that the general sat for a portrait in Givet. In that case, Wautier would have visited him in his army camp. While it is not impossible that he found time to pass through Mons and pose for her there, that does not answer the question as to what persuaded him to have his portrait done by her. Pierre Wautier may have vouched for his sister but, judging by the works she made that have been preserved and dated, her experience at the time was limited. The higher quality of the Cantelmo portrait, however, indicates that by then she had acquired some experience as a painter.[22] It is remarkable that at the beginning of her career, Wautier had already developed the skills necessary to depict male subjects as so energetic and virile.

Other factors may have played a role in Cantelmo's decision to commission a portrait from Wautier. If he had a special interest in artistic women, he may well have been following a family tradition. Margherita Cantelmo, one of Andrea's ancestors, was a Renaissance proto-feminist who, as a friend of Isabella d'Este, made a unique contribution to contemporary discourse on the position of women.[23] However it may be, the decision of this highly placed commander to have himself portrayed by Wautier must have made a huge difference for her. He doubtless took the portrait with him to Spain, where he died in 1645. We would expect the engraving from the portrait to take on a life of its own, but we cannot find any trace of it. Even worse, already in 1643, a 'pirated edition' appeared in which her signature 'Michaelina Wautier pinxit' had been shifted to the bottom right corner and was hardly perceptible. On a slightly later print, her name as the designer had been replaced by that of Coenraad Waumans as the maker ('Coenraad. Waumans fecit').[24] It not uncommon that the name of an unfamiliar designer who did not add any value gradually disappeared. That this occurred in the case of Wautier is telling. Not only was she not well known, she was also a woman, certainly an additional argument to elide her as the *pictor* to avoid gender bias in the marketing and purchase of the print. Such pirated editions were often made, but in the case of Wautier's portrait, the original engraving disappeared unusually quickly, which probably partly explains why there are only a few surviving examples of the version that bears her name.[25]

ADAM-PIERRE DE LA GRENÉ: A DANCE MASTER AS CLIENT

It is improbable that Andrea Cantelmo and Leopold Wilhelm knew one another personally, since the commander died as early as 1645. But the Archduke is likely to have been familiar with another early supporter of Wautier's work, the French dance master Adam-Pierre de La Grené (1625–1702). It is very well possible that Leopold Wilhelm himself brought De La Grené over from Paris to Brussels in 1649, to popularise the French *ballet de cour* much *en vogue* at the French court.[26] Given his position as a dance master, he played a crucial part in the numerous celebrations and parties at court. De La Grené kept a journal, a combination of an accounting report and a diary. This is a unique document and a good reflection of what went on at the seventeenth-century archducal court. Like a consummate bookkeeper, De La Grené recorded who was taking dancing lessons with him and what sum they had already paid. Thanks to his meticulousness, we know exactly who was living at court and who only visited for a few days. The list of De La Grené's pupils provided in the manuscript makes it immediately clear that Leopold Wilhelm's court was attractive to members of the whole European nobility. The son of the King of Denmark, the Duke of Bournonville, the Duke of Buckingham and 'les mesieurs baron de Breda' were as glad to be guests there as the Prince d'Arenberg or Mademoiselle d'Hovyne, virtually certainly the daughter of Charles d'Hovyne, the highest public servant in the Spanish Netherlands and a neighbour of the Wautiers. His mausoleum from 1671, made by Jan van Delen, is the most impressive to be preserved in the Church of Our Lady of the Chapel.[27]

De La Grené's journal provides important information about Michaelina and Charles Wautier (fig.14). For instance, on 17 January 1650, the author bought a Bacchus-themed painting by Michaelina for 15 guilders ('J'ay acheté de madamoiselle wautier 15 florins le 17 de Januier lan 1650 un baqus'; 'I have bought a Bacchus depiction by mademoiselle Wautier for 15 florins on 17 January 1650').[28] This work is no longer extant, but it is telling that De La Grené knew that it had been painted by a 'madamoiselle wautier'. Apart from Leopold Wilhelm and Cantelmo, De La Grené is the only collector known with certainty to have owned a painting by Wautier in her lifetime.[29] Whether De La Grené knew her personally remains to be established but must not be excluded, since the dance master was a crucial figure among the aristocratic and upper-middle-class circles in Brussels, where particularly her brother Charles had many contacts.[30] De La Grené's manuscript also indicates that he bought a 'portrait by Wautier' for 24 guilders ('J'ay acheté le portray de wautier 24 florins et la moulur 12 florins') and a depiction of the biblical figure of Nicodemus ('J'aij acheté le nicodème fait par M[o] Vautier 30 patacon et la moulur 9 florins').[31] Since he refers in the latter notation to 'Monsieur Wautier', this must have been a work by Charles. The interpretation of 'le portray de wautier' is more complicated. Did this concern a portrait made by one of the Wautiers or rather a portrait of a person called Wautier? The prices vary significantly and are not very high, apart from the Nicodemus painting, which was priced at approximately 87 guilders, and cost nearly 100 guilders including the frame.[32] On the other hand, their market value should not be underestimated. It is very important that De La Grené also entered the price for Michaelina's 'Bacchus' since this is the only mention of the value of a painting by her hand. Prices for paintings are a standard for the assessment of the works of an artist in their own lifetime, and thus are also socio-economically important.[33]

De La Grené is the only contemporary of Wautier who indicated the price of one of her paintings, but his diary is also proof that she sold her work. This situation was unusual, for there was a long tradition of women artists from the upper echelons who were supported by their family or husband and who never sold their artistic work. Rather, they donated it to prominent art enthusiasts, in the hope that they would spread the word about their talent. This mostly applies to amateurs rather than female painters with great expertise, but this kind of self-promotion had proved to be useful in the past, especially within the context of the court. The first generation of female artists in the Spanish Netherlands was proof of

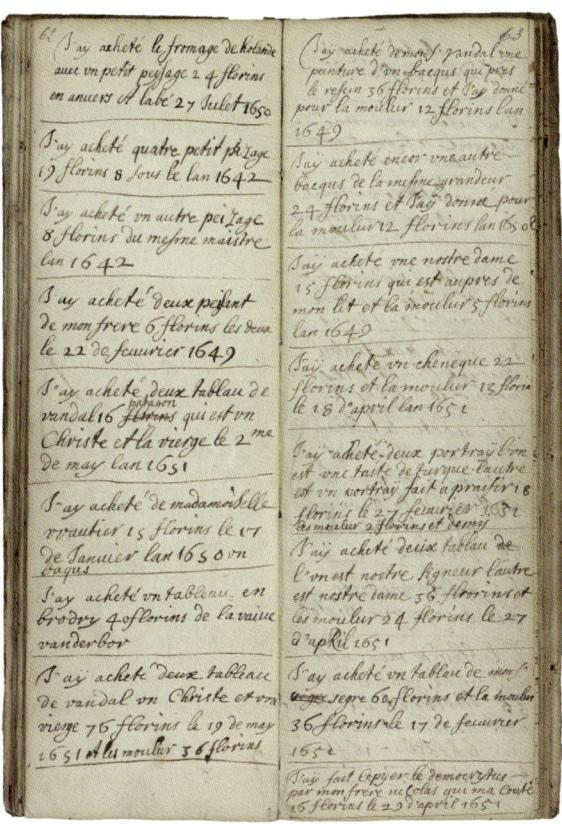

14 Account book of Adam-Pierre de La Grené, Dance Master at the Court of Archduke Leopold Wilhelm, c.1650, manuscript, 32.3 × 10.5 cm (12 ¾ × 4 ⅛ in), State Archives, Manuscript Collection, Brussels

this. Susanna Horenbout, Levina Teerlinck and to a lesser extent also Catharina van Hemessen were not paid per commission but were part of the entourage of the court as ladies-in-waiting. Anna Maria van Schurman, a learned woman from the lower nobility, was a prime example of the application of the humanist-inspired gift-giving culture. She handed out exclusive little portraits, cut-outs and calligraphed poems or added these to her correspondence to present herself, to extend her network or to personalise budding contacts (Chapter 4).

Leopold Wilhelm of Austria arrived in Brussels on 11 April 1647. His nephew, King Philip II of Spain, had appointed him as Governor of the Spanish Netherlands.[34] Leopold Wilhelm took up residence in Coudenberg Palace. His predecessors had been the Cardinal-Infante Ferdinand, who died in 1641, and Don Francisco de Melo and the Marquis Manuel de Castel Rodrigo, two Portuguese commanders who ruled for shorter periods in the service of the Spanish King. Leopold Wilhelm's *Joyeus Entry*, the official inauguration of the Prince, took place on 27 March 1648, in Antwerp.[35]

Like others in Brussels, Wautier must have known that the newly arrived Archduke had a reputation as an arts enthusiast. More than a year earlier, on 5 January 1646, a Brussels collector wrote to the Antwerp art dealer Matthys Musson with the news of Leopold Wilhelm's appointment, adding that he 'will help the love of the arts to flourish, as he is a lover of all curiosities and particularly of Italian art'.[36] On his way from Vienna, the Archduke bought tapestries and antiques and was elated with the ample supply available to him. Once in Brussels, he wrote of the abundance of paintings in Antwerp and that he planned to extend his collection with 'contemporary' art from the Low Countries.[37] In a letter of 4 January 1648, the court painter Jan van den Hoecke (1611–51), uncle of Musson, wrote to his nephew that the Archduke had told him personally that he would go to Antwerp to buy 'the most beautiful things that pleased him most, according to his own taste'.[38] Leopold Wilhelm attributed to himself the ability to select works of the finest quality. Indeed, during his time in the Spanish Netherlands, he assembled one of the most important collections of paintings in the early modern era.[39] He gathered 580 paintings from masters in the Dutch Republic and the German lands, 517 Italian works, 343 drawings and 542 sculptures. While staying in Brussels, he

collected Italian paintings from the Renaissance but bought even more that were made in the Low Countries, especially classically inspired history pieces and portraits. The way in which Leopold Wilhelm surrounded himself with paintings can be seen in the various depictions which he commissioned of himself, posing in his picture gallery, in the company of David Teniers II (1610–90), the supervisor of his collection, and other art connoisseurs (fig.15). In 1651, Teniers was appointed *ayuda da camera* (chamberlain) and painted Leopold Wilhelm's full-length portrait, for which the Governor posed in armour (fig.16).

We cannot know when the Archduke first heard or read the name of Michaelina Wautier, but we know that, at least by 1650, 'mademoiselle Wautier' was known to one of his courtiers. If an artistic dance master such as Adam-Pierre de La Grené knew who she was, it is obvious that, around that time, Leopold Wilhelm himself must also have been familiar with her name. Her brother Charles may have played a mediating role in this because of his reputation as a portraitist of the Brussels aristocracy, as will become clear later.

THE 1659 INVENTORY

On his return to Vienna, Leopold Wilhelm had a detailed inventory drawn up of all the works of art he had bought in the Low Countries, a list that included works by Michaelina Wautier. The inventory was compiled by the painter-chaplain Jan Anton van der Baren (1615/16–86), who had accompanied the Governor after he left Brussels. He finalised it in 1659.[40] In this inventory, all the works are meticulously described. The subject, the support, the dimensions, the nature of the frame – if any – were all recorded. And among these, three male saints are listed as original works by the hand of 'Magdalena Woutiers'. *Saint Joachim Holding a Book* (fig.17) is described as an 'Original von Jungfraw Magdalena Woutiers von Mons oder Berghen, Henegaw in Niderlandt' ('Original by Miss Magdalena Woutiers

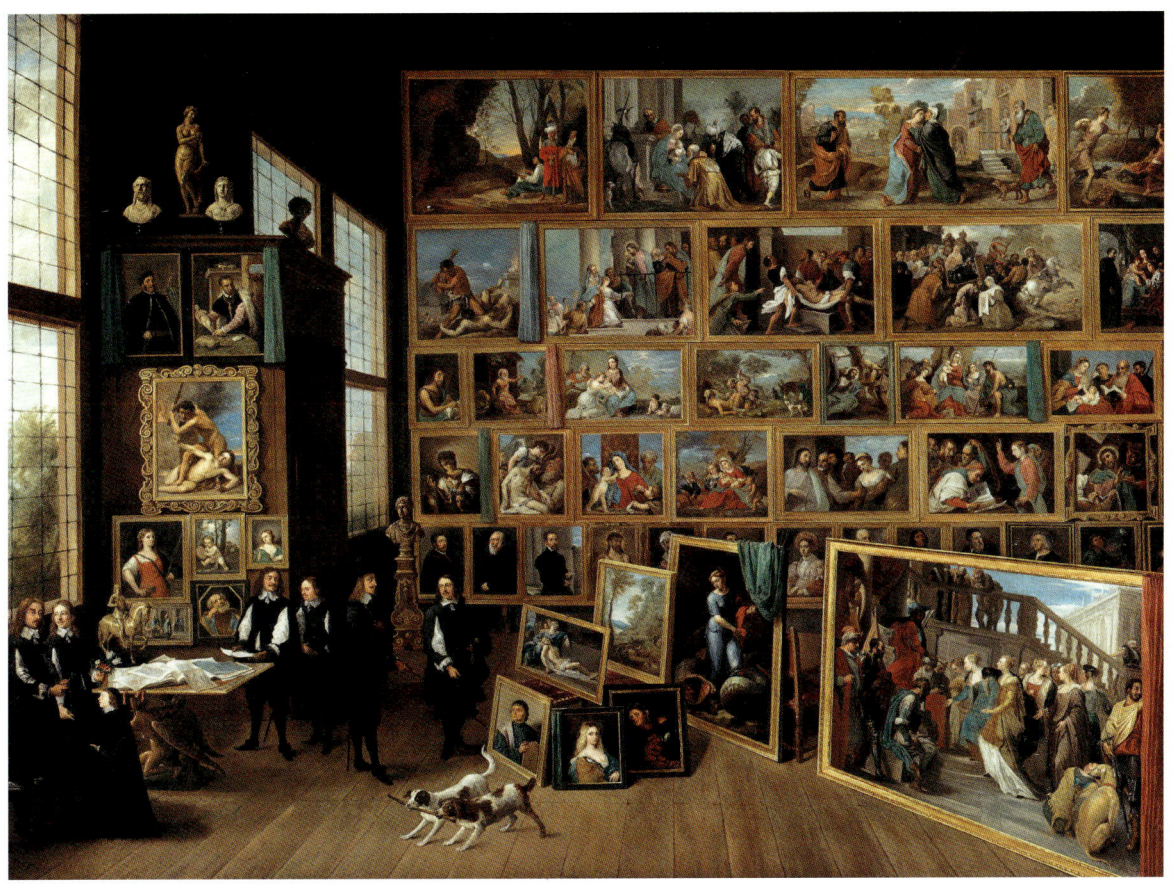

15 David Teniers II, *Archduke Leopold Wilhelm in His Gallery*, *c.*1650, oil on canvas, 124 × 165 cm (48 ⅞ × 64 in),
Kunsthistorisches Museum, Vienna

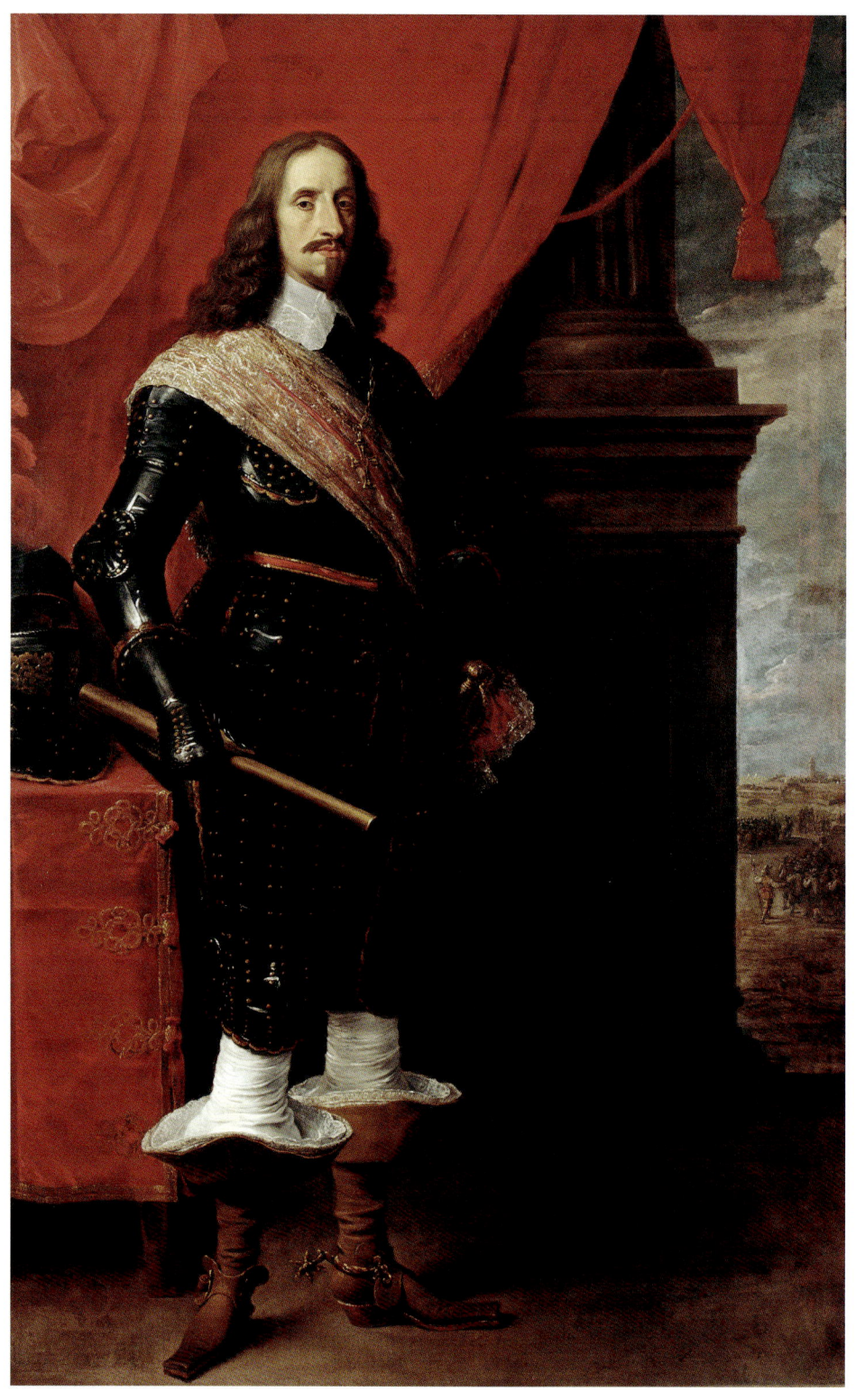

16 David Teniers II, *Portrait of Archduke Leopold Wilhelm in Harness*, *c.*1652, oil on canvas, 203.5 × 136 cm (80 ⅛ × 53 ½ in), Kunsthistorisches Museum, Vienna

from Mons or Bergen, Hainaut in the Spanish Netherlands'). Under no.87 is mentioned 'der heyl. Joseph' (*Saint Joseph*; fig.18) as an 'Original von der Jungfrawen Magdalena Woutiers'. Subsequently, under no.88, a second Saint Joachim (*Saint Joachim Reading a Book*; fig.19), no.75 in the list, is described as 'Original von Magdalena Woutiers'.[41] Additionally, a *Triumph of Bacchus* (see fig.63) is mentioned: 'Ein grosses Stuckh von Öhlfarb auff Leinwath, warin desz Bacchi Triumph. In einer schwarzen Ramen, hoch 14 Span 4 Finger und 20 Span 4 Finger braidt. Original von N. Woutiers' ('A large piece, oil on canvas, on which the triumph of Bacchus. In a black frame, 14 span and 4 fingers in height and 20 span and 4 fingers in breadth. Original by N. Woutiers').[42]

This contemporary information is an important source of knowledge about Wautier. She is described as a *jungfraw* (maiden) from Mons in Hainaut in the Spanish Netherlands.[43] This is the only known documentary reference to her origins. Once again, 'Woutiers' is given as her family name. Her first name is harder to interpret. As related in Chapter 1, Wautier had a sister called Marie Magdelaine who was born in 1604. The inventory implies that Michaelina's sister was the maker of these three paintings. In that case, there would have been three painters in the Wautier family: Marie Magdelaine, Charles and Michaelina, which would be highly unlikely. Moreover, there are no known paintings with the signature '[Maria] Magdalena Woutiers'. The only possible conclusion is that the name in the inventory of Leopold Wilhelm's collection must be erroneous. The compiler of the inventory entered an incorrect name by mixing up two names that were similar in both spelling and pronunciation.

Still, the question remains how it was possible that Michaelina's first name was not sufficiently known. Was this because the name '[Maria] Magdalena' occurred much more often in seventeenth-century Brussels and was thus more easily recognisable? It is more probable that these first names were hardly ever used in everyday life and that Wautier was usually referred to as 'Mademoiselle Wautier'. Dance master De La Grené also described the painter as 'Mademoiselle Wautier'. That an error had slipped into the inventory – and that it was recognised as such – is borne out by a label on the back of the painting of Saint Joachim with the book under his arm, in the Kunsthistorisches Museum in Vienna. In black paint, it is written: 'Michelline Wovteers'. This label itself is of a later date and very probably goes back to a note on the back of the original canvas. On recanvassing the painting, the old label must have been copied onto the new one, as was done with several other paintings from the Governor's collection.[44] It is hardly likely that the label in black paint is a transcription of a signature.[45] Wautier always signed on the front of the canvas and never used any other kind of signature. The spelling 'Michelline' is very important because it can be read as a francophone form of 'Michaelina' and thus more closely resembles the Latinate form she used as her signature. Therefore, it appears that the name in black paint on the back of the painting was intended as a correction to the inventory, in which the paintings were assigned to 'Magdalena Woutiers'. The variant 'Michelline' also corresponds to the way contemporary notarial sources refer to her, that is to say as 'Michelle' or the Dutch version thereof: 'Michielle'.[46] We do not currently know who made this correction on the back of *Saint Joachim Holding a Book*, and when.[47] It must at least have been someone who knew that Michaelina was the artist, and not 'Magdalena'. It is surprising that this person spelled her name 'Michelline' rather than 'Michaelina', giving rise to the suspicion that they were not familiar with the signatures on the paintings, which were always the same: 'Michaelina Wautier'. The spelling of her family name 'Wovteers' shows that this name occurred in many variations. In itself, this is not exceptional in the seventeenth century, when names did not have a fixed orthography, but in this case, the number of variants is very large: Wauthier, Wouteers, Wouters, Wauther, Votier and Vautier all occur.[48]

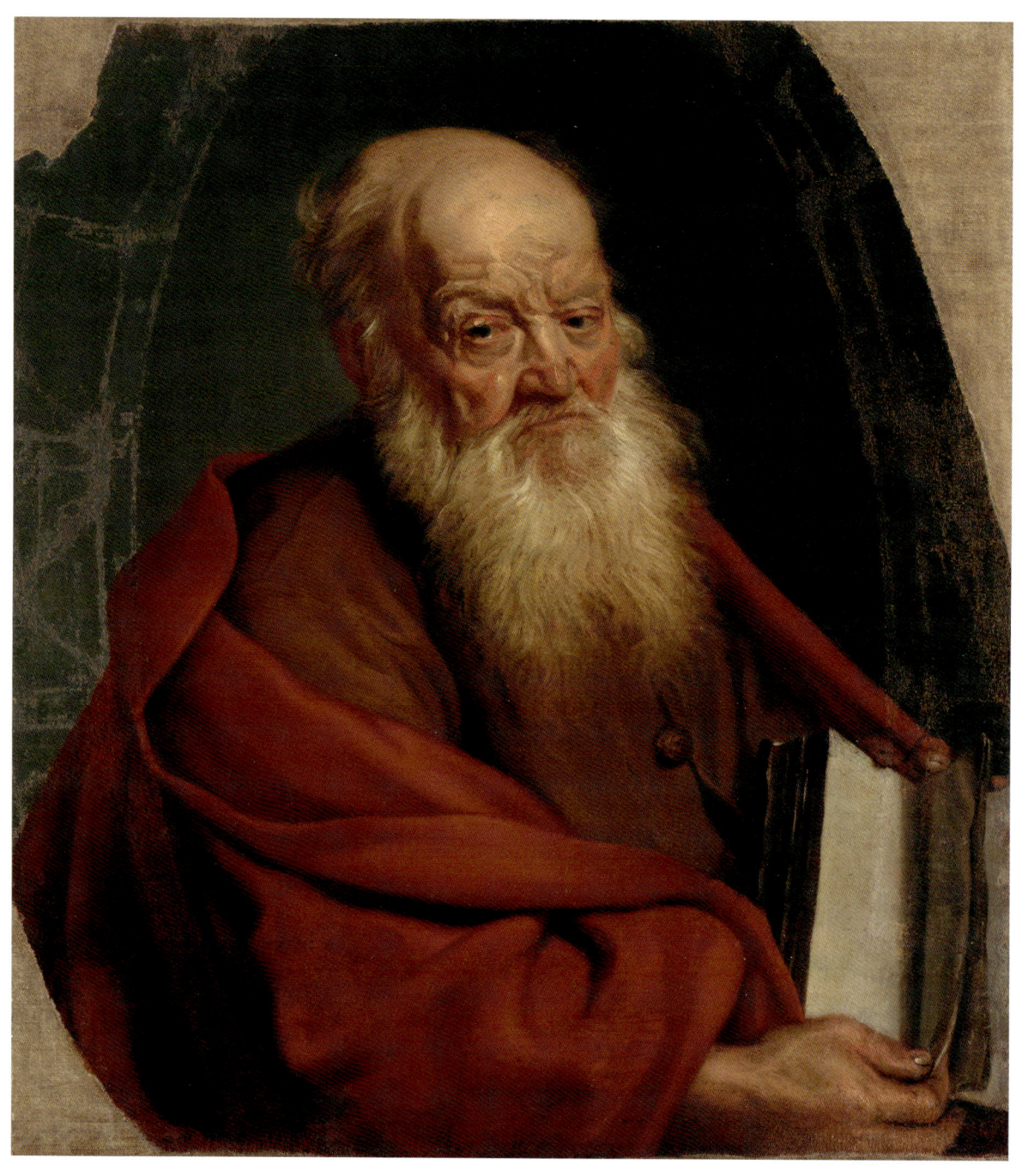

17 Michaelina Wautier, *Saint Joachim Holding a Book*, c.1655, oil on canvas, 76 × 66 cm (29 ⅞ × 25 in), Kunsthistorisches Museum, Vienna

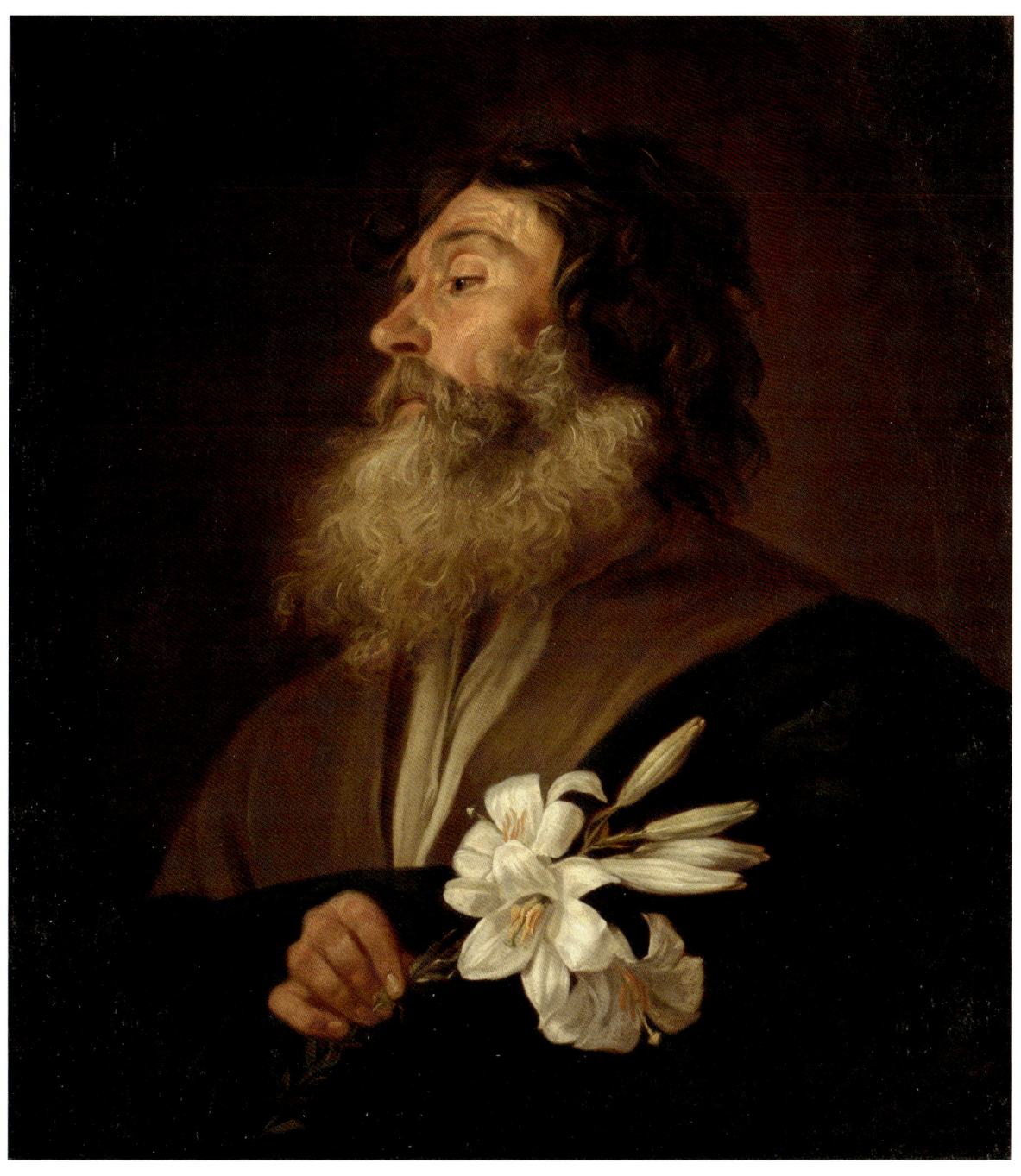

18 Michaelina Wautier, *Saint Joseph*, c.1655, oil on canvas, 76 × 66 cm (29 ⅞ × 25 in), Kunsthistorisches Museum, Vienna

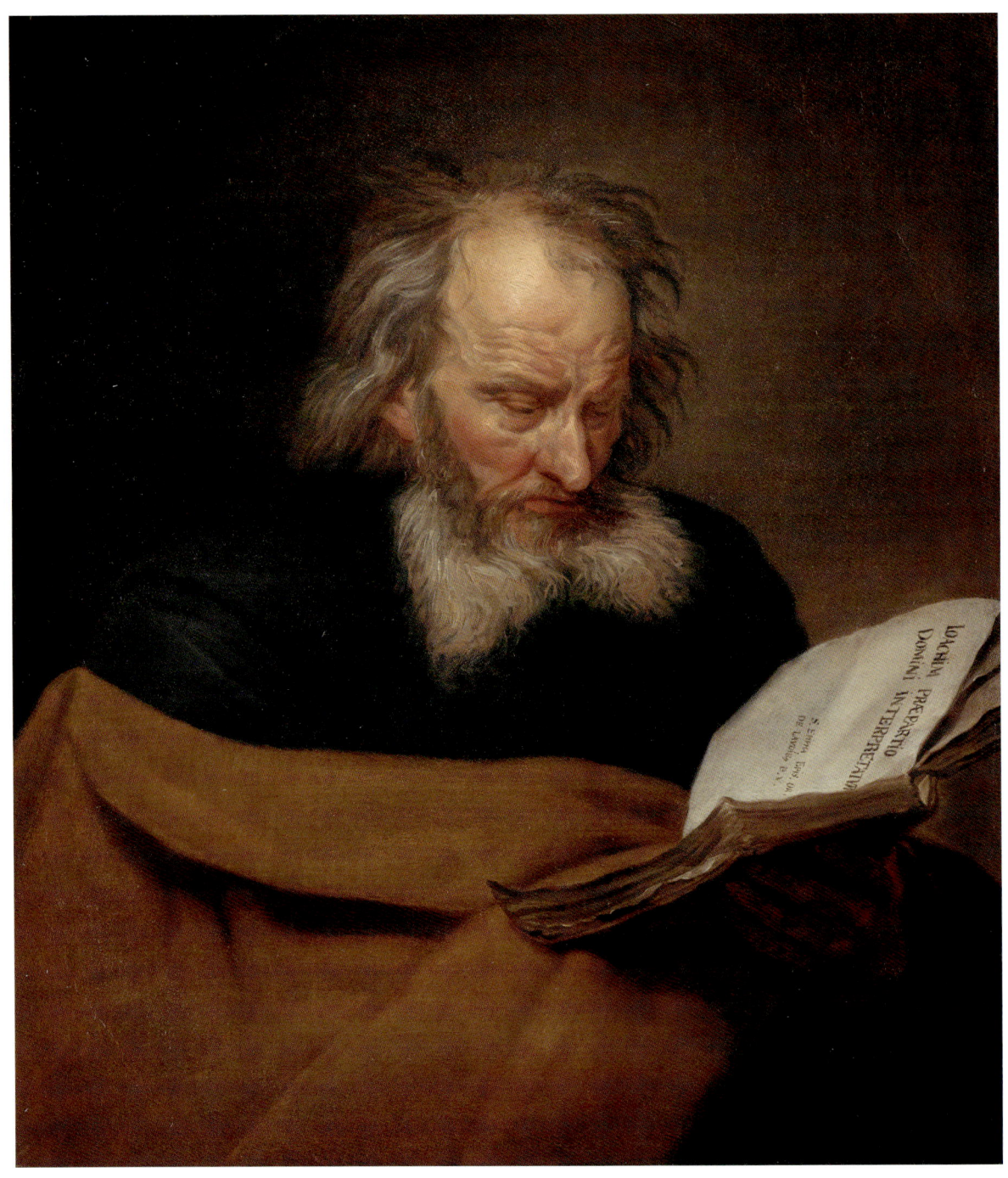

19 Michaelina Wautier, *Saint Joachim Reading*, c.1655, oil on canvas, 76 × 66 cm (29 ⅞ × 25 in), Kunsthistorisches Museum, Vienna

With this in mind, it can hardly surprise us that both first and family names have led to confusion in the attributions. That even in 1660, 'Magdalena' was maintained as the author of the paintings, also appears in another source. In that year, the already mentioned David Teniers, by order of Leopold Wilhelm, published a catalogue of the Archduke's collection under the title *Theatrum Pictorium*.[49] This deluxe folio publication features 234 engravings of paintings that the Governor had in his possession; it concerns predominantly prints based on Italian works. However, at the beginning of the book, there is an alphabetical list of 180 names of painters from the Low Countries whose works he owned. The name 'Woutiers' occurs twice, the first time under 'M' with a reference to 'Magdalena Woutiers' and the second time under the letter 'W'. There is no first name with the family name; it has been replaced with two hyphens: '- - Woutiers'.[50]

A PAINTING WITH 'A VERY STRONG, ALMOST CRUDE CONCEPTION' CANNOT BE BY A WOMAN

What does this mean and to what painting does it refer? When we look at the reference '- - Woutiers' in the 1659 inventory of Archduke Leopold Wilhelm's collection, we come to the fourth painting in his possession that is assumed to be by Wautier. Apart from the three saints, a *Triumph of Bacchus* is registered: 'Ein grosses Stuckh . . . warin desz Bacchi Triumph . . . Original von N. Woutiers' ('A large work depicting the Triumph of Bacchus. Original by N. Wautier'). Apparently, there was some uncertainty about the attribution of this monumental painting, for an 'N' was entered instead of a first name. The reason for this approach is not known.[51] Possibly, the maker of the inventory could not believe that a painting of such scale and such quality was made by a woman. Even in 1933, Gustav Glück, the famous connoisseur of seventeenth-century art and the director of the Gemäldegalerie in the Kunsthistorisches Museum

in Vienna, wrote that, even 'in a time of women's emancipation', as he characterised his own time, it was hard to associate a painting 'which shows a very strong, almost crude conception' with a woman. His successor, Günther Heinz, was the first to analyse thoroughly the 1659 inventory and to study the paintings associated with the name 'Woutiers'. In a groundbreaking article about Jan van den Hoecke and a number of other painters whose work was in the possession of Leopold Wilhelm, he noticed that no one had ever dared to think that the 'Bacchus procession' could be the work of Michaelina Wautier because of the size and the virtuoso execution. For Heinz, there was no doubt about the attribution. He recognised without any hesitation the same hand in all four paintings and came to the conclusion that a number of prejudices concerning the artistic capabilities of women had played a part.[52] The attribution of the painting to Charles Wautier, which has been proposed several times, would have offered no solution. No paintings by him feature in the 1659 inventory. He did paint a life-size portrait of Leopold Wilhelm, which bears the signature 'C. Wautier'. The Archduke himself did not commission it, but Johann Adolf von Schwarzenberg, his chamberlain-in-chief. Already in 1656, it had been registered in the inventory of the latter's collection,[53] which implies that Charles Wautier met the Archduke personally before that date. During Leopold Wilhelm's reign as Governor, Charles made dozens of portraits of courtiers, published as prints.[54]

Leopold Wilhelm admired the paintings of Michaelina Wautier highly enough to acquire four works by her hand for his collection. Of all the paintings he bought himself, hers are the only works by a woman. It is hard to draw any conclusions about the nature of the relationship between them. It is possible that the Governor purchased these four works directly from her, as the dance master De La Grené had done in 1650. In the case of the three depictions of saints, which were an easy fit in any interior, this may well have been the case. But the *Triumph of Bacchus* (see fig.63) is different. The unusual theme and the size of the painting make it impossible for Wautier to have painted it on her own initiative: it must have been very expensive and a great risk to paint on speculation. In my opinion, it is unlikely that another client had anything to do with the project since it appears in the 1659 inventory (see Chapter 5). Did Leopold Wilhelm and Wautier know each other personally? Had he met her brother Charles but did he find him a less interesting artist because he, around 1650, was mostly known as a portraitist, as appears from Florent du Rieu's poem of 1658: 'Pour Wautier, Peintre en Portrait dans la ville de Bruxelle' ('To Wautier, Painter of Portraits in the City of Brussels')?[55] The extent of Charles's contacts with the nobles at the Brussels court[56] makes it virtually impossible that the Governor was not familiar with him. Did Leopold Wilhelm get to know Wautier via her brother or did members of the court point out her exceptional talents to him? Even then, the question bears repeating why he, like some of his predecessors, bought work by a female painter. Was it because of their curiosity value or because he was truly impressed by their exceptional artistic merit?

DEVOTION, ART AND OPERA

What could have inspired Wautier to undertake such an ambitious painting as the *Triumph of Bacchus* (see fig.63)? To contextualise the worldly atmosphere and interest in profane festivities at the Brussels court, it is important to be aware that Leopold Wilhelm's passion for the visual arts was just one facet of his personality. Eight years after his death, a biography appeared which describes him as 'un prince dévôt et guerrier' ('a devout prince and commander') and in which his religious convictions, his pious life and the role in it of the Jesuits are expounded.[57] Music also played a huge part in the Archduke's daily life. For his private music ensemble, called the *musica da camera*, he had engaged the best musicians from Vienna and Italy. Religious feasts and church services in the court chapel, and also in other Brussels churches and monasteries, were graced with this ensemble and celebrated with processions. For the Governor, this was a way to put the Counter-Reformation into practice and to establish himself as a devout benefactor. At the court itself, he spent even more resources on the practice of profane music. To this aim, the genre of opera was especially suitable.[58] In 1650, the first *grand opéra à machines* was performed, *Ulisse all'isola di Circe*. The first performance on 24 February was of great historical significance, since it was the first time an 'opera' was performed in the Spanish Netherlands. The Archduke commissioned the libretto from the Italian poet Ascanio Amalteo, and his court composer Giuseppe Zamponi supplied the music. The Venetian choreographer Balbi staged the interludes, conceived as a *ballet du monde*. The performance was played against seven different backgrounds in which the carriages of Neptune and Venus, and Odysseus's ship, moved across the boards and Jove's eagle descended from the clouds. At the end of the prologue, Bacchus entered the scene, followed by Thetis and Saturn. In 1651, a book was published in Paris about the *Ballet du Roy aux festes de Bacchus*, which Louis XIV performed at the age of 12, on 2 May 1651.[59] To the printed book, which is preserved at the Bibliothèque nationale de France, coloured drawings were added and in one of these illustrations, a dancing bacchant(e) was featured, adorned with vine branches and with a tambourine in hand (fig.20). The pictures, enhanced with watercolours, give an impression of the participants' costumes. The presence of mythological figures in both the *grand opéra* and the *Ballet du Roy* indicates a familiarity among courtiers with these profane narratives and shows that Bacchus, as the god of wine and entertainment, played a central part in their imagination. When Queen Christina of Sweden arrived in Brussels in December 1654,[60] she expressed a desire to attend 'la rare et magnifique comedie chantée' ('the unique and magnificent sung comedy'). Leopold Wilhelm made sure that the theatre and the moving scenery were updated and, at the beginning of February 1655, the opera was performed for a second time. To facilitate the performance, 'un grand Theatre' ('a large theatre') was installed 'sur la grande sale de la Cour' ('in the big hall of the court'). It is unknown whether Wautier witnessed these performances, but the purveyor of the court, Francisco Alonso Lozano, mentions that this performance was attended not only by the nobility but also by the Brussels magistrates 'et plus bas les comuns, gens de distinctions' ('and lower down, citizens of distinction').[61] The performance of 1650 was concluded with a grand gala, when 'un cavalier venoit prendre une Dame pour Danser, et puis elle un Cavalier' ('a gentleman invited a lady to dance, and then she [invited] a gentleman'), a significant remark about the progressive gender patterns governing the entertainment at court.[62]

The exuberant yet sophisticated entertainment culture, characteristic of the Archduke's reign, may have been an excellent inspiration for ordering paintings with mythological subject matter. One could ask whether Wautier was inspired by these lively stagings, including those involving the figure of Bacchus, and the opera may have given Leopold Wilhelm ideas for commissioning a bacchanalia painting, assuming that he himself was the client for the *Triumph of Bacchus*. In fact, it seems that the Governor regularly discussed matters of the arts with visitors to the court. For example, a few days before his return to Vienna, he was visited by the Dutch poet-diplomat Constantijn Huygens, who needed to arrange some business matters at the Brussels court but who also, as a musician and a composer, fully enjoyed the sublime music to be heard there. He described his visit with Leopold Wilhelm as an informal meeting. Between the music, the Archduke addressed him two or three times and was pleased to see how impressed his guest was by the music performed.[63] Huygens's report tells us much about Leopold Wilhelm's fascination with music and, even more importantly, the informal manner in which one

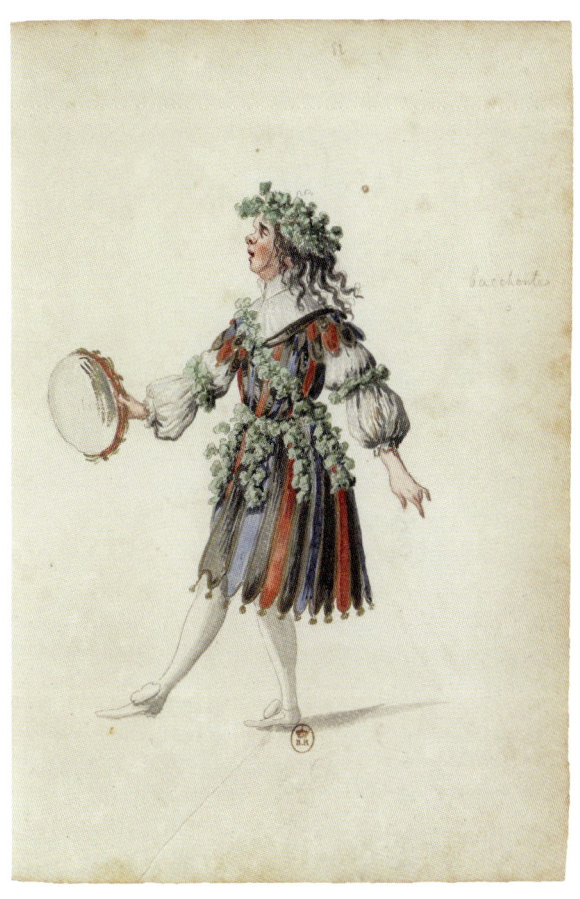

20 'Bacchante', in *Ballet du Roy aux festes de Bacchus, dansé par sa Majesté au Palais Royal, le 2ième jour de May 1651*, R. Ballard, Paris, 1651, 33.4 × 22.1 cm (13 ⅛ × 8 ¾ in), Bibliothèque nationale de France, Paris

could have access to his immediate circle at court. This raises the possibility that similar communications took place regarding paintings. The Governor was not only the untouchable 'prince dévôt et guerrier', but also a passionate collector and music lover who appreciated sharing his experiences with 'kindred spirits'. It is possible that Wautier was among those with whom he communicated his interest in bacchanalia, resulting in the commission of the painting by her in his collection.

3

Charles as the Elder Brother

There can be no doubt that Michaelina Wautier's older brother Charles was important to the advancement of her career as a painter. As the sources reveal, he was her faithful *compagnon de route*. As a painter in Brussels, he provided Michaelina with ongoing support as an artist, including providing studio space and facilitating advantageous connections with important figures in the art world. A certain reciprocity marks their history, however, for in an unusual reversal of gender norms, the recent interest in Michaelina and her work has prompted a recovery and re-evaluation of Charles's oeuvre.

As noted above, no painters were among the ancestors of Michaelina and Charles, so that the choice to become an artist was far from obvious for the Wautier siblings. This may have had consequences for Charles in the age at which he began his training as an apprentice. He would naturally have started looking for opportunities in his hometown. But in Mons, there are no known artists for this period. A possible connection for painterly activity there can be found in the biography of the painter Philippe de Champaigne (1602–74), who would later gain fame in Paris. He was born and educated in Brussels, but some sources claim that, before he departed from the Spanish Netherlands in 1619, at the age of 17, he was the apprentice to a painter in Mons.[1] The name of his master has not come down to us, but the fact that De Champaigne moved from Brussels to Mons supports the assumption that he must have been an artist of some note. It is natural to assume that Charles initially went to school in Mons, for instance, in line with the intellectual orientation of the Wautier family, at the Jesuit College there.[2]

To appreciate their artistic influences, it is important to consider the nature of the artworks the brother and sister were exposed to growing up in Mons.[3] Only recently, it has been pointed out that, as early as the 1630s, the no longer extant Jesuit church held three paintings representative of the then prevalent Italianate school from Antwerp. All three testify to the influence of Caravaggio (1571–1610), whose style the painters had seen in Rome. Two of the paintings are *Saint Francis Xavier Performing Communion in the Far East* (1630s), by Cornelis Schut, and *Christ Appearing to Saint Ignatius* (*c.*1630–35), which was attributed to Gerard Seghers (1591–1651) but no longer exists. On the high altar, doubtlessly the most influential of the three, the *Elevation of the Cross* (*c.*1623) by Abraham Janssens (1575–1632) was displayed; it is now preserved in the Saint Waltrude Collegiate Church in Mons.[4] These three paintings were surely acquired by the Jesuits while both Charles and Michaelina were still living in Mons, and they must have made a deep impression on them. It is possible that the dramatic visual language of these paintings persuaded them to go to Italy, the cradle of this sculptural and emotional Baroque style, characterised by dramatic chiaroscuro. Just outside the city of Mons was the Chapel of Our Lady of Goodwill, adorned with the *Assumption of the Virgin* (1631) by Anna Francisca de Bruyns. This painting, the only known altarpiece by a woman's hand in the early modern Low Countries, will certainly also have caught Michaelina's attention.[5]

A RESILIENT FOREIGNER IN BRUSSELS

Where did Charles think he might find the opportunities to start or finish his training? When did he leave Mons? Sadly, in this regard, we know nothing. The connection to Mons remained, since on 4 September 1642, Charles paid his *poortersrecht* (citizenship tax) in Mons, for the period of two years.[6] At that time, he was still registered in the Rue d'Havré, but that does not mean that he had actually lived in Mons during the preceding years.[7] There is a gap of at least ten years in his biography. In this period, Charles was between 20 and 30 years old and his younger sister was between 15 and 25. What country, what city may have attracted him? Not yet Brussels, since he would settle there only later. A document from 1651, which will be discussed below, states that he had 'buytens lants gheleert'; that he had received training abroad.[8] For any ambitious artist – who moreover had an intellectual background – Italy was the cradle of the Renaissance and the inspiration for contemporary art. Research for the Wautier exhibition at the Kunsthistorisches Museum in Vienna has yielded several clues which make it more probable, but by no means certain, that she did indeed travel to Italy.[9] It would not have been feasible for her to travel there alone but this does not preclude the possibility that she travelled in the company of other artists or companions. The fact that women were permitted to travel in a group is supported by a notarial deed of 11 May 1685 in which Marie Jeanne Françoise Wautier's father granted Jacques Bartolomé,

Count of Strasoldo, permission to have his daughter accompany the Count on his journey to Italy as 'dame d'honneur pour servir sa compagne' ('lady-in-waiting to serve her companion').[10] If Michaelina had wished to travel to Italy, the company of her brother Charles, who could serve as a chaperon, would have made the journey possible. Given his age, born in 1609, his sojourn abroad could be situated somewhere in the years 1625/30–1635/40. It seems unlikely that Michaelina would make the trip before she was 20. This suggests that if Charles and Michaelina crossed the Alps together, they did so between 1635 and 1640. Such a journey would be rather hazardous and could be made on horseback, by (stage) coach and partly across water.[11] In any case, it must have been an adventurous undertaking.

In 1642, by whatever route, Charles had arrived in Brussels, for that year he rented a house in the Gasthuisstraat, in the prestigious Court District, within walking distance of Coudenberg Palace.[12] His residence there is confirmed by a demand note he received on 15 December 1642 from the Brussels Guild of Painters, Goldsmiths and Glass-Blowers. This is the first occasion he is referred to as 'a painter': 'verscheyden vreemdelingen schilderen zonder te weesen poorteren oft meesters: eenen jonckman van Bergen in Henegouwen genoempt N. Woutier wonende in de Gasthuysstraete tegen over den Arent' ('several strangers are painting without being registered as citizens of the city of Brussels or masters of the guild: a young man from Mons called N. Woutier, who lives in the Gasthuisstraat opposite the house called the Eagle'). Charles Wautier therefore had not registered as a *poorter* (citizen). Even worse, he had also neglected registering as a painter with the guild. Registering as a *poorter* and as a painter required that he pay a considerable sum. Charles refused to comply with the registration requirement, for five months later, he was, together with three other painters, again reprimanded for not having paid the dues: 'M[onsieur]: Wautier, Item Peeter François, Item Jacques Boesdonck[13] ende Jaspar vanden Bemde' should act according to the rules of the trade. As long as they were not registered as *poorters* and with the guild, they could not execute their trade.[14] The regulations of the trade were once again confirmed on 11 October 1647 and on that occasion as well, Charles Wautier is explicitly mentioned as an offender. It seems he was not concerned, since four more years passed before he fulfilled this obligation. He registered on 14 March 1651: 'ontfanghen als meester monsieur Wauti buytens lants gheleert ende heeft betaeylt de rechten van het ambacht over vyf jaer . . .' ('admitted to the guild as a Master, Mr Wauti, who has been trained abroad'). Added in the margin is: 'gheboren tot berghen henegau' ('born in Mons, in Hainaut').[15] Charles never did register as a *poorter* of Brussels. Returning to the first reference to Charles in the guild registers, it is striking that Michaelina's brother is described as 'N. Woutier'. Surprisingly, the initial 'N' also appears in Leopold Wilhem's inventory of 1659 as discussed in Chapter 2. Furthermore, Charles is mentioned again in 1770 as 'N. Woutier', the painter of a Crucifixion in Mechelen. As many aspects of the biographies of the Wautier siblings are still unresolved, the reason for the replacement of the initial 'C' by 'N' remains another mystery.[16]

Two aspects of the document of 1651 are noteworthy. First, Charles Wautier is respectfully described as 'Monsieur' and, second, his training abroad and origin in Mons in Hainaut are emphasised.[17] He paid his dues to the guild for the preceding period of five years, which is to say the for period from 1646 to 1651. Does this mean that he was abroad between 1646 and 1651 and therefore had to pay five years of back duties on his return? It is more likely that the amount he had to pay was a lump sum, to compensate for his negligence. The guild was obviously eager to resolve the situation and turned a blind eye to his resistance, for Charles Wautier was a 'Monsieur' who had trained abroad and doubtlessly contributed to the prestige of the Brussels guild. Around 1650, he painted several portraits of

nobles connected to the Brussels court. This will have provided him with a protection of sorts when it came to the enforcement of guild membership.[18]

ONE OF THE 'MASTERS' OF THE BRUSSELS BAROQUE

Charles's oeuvre is characterised by both Caravaggesque and classicist traits. These may, of course, have reached him via other channels than a journey to Rome. Italian paintings and prints circulated widely in the Spanish Netherlands and were popular collectables. The collection of Archduke Leopold Wilhelm offered a rich sampling of works from the Italian Renaissance. In addition, from 4 to 15 May 1635, the collection of Anne de Croÿ, widow of Charles van Arenberg, was brought under the hammer in Mons. The auction had 520 lots. At that moment, both Charles and Michaelina were still living in the city, and were 26 and about 21 years old.[19] Given their artistic ambitions and their social position in town, they may have heard about the auction and may have visited the collection of goods to be sold.[20] Furthermore, Charles's expressive style, and also Michaelina's which will be discussed later on, has many similarities with that of the Spanish-Netherlandish Caravaggisti painter Theodoor van Loon (1581/2–1649). Van Loon was a Brussels artist who lived in Rome from 1602 to 1608 and again in the 1620s for two years, a sojourn from which he returned in 1629. In Brussels, he was, next to Gaspar de Crayer (1584–1669), the pre-eminent painter. He developed his own visual language, with volumetric figures wrapped in loose garments, subtle human expressions and the use of chiaroscuro effects.[21]

The iconography of Charles's oeuvre is varied.[22] He predominantly painted portraits but also religious scenes and, now and then, a mythological or allegorical painting. The completely atypical *Allegory of the Triumph of Wisdom* recently appeared on the market. This fully signed painting is dated 1678 and bears the Latin inscription: 'Sapientia fulget / (Imperiis); latet ignorantia vilis. Carolus Wautier fecit 1678' ('The wisdom of a prince operates in the light; ignorance lies in darkness. Charles Wautier made this 1678'). The iconography and execution differ greatly from the rest of his oeuvre. It was most probably commissioned by a humanist patron who preferred the classicist, French-oriented style. As far as we know, it is the only occasion on which he signed with his full name in a Latinised form.[23] The flower still lifes and the genre paintings that were so very important for Michaelina are almost completely absent from Charles's output. Only one genre painting by Charles is known: a portrait of a boy with a pipe. The small canvas is signed and dated in the upper right corner: 'C. Wautier 166[?]'. Based on the theme, it could be part of a series depicting the Five Senses, comparable but inferior to Michaelina's ensemble (see figs 39–43).[24] The fact that it was made in the 1660s may suggest that Charles wanted to emulate his sister's successful formula. The quality of his paintings varies sharply and only in his best works does his style closely resemble that of his sister. His paintings are thematically more limited and 'they lack the introspective depth that gives Michaelina's art its distinctive flavour'.[25]

Little is known of Charles's early oeuvre. His first known and dated work is a portrait bearing the monogram 'CW' and the date 1650. This does not mean that he had not been active as a painter before that, since he did not always date his paintings. His last dated work is from 1685, which means that his career spanned at least 35 years. Michaelina's dated paintings are from the years 1643 to 1659, surprisingly a period of only 16 years.

Probably during the late 1640s and the beginning of the 1650s, Charles was first and foremost a portraitist with a preference for aristocratic models, mostly from the Hainaut region or from the entourage of the Brussels court, some of whom also followed dancing lessons with dance master Pierre-Adam de La Grené.[26] Many of these portraits were

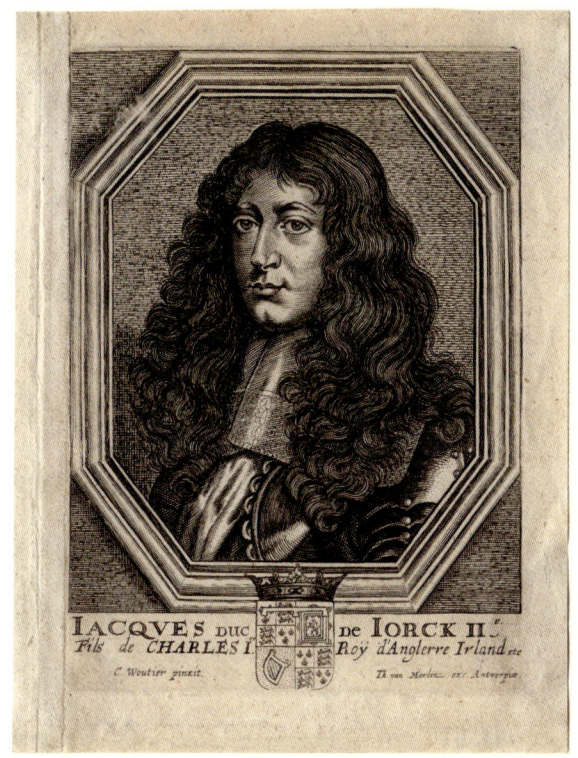

21 Theodoor van Merlen II after Charles Wautier, *c.*1655, *Portrait of the Duke of York, later James II*, engraving, 16.3 × 11.6 cm (6 ⅜ × 4 ⅝ in), National Portrait Gallery, London

also published as prints, such as those of Isabella van Arenberg or Eugène de Berghes. Such a print also exists of the portrait of James, Duke of York, and later King James II (fig.21).[27] Interestingly, all of the engravings for the prints were made by Antwerp engravers, which points to Charles's contacts in the most important city of the Flemish Baroque.[28] Even though most of these portraits are traditional busts that do not seem inventive, Charles enjoyed an international reputation, as is apparent from two letters mentioning these portraits. In 1653, Daniël Conrad wrote a request to Matthys Musson, the art dealer who already in 1646 anticipated the appointment of Leopold Wilhelm (see Chapter 2).[29]

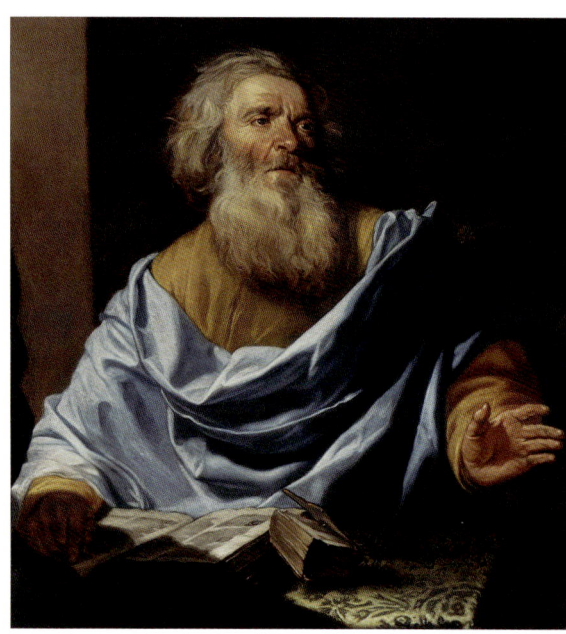

22 Charles Wautier, *Prophet*, 1652, oil on canvas, 100 × 92 cm (39 ⅜ × 36 ¼ in), signed and dated: 'c. WAVTIER F / 1652', Musée des Beaux-Arts, Cambrai

In Brussels, Musson should ask 'Monsieur Votier, schilder aldaer' ('Monsieur Votier, painter there') to forward to Amsterdam 'de conterfeijtsels' ('the paintings') intended for Prince Radziwill (possibly meaning the Polish Prince Bogusław Radziwiłł (1620–69)).[30] Even more interesting is Charles Wautier's own letter of 8 August 1668, which he sent, together with a portrait, in a chest to the Antwerp art dealer Henri François Schilders. He had made the portrait by order of the Prince of Tuscany, later Grand Duke Cosimo III de Medici. This no doubt concerned a portrait of the client himself.[31] These paintings, and the engravings made from them, carrying his name, followed by 'pinxit' or 'delineavit', spread his fame in the highest circles.

It seems that in the period from 1650 to 1655, Charles painted mostly half-length portraits or single figures that are striking in their individualised physiognomy. Characteristic examples are *Prophet*, with its dynamic, diagonal position in the field, fully signed and dated to 1652 (fig.22), and *Bacchus* (fig.23), in which the young, naked Bacchus impresses with his melancholically inclined head crowned with vines and his torso painted from life. Also on this latter work, the signature is clearly visible: 'c. WAUTIER', the initial 'C' followed by the name in capitals, as opposed to that of his sister, who systematically wrote her name in cursive with her full first name: 'Michaelina Wautier'.

After 1655, Charles specialised in religious paintings in addition to portraits. A beautiful and very decorative example is *Christ among the Pharisees* (fig.24), dating from *c.*1650–65. It is a colourful and expressive scene with splendid, distinctive heads. The young, vulnerable Jesus sharply contrasts with the obtrusive scribes by way of an ingeniously executed chiaroscuro. The psychological interaction is both sophisticated and bold. It is one of the few paintings in which Michaelina's influence can clearly be seen. The palpable intimacy here is lacking in the larger altarpieces, which Charles would paint from the beginning of the 1660s until the 1680s. The canvas with the painting of Saint Eligius, signed and dated 1659, in the Church of Saint-Servais in Gimnée, is a typical example of his monumental altarpieces.[32] The use of light reveals a Caravaggesque approach that would have struck a contemporary viewer as slightly old-fashioned.[33] Indeed, Charles seems not to have established great fame in this genre. There is hardly any information about the provenance of these paintings, but they are not from the most prominent churches. They are composed according to the same principle, with one or several monumental figures in the foreground, dominating the scene. Locally, however, Charles remained in demand as a history painter. Even in 1685, when he was 76 years old, he received a commission from the chapter of Saint Peter's Church in Leuven for a painting, destined for the high altar, of Jesus handing over the keys of

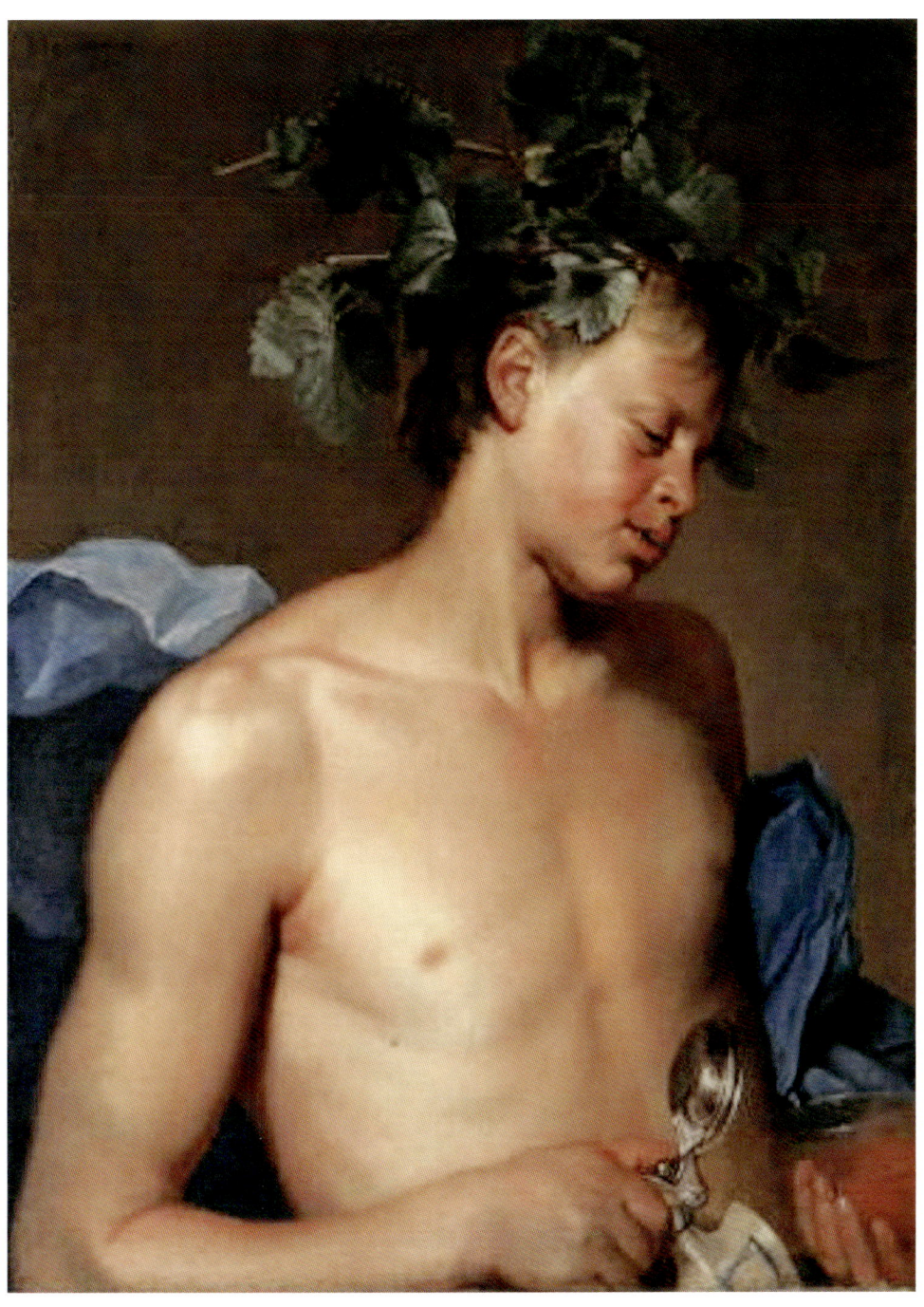

23 Charles Wautier, *Bacchus*, 1652, oil on canvas, 86.5 × 61.5 cm (34 × 24 ¼ in), National Gallery, Prague

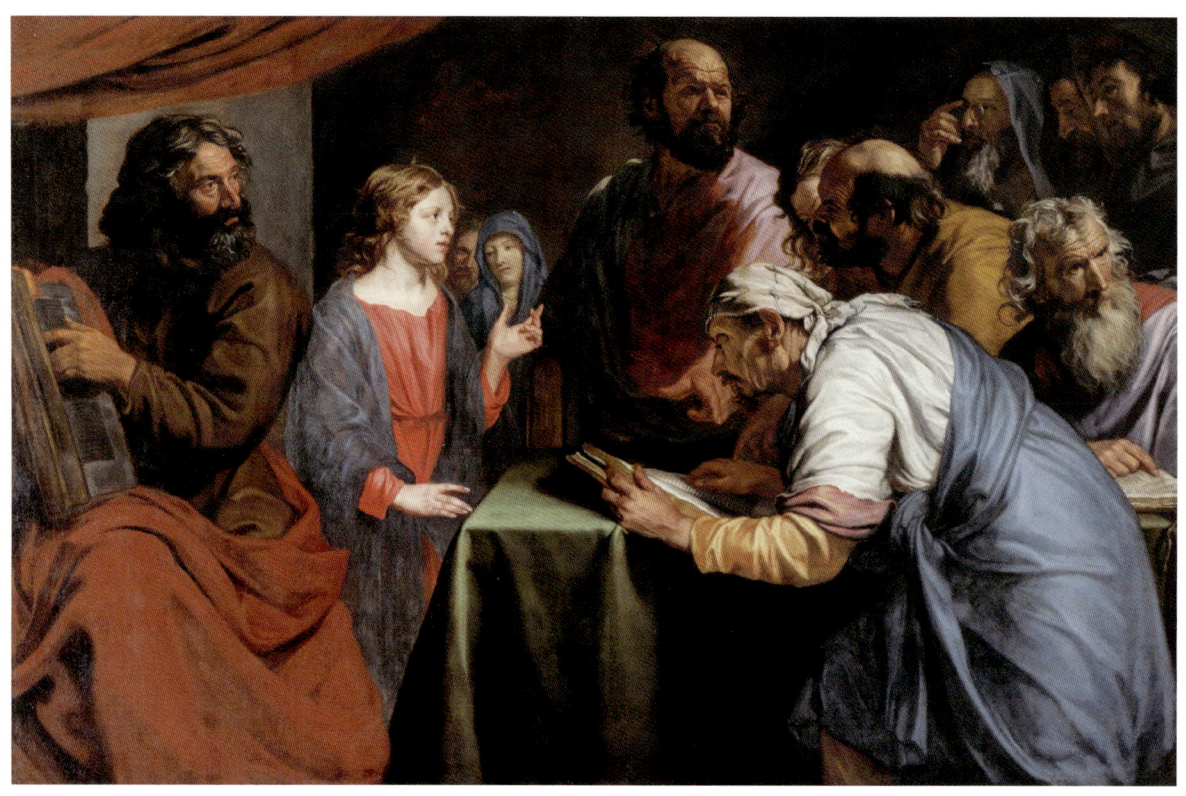

24 Charles Wautier, *Christ among the Pharisees*, c.1650–65, oil on canvas, 166.5 × 249.5 cm (65 ½ × 98 ¼ in), private collection

heaven to Saint Peter.[34] Four years later, Michaelina Wautier died. It is most surprising that no paintings by her are known from the period between 1659 – the date of her last known painting (see fig.34) – and her death in 1689. During that time, her brother had been constantly productive. It seems improbable that Wautier had no artistic output for 30 years.

Charles Wautier's unwillingness to become a member of the Brussels guild in the period from 1642 to 1651 suggests that he kept his distance from painters in the association whom he deemed to be less skilled and less prestigious than himself. That he was taken seriously by the most celebrated and well-connected painters in his trade, we can conclude from the appendix to a letter that the famous painter Peter Snayers wrote to the city council of Valenciennes on 11 August 1662. As regularly happened, fellow artists were willing to confirm the value of a specific painting that was under dispute. When the Valenciennes city council hesitated to pay the asking price for Snayers's painting *The Siege of Valenciennes*, Snayers called in the help of the five 'most prominent' painters of the city: 'les plus princepaus mestres del arte de paintures'. These were Gaspar de Crayer, David Teniers, Louis Primo alias Gentile (1606–67), Daniel van Heil (1604–62/4) and 'monsieur Woutier'. Here, we see Charles Wautier referenced together with the prime exponents of the Brussels Baroque. Snayers's request to the city magistrate of Valenciennes is written in French. The consulted painters each evaluated the painting in Dutch, with the exception of Wautier, who wrote in French that he 'has seen the piece by Mr. Snayers' and thinks it 'has a value of 2,000 guilders or even more'.[35] The Dutch-speaking painters testified together on 7 August, while Charles Wautier gave his approval on 10 August. Charles Wautier was alone. While the other painters signed their testimony with their family name and first name, Charles is the only one to sign with just his initial 'C'. We get the impression that Wautier was highly esteemed but did not quite belong to the same circle.

MICHAELINA AND CHARLES AT WORK SIDE BY SIDE?

Between 1653 and 1668, Charles registered seven apprentices at his studio in Brussels, where Michaelina also likely worked. In 1653, Tomas Monnorino, a son of the late Huybrecht, was officially registered as Charles's apprentice, and in 1657, he took on the 'apprentice Pier Vyvier', the son of a late Brussels master. On 6 July 1661, an 'Ambrosius' about whom we know nothing further, became the apprentice of 'Caerles Wautier', and François Volsom, the son of Brussels citizen Nicolaas, was taken on as an apprentice on 14 August 1664. Jan Baptist Tel and Peter van der Bellen became apprentices of 'Saerle Wateer' on 15 February 1681. Finally, Gilles Wauters was the seventh apprentice, in 1686.[36] Given Charles's output, having trained just seven apprentices over a period of more than thirty years is extremely low. Furthermore, it is notable that in some cases he produced several versions of the same composition. For example, no fewer than six versions of the signed *Calling of Saint Matthew* (c.1660), formerly at Osterley Park in London, exist, all of which are of a high quality. The question is whether they were all painted by Charles alone. It is unlikely that they were fully executed by one of his known pupils, as none of them went on to become a master in Brussels themselves.[37] It was only in 1681, towards the end of his career, that he had two apprentices at once. This was an exception to the rule, as the guild regulations of 1647 stated that a painter could only have one apprentice at a time. Officially, Michaelina was unable to hire pupils as she was not a member of the guild. Assuming that Charles shared his studio, and also his pupils, with his sister, the number of apprentices per master was even lower. Given that Charles contravened the rules by hiring two apprentices at the same time, it is possible that he may also have done so in other ways, such as not officially registering pupils. In the period that Michaelina Wautier dated her works (1643–59), Charles took on two apprentices consecutively: one in 1653, when Michaelina painted *Study of a Young Man* (see fig.54), and another in 1657, the year in which she completed *Education of the Virgin* (see fig.59). Apprentices usually worked at the same studio for about four years, which would imply that there was at least assistance in the Wautier studio between 1653 and 1668, and again between 1686 and 1690. Charles was by then 81 years old, Michaelina about 76.

We have Michaelina's art to thank for the recent interest in Charles Wautier, and this is highly exceptional. Nearly all early modern female artists in the Low Countries owe their fame to their artistic family members or to a painting husband. Examples are Catharina van Hemessen; Magdalena de Passe (1596?–1638); Maria de Grebber (*c.*1602–80); Susanna van Steenwijck-Gaspoel (*c.*1610–after 1653); Catharina Pepijn (1619–88); Geertruyd Roghman (1625–51/7); Maria Theresia (1640–1706), Anna Maria (1641–after 1664) and Francisca Catharina van Thielen (b.1645); Cornelia de Rijck (1653–1726); and Catharina Ykens II (1659–after 1689). They initially attracted attention as part of a family network from which they received their training and contacts.[38] The only woman who gained greater fame than her elder brothers (Hendrik and Antoon) is Maria Faydherbe (1587–after 1633), a sculptor from Mechelen who on 7 December 1632 addressed the aldermen of the city, scoffing at several members of the guild, accusing them of being simply 'dozijnwerkers' ('mass producers of art'). On 12 January 1633, the accused guild members tried to defend their names and proposed sculpting in competition with Maria. Nothing is known about the outcome of the competition. There is no evidence that she wanted to become a guild member but, apparently, she was trying to obtain official commissions. Maria Faydherbe felt threatened by the guild members who had vilified her to prevent her from getting a commission from the Mechelen Jesuits. Only a few sculptures of boxwood, such as *Maria with Child* and a *Crucifix*, have been signed in full, 'MARIA FAYDHERBE', and show her great talent. Furthermore, she sculpted in boxwood, alabaster and marble, at small and large scale, another proof of her craftsmanship.[39] This confrontation dates from a generation before Wautier and shows that great self-confidence in women is not an anachronism. It is entirely possible that Wautier, just as Faydherbe, was fully conscious of her superiority. Her peers were no 'mass producers' but artists of fame who were also working for the archducal court, which would have made the challenge all the greater.

4

Wautier and Her Female Colleagues

Wautier was surrounded by manifold sources of artistic inspiration. Among them were her brother Charles, the works of art circulating in her domestic environment, those on display in the churches in Mons and Brussels, the conceivable connections with the court of Leopold Wilhelm and possibly a journey to Italy (see Chapter 5). But what was her fundamental motivation? Was it the urge to explore her talent, to prove herself and match her brother? Or did she want to achieve something professionally and were male or maybe rather female colleagues her perceived competitors? No genre within the art of painting triggers painters' ambitions as much as the self-portrait. It summons all their available powers, craftsmanship and finesse, originality and innovation, and ultimately, the singularity of the self.[1] Who am I, how do I look and what will be my legacy? Wautier's *Self-Portrait* (see fig.1) is groundbreaking. It surpasses earlier examples from the Spanish Netherlands and distinguishes itself expressly from contemporary innovations in the Dutch Republic and Italy.[2]

To establish Wautier's starting point, we need to investigate the origins of the iconographical category. On what basis did she arrive at this representation of herself? What portraits inspired her? What self-portraits could she have seen herself and studied closely? Or was she familiar with engravings of self-portraits that were circulating? There is, for instance, an

engraving by Jérôme David of Artemisia Gentileschi's self-portrait, a print that must have spread her name throughout Europe (fig.25). The portrait came with a challenge in the form of an ambiguous legend: 'En Picturae Miraculum / Invidendum Facilius Quàm Imitandum' ('In the miracle of painting, it is easier to envy than to imitate'). Was there a difference for Wautier between self-portraits by male and by female artists? Of Northern European or Italian origins? These questions can be answered only partially, but a contextual analysis can shed new light on the innovative way she designed her self-portrait. Wautier's *Self-Portrait* is part of a centuries-old tradition in which women, and to a lesser extent men, have strived to immortalise themselves as painters. If we analyse this unique form of self-representation, we can compare Wautier with other women who applied similar strategies to secure their legacy.[3] What was so appealing about this formula to Wautier? Did she, like all painting women from antiquity up to the sixteenth century, feel the need to show who she was? Did she also want to expel the fear of her own non-existence?

'EGO ME PINXI': I PAINTED MYSELF, 1548

Posing as an artist at the easel is part of the portrait tradition in the Low Countries. Indeed, Wautier's painting closely corresponds to the self-portrait

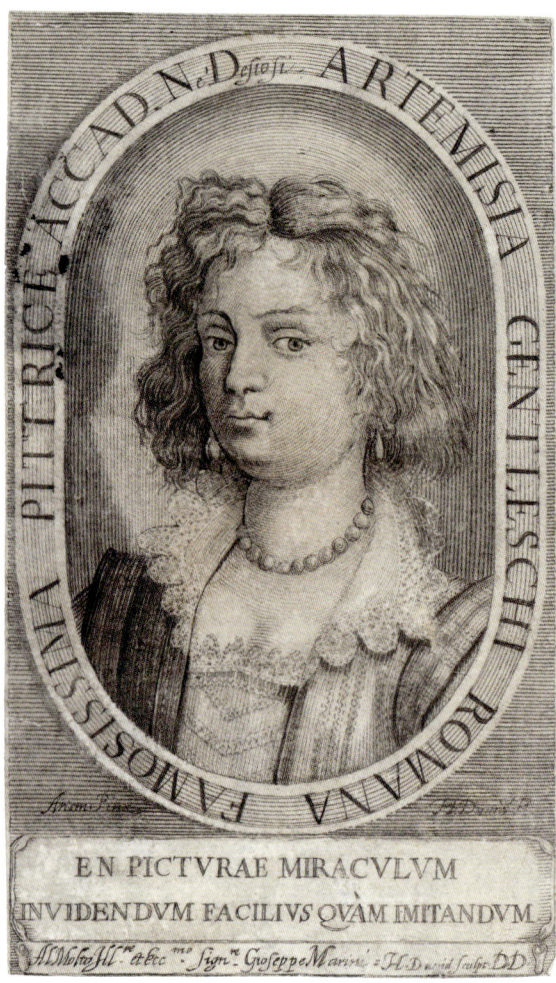

25 Jérôme David after Artemisia Gentileschi, *Self-Portrait*, 1627, engraving, 14.1 × 8 cm (5 ½ × 3 ⅛ in), British Museum, London

Catharina van Hemessen painted in 1548. This is the oldest known European self-portrait, whether Northern or Italian, of a painter at the easel, with a palette and brushes in hand (fig.26). Italian artists were earlier in depicting themselves, but not in their capacity as painters.[4] This makes Van Hemessen's self-portrait unique, and her awareness of her own exceptionality appears from her expansive

signature: 'EGO CATERINA DE / HEMESSEN ME / PINXI / 1548 / ETATIS / SVAE / 20'. The portrait's success is evident from the fact that she painted two versions of it herself and at least one copy was made.[5] The young woman no doubt used a mirror to paint herself from her reflection and thus gives the viewer the impression that she looks them straight in the eyes. As the daughter of a father schooled in the humanist tradition, Van Hemessen no doubt enjoyed a broad education.[6] In Antwerp's middle and upper classes, the education of girls in several languages, mathematics, handicrafts and music was not at all exceptional, influenced especially by the Spaniard Juan Luis Vives. The first Latin edition of his *De institutione feminae christianae* was issued in 1524; shortly thereafter, translations in six languages appeared, among others in Dutch, French and English. He defended the position that girls were intellectually equal to boys and should therefore receive equal education and schooling.[7] It probably goes too far to assume, on the basis of the signature, that Catharina van Hemessen knew Latin.[8] And although Van Hemessen's self-portrait is a testament to her originality and 'ingenium', as will be elucidated, she did not invent the elements of this artistic category.[9]

PLINY & BOCCACCIO: CONCERNING FAMOUS WOMEN

The genesis of this category of design goes back to antiquity. In his *Naturalis Historiae*, Gaius Pliny the Elder mentions five female artists famous in their own time. Within this context, especially important is Iaia of Cyzicus, for Pliny writes that she 'worked at Rome in the youth of Marcus Varro . . . She painted chiefly portraits of women . . . and a portrait of herself, executed with the help of a mirror' ('suam quoque imaginem ad speculum'). She was active around 90 BCE and Pliny notes that '[she] remained single all her life' ('perpetua virgo').[10] It is remarkable that she is also the only artist of whom he mentions a self-portrait and whom

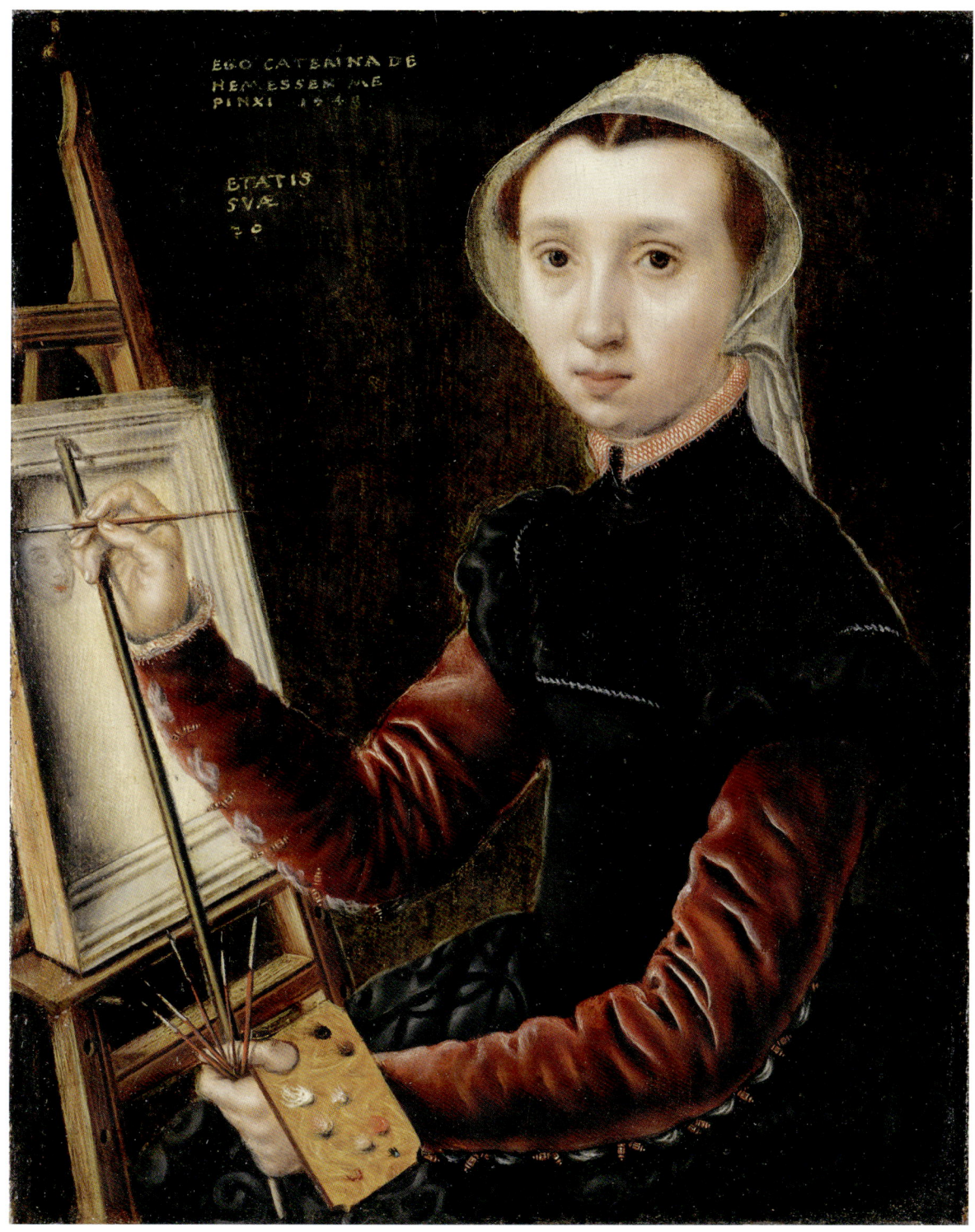

26 Catharina van Hemessen, *Self-Portrait*, 1548, oil on panel, 35.2 × 25.2 cm (13 ⅞ × 9 ⅞ in), Kunstmuseum Basel, Basel

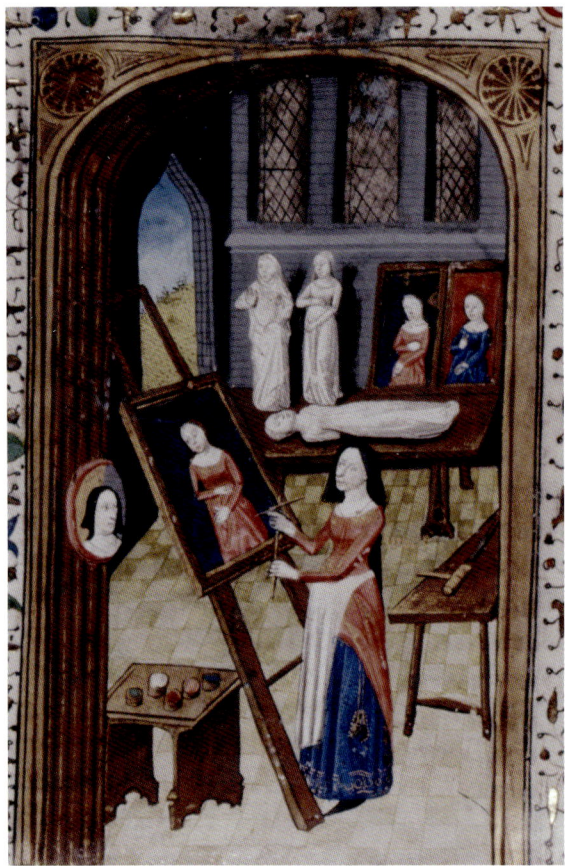

27 Miniature showing Marcia before an easel, in Giovanni
Boccaccio, *Des cleres et nobles femmes*, c.1450, New York
Public Library, Spencer Collection

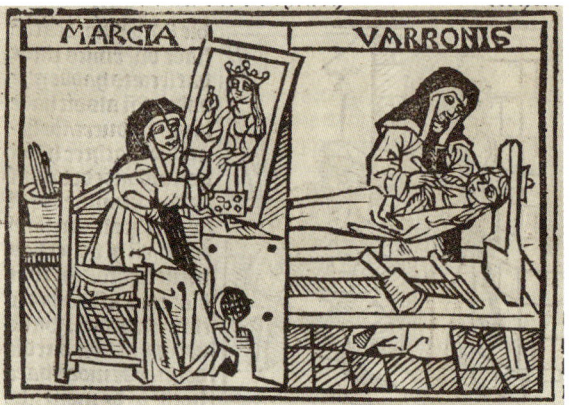

28 Johannes Boccatius van Florentien, *Bescrivende van den
doorluchtighen, glorioesten ende edelsten vrouwen ende van
haren wercken ende gheschienissen die si gedaen hebben
binnen haren leven in den ouden voorleden tiden, ende is
ghenuechlick om te lesen*, Claes die Grave, Antwerp,
1525, p.115

he praises for her exceptional abilities, not only in
painting but also in sculpture.[11] Boccaccio copied Pliny's
text about Iaia of Cyzicus in his *De mulieribus claris*
(*Concerning Famous Women*), written c.1360–70.[12] Due to
a transcription error, her name was changed from 'Iaia'
to 'Marcia' and under this guise she led an independent
life as a female artist in medieval literature.[13] There are
many versions and copies of Boccaccio's manuscript,
and in the French translation, titled *Des cleres et nobles
femmes*, the text became a reference point in the
proto-feminist discourse of the fifteenth century.[14]
It is important for the iconographic tradition that

manuscripts were illustrated and that Marcia's story
acquired its own visual tradition. Boccaccio added
anecdotal details that inspired illustrators. In many
miniatures, Marcia is depicted while painting with
a mirror in her left hand, a brush – and sometimes a
palette – in her right hand. Mostly, the miniaturists
depict Marcia in a contemporary medieval studio,
where all sorts of painting utensils are exhibited. A great
example of the recuperation of the antique prototype
can be seen in a manuscript from c.1450 (fig.27).[15]

We cannot rule out the possibility that Van
Hemessen saw such a miniature, but insufficient
consideration has been given to printed versions of
Boccaccio's text, many of which were illustrated. In
1525, for instance, a Dutch translation with images
appeared in Antwerp (fig.28).[16] Even though the
colourful miniatures were replaced by monochrome
woodcuts, the subject of the painter Marcia at work in
her studio was retained. In the woodcut devoted to her,
Marcia does not paint a self-portrait but a portrait of
a woman, and she is also represented as a sculptor. The

illustrations were copied from the Latin edition that was printed in 1473 in Mainz by Johann Zainer.[17]

Van Hemessen would certainly have taken notice of contemporary discussions on women's education, and the female prototypes in word and image would have served her as role models. Her self-portrait is a unique manifesto of self-esteem, an appeal to be appreciated as an artist. She was the first artist known within European borders to develop such a daring composition. No male artist had shown her the way, and her ingenuity may have advanced her social status and historical notoriety. Even before her death, her name is mentioned as the daughter of the painter Jan van Hemessen, in Lodovico Guicciardini's *Descrittione di tutti i Paesi Bassi* (*Descriptions of the Whole of the Low Countries*) from 1567. In the second edition of *Le Vite* (*The Lives*) by Giorgio Vasari, she is identified as an excellent miniature painter (1568).[18] In 1643, the physician Johan van Beverwijck published a book titled: *Van de uitnementheyt des vrouwelicken geslachts* (*On the Excellence of the Female Sex*), an ode to exceptional female contemporaries, in which he indicates female artists 'with whom our country abounds'. The name 'Catharyn van Hemssen' is mentioned as the daughter of the painter Jan van Hemessen and the wife of the organ player and musician Chrétien de Moriën. Mary of Hungary invited the pair, 'per la loro rara virtu' ('because of their exceptional virtue'), to follow her to Spain and, after her death, they received a 'provisione' ('pension') for the rest of their natural lives.[19] Only Van Beverwijck expressly points to 'her great virtues and arts'. It is unclear whether this description concerns drawing and painting because it could equally well refer to her music, for Catharina appears to have been a good musician as well.[20]

'VIRGO SE IPSAM FECIT': THE VIRGIN PAINTED HERSELF, 1554

The same debates that would later occupy Antwerp also raged around 1550 in Italy and yielded similar women's self-portraits. The little *Self-Portrait* by Sofonisba Anguissola from 1554, for instance, was painted no more than six years after the one by Van Hemessen. She does not show herself at an easel but holds a book in her hand with the text 'Sophonisba Angussola Virgo se ipsam fecit 1554'. The inscription appears to be a variant of the one by Van Hemessen. Anguissola mentions her full name, stresses her unmarried state and the fact that this is a self-portrait. She does not show herself in the act of painting but rather identifies as a painter through the inscription. Moreover, she holds the book in her left hand, which indirectly suggests that she used a mirror to paint herself, which she ostensibly held with her right hand.[21] This *preciosum* is held in the Kunsthistorisches Museum in Vienna and originates from the collection of Rudolf II.[22] Even more interesting in relation to Van Hemessen and Wautier is the self-portrait in which Anguissola depicts herself while painting a Madonna and Child (Muzeum Zamek at Łańcut Castle, Łańcut), dated *c*.1556.[23] The portrait is a milestone in this young tradition because the image on the easel is not a self-portrait but a finished devotional painting, and, unlike the portraits discussed thus far, the figure is life-size rather than of smaller dimensions. In a different approach, in 1579, approximately thirty years after Van Hemessen, Lavinia Fontana painted a small, round self-portrait. She sits at a table, with a pen in hand and a blank sheet in front of her, to draw the classical objects surrounding her.[24] This is a strikingly intellectual self-portrait of a woman who, in the humanist tradition, is working in her *studiolo*. Just as in Van Hemessen's self-portrait and the two early self-portraits by Anguissola, the artist looks the viewer solemnly in the eye. These women represent themselves as *inventors*, they demand attention for their accomplishments and decline to appear agreeable. Such an expression emphatically contrasts with how women were usually portrayed in the early modern period. A pleasant smile was typical for women adapting to social expectations.[25]

Strikingly, in this area of self-representation, women led the way, for male painters both in Italy and in the Low Countries also began to portray themselves at the easel.[26] Both the self-portrait by Crispijn van den Broeck from 1557, and the one by Antonio Moro from 1558, fit in well with this self-reflective phase.[27] Moro's intellectual aspirations are shown in the painting by a Greek inscription that compares him to Apelles and Zeuxis, the greatest painters of all time.[28] A similar audacity is absent in the contemporary self-portraits of women. The earliest self-representations of women demonstrate an ambitious yet relatively modest sense of introspection. Unlike Moro, who compared himself explicitly to the prototypes of ideal artists in antiquity, none of them dared to do the same with their classical female predecessors.

ROLE MODELS NEAR AND FAR

It is unlikely that Wautier ever saw Van Hemessen's self-portrait, but through publications by Guicciardini, Vasari and Van Beverwijck, she may have been acquainted with her fame. The portrait engravings of female artists or authors may also have inspired her.[29] Wautier must certainly have known the 1629 portrait of Anna Francisca de Bruyns, *De sua Effigie à se depicta*, from which both Wenceslaus Hollar and Frederik Bouttats produced engravings in 1648.[30] De Bruyns (fig.29) almost certainly was a role model to Wautier, who could easily have seen the artist's *Assumption of the Virgin*, which was installed on the high altar in the Chapel of Our Lady of Goodwill, 5 km from the Rue d'Havré where Wautier grew up.[31] De Bruyns was married to Isaac Bullart, the author of *L'Académie des sciences*, and she was the niece of architect-painter Jacques Francart (1583–1654) who educated her in his house in Brussels. In the handwritten biography of his mother, Jacques Ignace Bullart testified to this: 'C'est de luy [Franquart] qu'Anne Françoise de Bruyns … a apris la Peinture'.[32] On 30 May 1628, Bullart and De

Bruyns married in the Church of Saint-Germain in Mons,[33] where Wautier's parents also had married.[34] Another possible female role model for Wautier was Virginia de Vezzo (1600–38; fig.30), wife of Simon Vouet, whom Bullart described in *L'Académie des sciences* as a 'Dame Romaine d'une beaute singuliere, & si bien instruite en l'Art de peindre' ('Roman Lady of singular beauty and well trained in the art of painting').[35] Interestingly, Bullart did not mention his own wife in this work.

Anna Maria van Schurman also may have influenced Wautier. Published in Leiden in 1641, Van Schurman's *Dissertatio de ingenii muliebris ad doctrinam, & meliores litteras aptitudine* (*Treatise on the Talent of Women for Study and their Aptitude for Literature*) was translated from the original Latin into various languages for wide circulation.[36] Importantly, Van Schurman approached the subject as a 'problema practicum' and asked herself what requirements a woman must meet to apply herself to science and the arts: 'a woman must have at least a moderate intellect' and have 'the aptitude for learning'. Furthermore, she should have 'the necessary financial resources' and 'not be distracted by domestic obligations'.[37] Consequently, 'a woman should not marry and should employ servants'.[38] If Wautier read this treatise, she must have realised that she was in the ideal position to apply herself to the practice of the arts. Being unmarried and having sufficient financial means at her disposal gave her the freedom she needed. In view of her social position, there is no reason to assume that she did not have opportunities to marry. Possibly, she realised the price she would pay if she became a wife. That people at the time understood what marriage meant for a woman with artistic interests is described by Jacques Ignace Bullart in his biography of his mother, Anna Francisca de Bruyns: 'After her marriage, it became much more difficult for her to find time to practice her art. Although she lamented it, taking care of her large family frequently forced her to put down her paintbrush.'[39] Although it is often assumed that, in the past, female artists

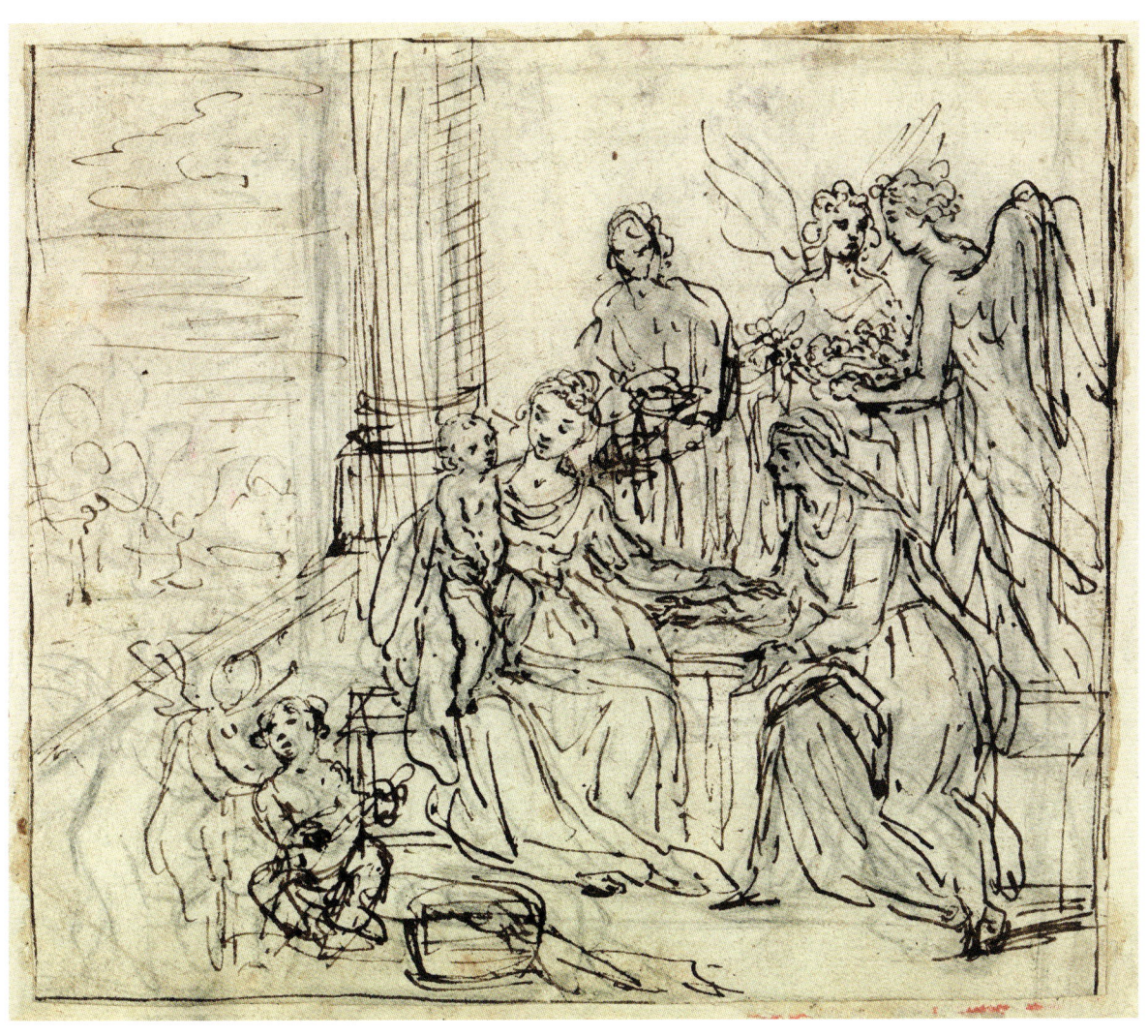

29 Anna Francisca de Bruyns, *Mary, the Christ Child and Saint Anna*, c.1630–40, pen on paper, 15 × 9 cm (5 ⅞ × 3 ½ in), Royal Museum of Fine Arts, Department of Prints and Drawings, Brussels

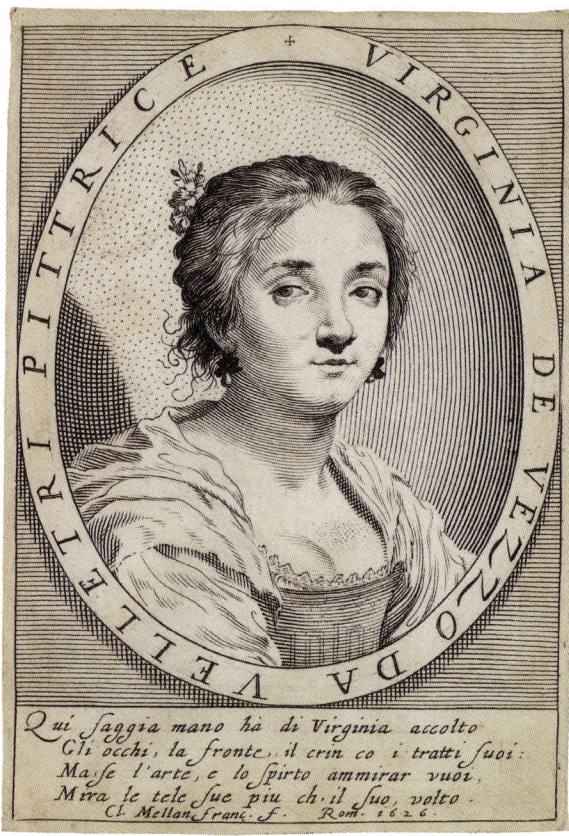

30 Claude Mellan, *Portrait of Virginia de Vezzo*, 1626,
engraving on paper, 11.5 × 8 cm, inscribed: 'VIRGINIA DE
VEZZO DA VELLETRI PITTRICE'; along the bottom:
'*Qui saggia mano hà di Virginia accolto . . . / Mira le tele
sue piu chi'il suo, volto.*'; at lower centre: '*Cl. Mellan franç.
f. Rom. 1626*', Royal Collection Trust

throughout the seventeenth century, with artists
such as Clara Peeters, Margaretha de Heer (before
1603–before 1665), Maria de Grebber and Susanna
van Steenwijck-Gaspoel.[40] It should be added that
it is often unclear to what extent these artists were
still active after their marriages, if their family indeed
'took the brush from their hand'.[41]

As appears from the also unmarried Van Schurman's
correspondence, which she conducted in the same
period when Wautier was artistically active, exceptional
women tried to contact other women in the public
sphere. For instance, Van Schurman exchanged
letters with the scholars Marie Du Moulin, Marie de
Gournay and Dorothy Moore and with two female
artists, the portraitist 'Madame Coutel' and the singer
Utricia Ogle.[42] She often sent self-portraits with her
letters by way of introduction.[43] Van Schurman was
a learned polyglot and a versatile artist. She painted
and drew portraits, sculpted in wax and boxwood,
calligraphed on glass, made ingenious cut-outs,
embroidered, engraved a number of portraits and
experimented with pastels. In various materials and
techniques, she made at least 12 self-portraits. Her
engraved self-portrait from 1633 enjoyed great fame
within a small circle. In the collection of her letters
published in 1648, entitled *Opuscula*, a self-portrait is
printed opposite the frontispiece, which was copied
dozens of times until far into the nineteenth century.
She exchanged letters and artistic works – such as
drawings, miniature portraits, small wax or boxwood
sculptures and elegantly calligraphed poems or
proverbs – with intellectuals, musicians and learned
women from all over Europe. This was her way of
spreading her fame within an exclusive network.[44]
However diverse her artistic production was, she
never attempted to make any large-scale works of
art. Her excellence was expressed in the many artistic
techniques she mastered. The reverse applies to
Wautier. Her artistic ingenuity was directed at the most
prominent of the visual arts: according to the order
of artistic expression dictated by men, the painting of
large history pieces was the highest endeavour.[45]

had to remain unmarried to fulfil their ambition,
this view does not completely adhere to reality. It
is noteworthy that during the sixteenth century,
numerous female artists in the Low Countries were
married. Agnes van den Bossche (*c*.1440–after 1502),
Susanna Horenbout, Levina Teerlinck, Mechtelt van
Lichtenberg toe Boecop (*c*.1520–98) and Catharina
van Hemessen were all married even as they actively
pursued their art. Moreover, this tradition continued

5

Wautier as a Painter

What situation did Michaelina Wautier face when she arrived in Brussels in the 1640s? Likely, she immediately moved in with her brother Charles, who with his studio could offer her room to work as well as a place to live. Michaelina's name is nowhere mentioned in the guild registers. At this time, no names of women were entered, so their contributions must be gauged in other ways. It may therefore surprise us that, in a decree from 1647 by the Brussels Guild of Painters, Goldsmiths and Glass-Blowers, mention is made of both male and female apprentices and masters. The Antwerp Guild of Saint Luke makes no explicit reference to women, with the exception of a few painters' widows and daughters, who were also required to pay (part of) the master's fee.[1] 'In Brussels, no painter or any other person can have any male or female apprentice working for him', unless 'this abovementioned male or female apprentice' had been trained in the trade by a free master.[2] Subsequently, it is advised that 'any male or female master should have only one apprentice' at one time[3] and that the sons of 'free male or female masters' should pay a different admission fee.[4] Such a decree was mostly issued to adjust prevailing practices. Thus, it is natural to conclude that there were indeed *meijsens* (girls or female apprentices) and *meesterssen* (female masters) active in the trade.[5] This decree was issued in 1647, when Wautier had already been working as a painter

for several years. The records of the Brussels guild are devoid of women's names prior to 1702. In that year, two women were registered as *Schilderesse* (female painter): Miss Elisabet Celdrin and Miss Cattharina van Stichel. They were charged only half of the usual membership fee.[6]

The earlier part of this chapter aims to provide an overview of the artistic context in Brussels, referring to fellow artists whose art may have influenced Wautier and contributed to the development of her unique style. Unfortunately, there is little evidence of direct contact, but the broader context of the court city enabled her to create a body of work that no other Northern European female artist had achieved before. The defining characteristic of her oeuvre is its astounding versatility. In this respect, she surpasses not only her brother, but also almost all of her painting contemporaries. It was unprecedented in the artistic climate of seventeenth- and eighteenth-century Antwerp and Brussels for a single artist to practise in four different genres. Most painters specialised in one genre, such as history painting, portraiture, still life or landscape painting. History painters, whose work was based on written sources such as the Bible or mythology, tended to be more versatile. They also painted portraits, for example. In contrast, painters who specialised in everyday scenes or flower still lifes were rarely persuaded to depict other subjects.[7] Wautier's adaptability is one aspect of her talent, but the outstanding quality of her work in different genres is even more impressive. In addition, Wautier loved to paint on supports of various sizes, ranging from medium-sized panels to large-scale canvases originally measuring more than four metres in width.[8]

THEODOOR VAN LOON AND JACOB VAN OOST

The earliest known work by Wautier, the portrait of the artillery general Andrea Cantelmo, is from around 1643. The decisions of the Guild of Painters, Goldsmiths and Glass-Blowers were doubtlessly far removed from the environment in which she circulated. At that moment, her brother Charles was still not inclined to join the guild. Possibly, he followed the example of Theodoor van Loon, in this period the most important painter to be active in Brussels, albeit with many interruptions. Although he joined, as a matter of course, the Accademia di San Luca in Rome, he never was a member of the Brussels guild. In a letter of 21 November 1612, written while in Brussels, Van Loon's loyal friend, the Leuven professor Erycius Puteanus, praised him for 'his talents as a painter, his elegant manners and his erudition'.[9] Between 1617 and 1631, Van Loon made several trips to Rome and from c.1639 until Puteanus's death in 1646, he regularly stayed with him in Leuven. Cantelmo was also an acquaintance of Puteanus's and paid him a visit in August 1642.[10] At Puteanus's house, Cantelmo must have heard about Van Loon or have met him. A compliment such as Puteanus paid Van Loon would no doubt have pleased the Wautier siblings. Not only did he have 'talents as a painter' but also 'elegant manners' and 'erudition'. Michaelina especially would have considered this a challenge. For a woman, it was considered even more exceptional to have such qualities than it was for a male colleague.

A direct link between Van Loon and the two Wautier siblings cannot be proven, but there are striking similarities between the work of this Caravaggisti contemporary and Michaelina's expressive style. He must have had a far-reaching influence on her, even more than on Charles. The Wautiers could have admired a number of examples of his work in their immediate environment. In 1626, he had painted the impressive *Saint Ursula Crowned by the Child Jesus* (fig.31).[11] In addition, the Wautiers would doubtless have visited the Basilica of Our Lady at Scherpenheuvel, for which Van Loon had painted a cycle of seven paintings with scenes from the life of the Virgin (c.1616–21) which Puteanus described as a 'miracle scene'.[12] Their interest in this cycle would have been stimulated by the avant-garde architecture of the domed church which the Archdukes Albert and Isabella commissioned from Wenceslas Coeberger (1557/61–1634). It was consecrated in 1627.[13] The possibility cannot be ruled out that Wautier also knew this architect. Coeberger closely collaborated with Van Loon, and furthermore, was the brother-in-law of Jacques Francart, who in his turn had trained his niece Anna Francisca de Bruyns as an artist. As mentioned in previous chapters, De Bruyns lived in Mons for some time and may have been a role model to Wautier.[14]

Van Loon's art also, in some way, influenced Jacob van Oost the Elder (1601–71), whose work is related to Wautier's in both form and content (fig.32). Van Oost learned his compositions and chiaroscuro from Caravaggio but he gave them his own cachet through the stylisation of the figures, the intimate setting and the natural expressions. In the past, the similarities between his style and Wautier's have led to some false attributions.[15] Since Van Oost is known as an established 'local' Baroque painter, Wautier's works have been identified as his. We cannot now pinpoint the reason for the correlation of their paintings. Are Wautier's works similar to Van Oost's because they were both influenced by Van Loon? Or were there more immediate contacts between Wautier and Van Oost? Van Oost may have met Van Loon in Rome in 1628, but after his return from Italy, one year later, he stayed in his native city of Bruges for

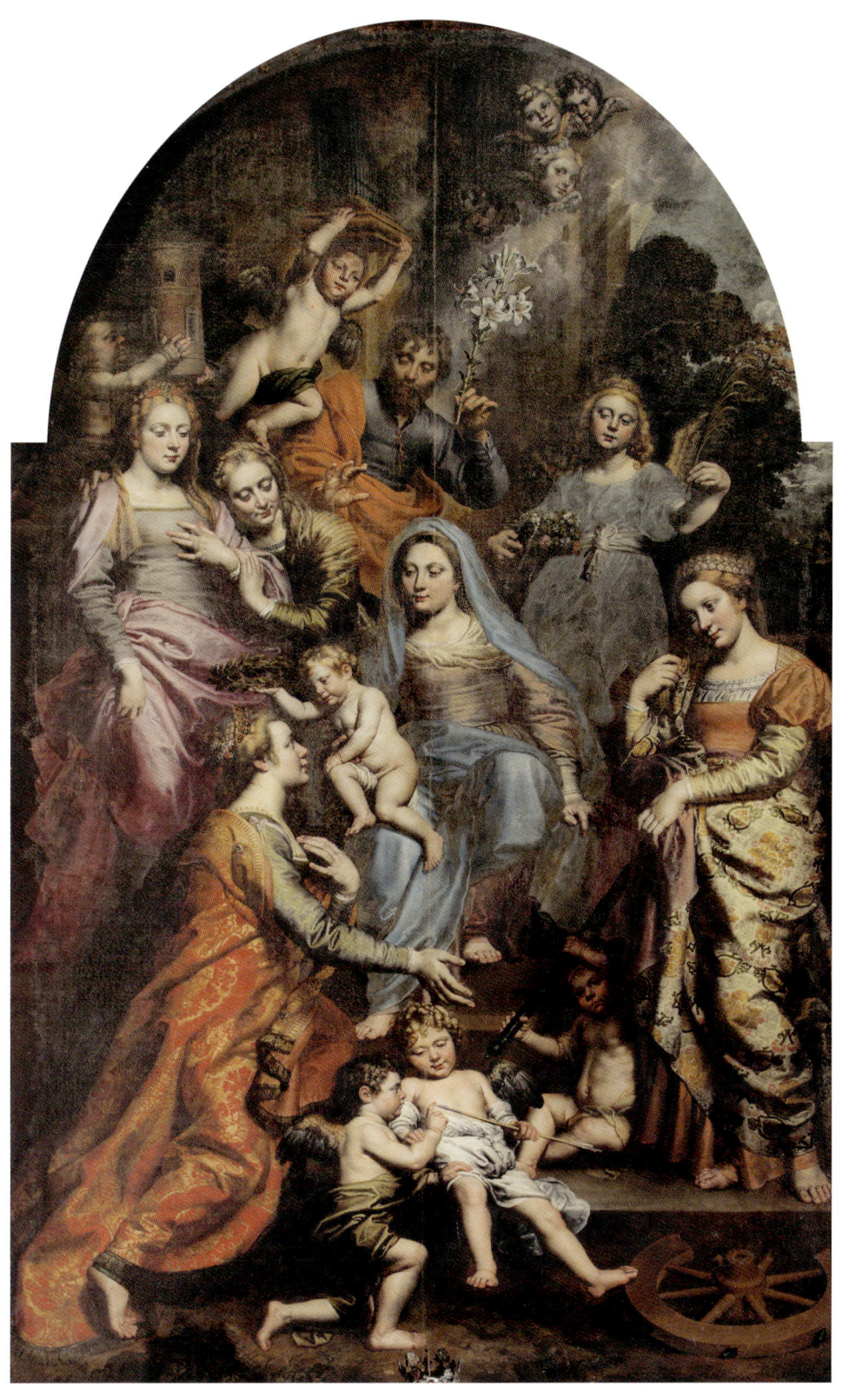

31 Theodoor van Loon, *Saint Ursula Crowned by the Child Jesus*, 1626, oil on canvas, 350 × 220 cm
   (137 ¾ × 86 ⅝ in), Church of Saint John the Baptist at the Beguinage, Brussels

the rest of his life. It is possible that Cantelmo may have introduced Wautier to Van Oost. The series of tapestries *The Seven Liberal Arts*, for which Cantelmo commissioned Cornelis Schut to design the cartoons, were woven in Bruges at the beginning of the 1640s (see Chapter 1). Much more important is that Cantelmo was Governor of Bruges and had a channel constructed there to supply his troops. In March 1642, he commanded an attack against Sluis from the city.[16] It is hardly surprising that, in 1644, the Bruges poet Petronella Keysers wrote in her 'Conversation in Heaven on the Occasion of the Bruges Holy Blood Procession', 'Cantelmo here returns? My poor heart turns to lead. / If that chap comes once more, he sure will leave me dead.'[17] All of this leads us to conclude that Cantelmo regularly visited Bruges for several years. Since Van Oost was the only painter of note in the city, Cantelmo must have known of him and may have introduced Wautier to him.

The style of Philippe de Champaigne, born and trained in Brussels but active in Paris from 1621 on, also shows elements that characterise Van Loon's work and may in turn have influenced Wautier's style.[18] As the preceding speculations make clear, the development of her style is hard to trace. We can only indicate similarities with artists who moved between the Low Countries and Italy.

ARTISTIC INFLUENCES, AT HOME AND FURTHER AFIELD

When we look at the diverse influences on Wautier's oeuvre, it is curious to see how little the painters active in Brussels during the period she lived there influenced her. Gaspard de Crayer, for instance, was not a direct inspiration to her, even though he had been a member of the Brussels guild since 1607, and many paintings by his hand were on display in the city.[19] His style was primarily influenced by the Antwerp master Peter Paul Rubens, an idiom that apparently appealed less to Wautier than other options available to her. The Church of Our Lady of the Chapel, whose choir was not ten metres removed from the Wautiers' house,[20] held three paintings by Rubens. Among those was *Christ Giving the Keys to Saint Peter* (c.1613–15; Gemäldegalerie, Berlin), a work commissioned by Jan Brueghel the Elder (1568–1625) for the decoration of the memorial stone to his parents, Pieter Bruegel the Elder and Maria Coecke van Aelst, who were married in the Church of Our Lady of the Chapel and were also buried there. Over the years, Wautier must have visited her parish church hundreds if not thousands of times. She must have been aware that one of the most famous sixteenth-century painters was buried in the church that she could see from the window of her house. Furthermore, no fewer than six Mannerist, sharply defined and often theatrical paintings by the court painter Hendrick de Clerck (1560–1630) decorated the walls of this church. These mostly date from the first decades of the seventeenth century. To Wautier, they would no doubt have seemed, for all their decorative Italianate flourishes, rather old-fashioned.[21] The *Appearance of Christ to His Mother* (1624) by Gaspar de Crayer (fig.33) was one of the star attractions of the church.[22] De Crayer remained in Brussels until he moved to Ghent in 1664. He is the only painter of distinction active in the city during the whole period the Wautier siblings were working. That is not to say that they considered him as a competitor. It is noteworthy that the Wautiers are not known to have painted any altarpieces for Brussels churches or monasteries, but it should be noted that little is known about the provenances of their altarpieces. However, Michaelina did paint several huge religious works. Originally measuring 316 × 211 cm, her *Annunciation* is now in the Musée-Promenade de Marly-le-Roi in Louveciennes (fig.34). In 1686, it was installed in the chapel of the Château de Marly, which was commissioned by Louis XIV and built by Jules Hardouin-Mansart. As the *Annunciation* is dated 1659, it is obvious that it could not have been commissioned for this chapel. Evidently, it must have been painted for another

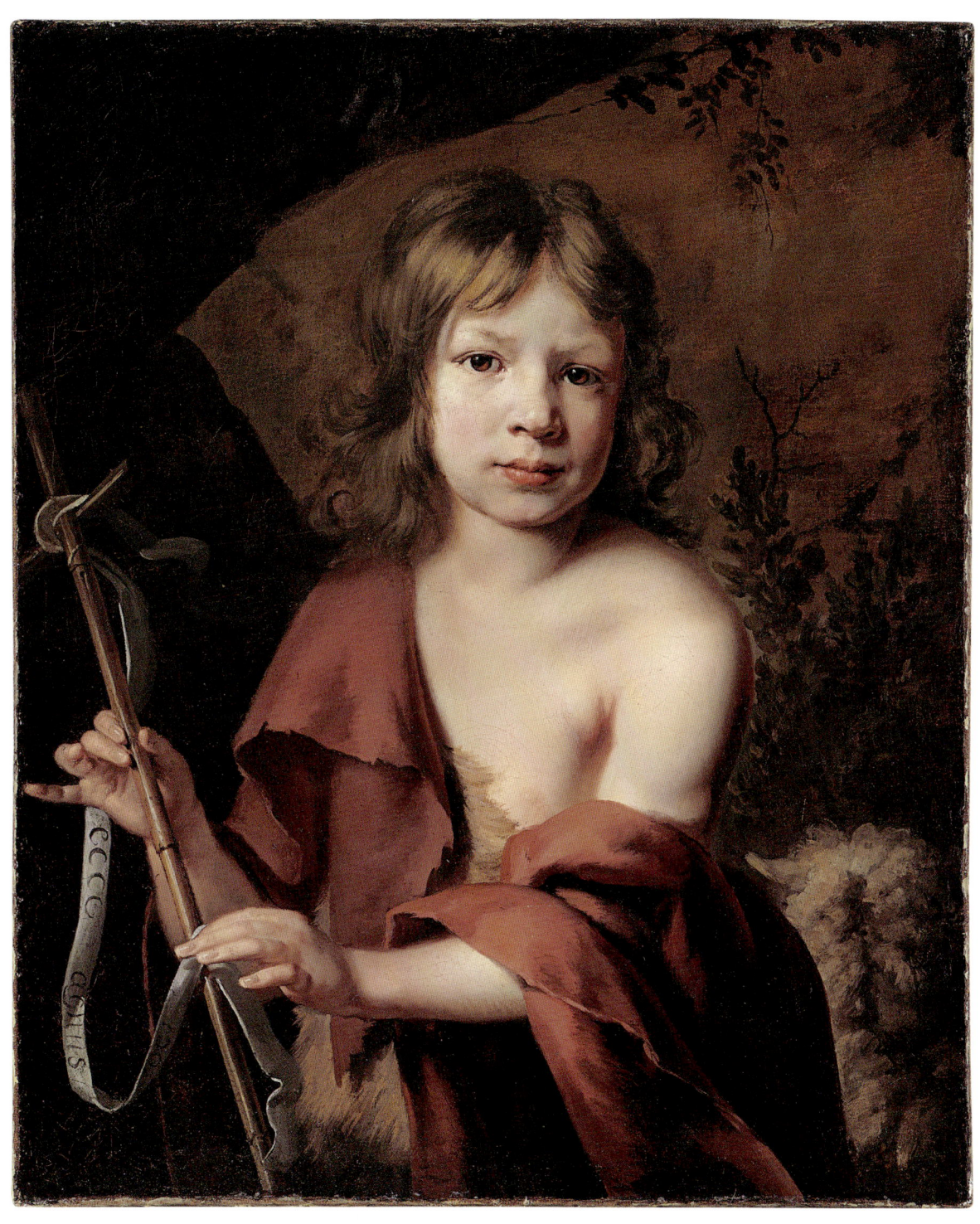

32 Jacob van Oost the Elder, *Portrait of a Boy as St John the Baptist*, c.1635, oil on canvas, 71.8 × 58.1 cm (28 ¼ × 22 ⅞ in), private collection

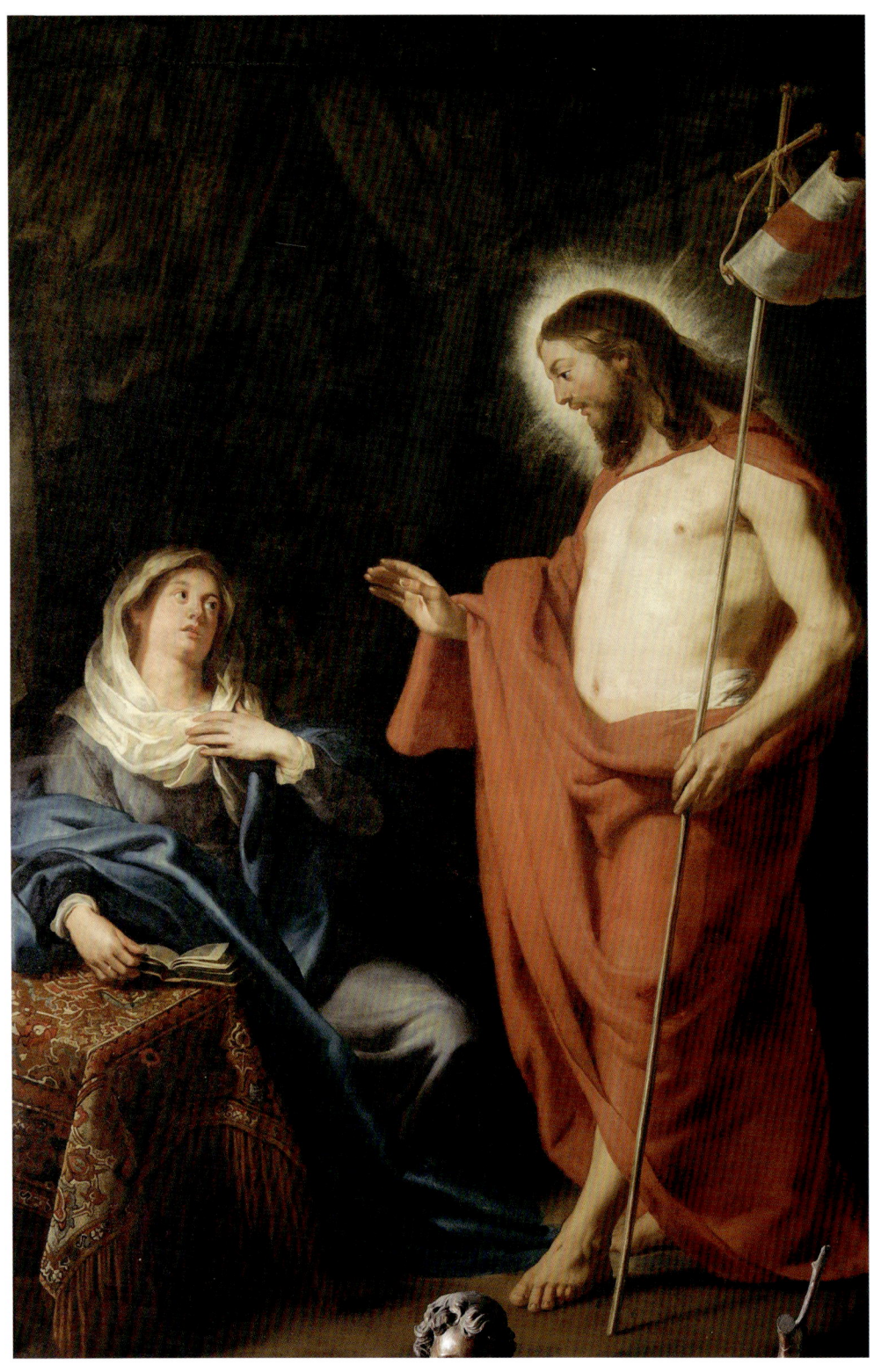

33 Gaspar de Crayer, *Appearance of Christ to His Mother*, 1624, 275 × 180 cm (108 ¼ × 70 ⅞ in),
Kapellekerk, Brussels

location, as it is inconceivable that Wautier would have embarked on a painting measuring over three metres in height purely for her own satisfaction. In 1686, she was still alive, so if it remained unsold for any reason, she could have facilitated a sale.[23] A second altarpiece, also an Annunciation, was sighted in 1770 in the church of the Discalced Carmelites in Mechelen. After describing several gravestones in the aisles of the church, Cuypers van Alsinghen turns to the portal: 'on either side of the west door, above the aisles, are two paintings: one, by N. Woutiers, depicts the Crucifix, and the other, by his sister, depicts the Annunciation'.[24] This remark is of crucial importance because the author was aware that Charles's sister had painted the religious scene opposite his work in the doorway of the church. The church was only consecrated in 1707, which excludes the possibility that Michaelina's 1659 *Annunciation* was painted for this location. But there is archival evidence that in about 1760 the two paintings were donated by Maria-Theresia de Bette, daughter of Ambroise Auguste de Bette, 2nd Marquis of Lede. She was the widow of François Claude Coloma, 2nd Count of Bornem, and a 'former canoness of Bergen in Henegauw' (that is, Mons in Hainaut).[25] She probably also played a role in acquiring the two paintings and knew the Wautiers from local tradition in the painters' native city. During the 1650s and 1660s, Charles was the artist behind a series of altarpieces, all for the decoration of less prestigious churches in the periphery and none for the court city itself.

The importance of Michaelina and Charles's exposure to works of art in Brussels and its vicinity should not be underestimated, but other options were also available to them. In Antwerp, the hub of the seventeenth-century art trade, enough paintings circulated to make Italian, French and Dutch artistic ideas accessible. A journey to Italy would have exposed her more intensely not only to early modern art but also to the relics of antiquity. Above, we have seen that, if there was indeed such a trip, it would have been made between 1635 and 1640.[26] Archival

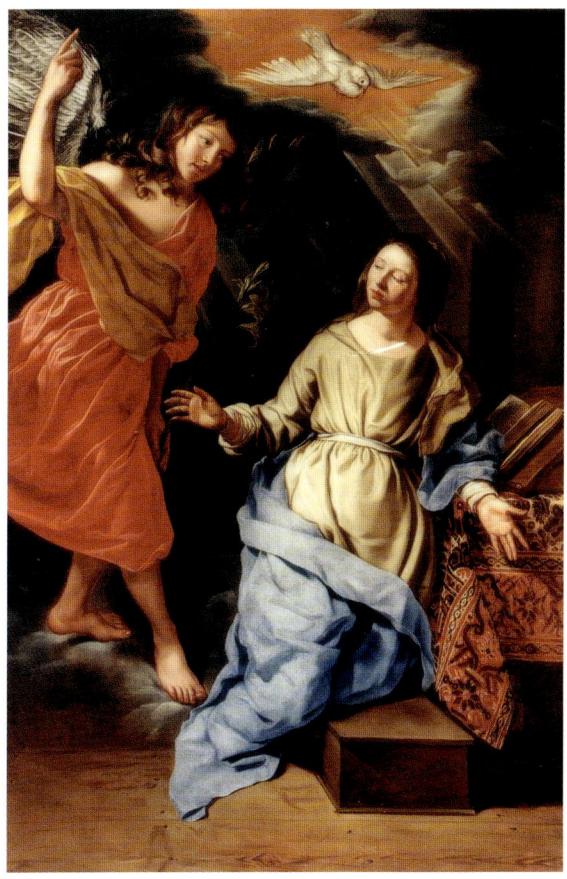

34 Michaelina Wautier, *Annunciation*, 1659, oil on canvas, 200 × 134 cm, (78 ¾ × 52 ¾ in) Musée-Promenade de Marly-le-Roy, Louveciennes

evidence for such a trip for Charles has been located. When he registered with the Brussels guild in 1651, it was recorded that 'monseur Wauti buytens lants gheleert [heeft]' ('Mr. Wauti was trained abroad').[27] This at least indicates that he spent some time outside of the country, and does not rule out that Michaelina also had that opportunity. Women could not travel alone but it was feasible for them to travel in the company of 'decent' companions.

Recent research shows that Wautier's oeuvre contains some references to works of art which were in Rome in the middle of the seventeenth century and had not yet been reproduced in any way.[28] Furthermore, technical research into Wautier's paintings has revealed an Italian influence in the composition of the paint layers on the canvas. Many of Wautier's paintings have a beige or buff-coloured ground layer. Her self-portrait (see fig.1) was indeed painted on a buff ground, as is also the case for the canvas exposed on her easel in front of her. Moreover, she used red ground layers in quite a number of her paintings, including *The Five Senses* (see figs 39–43), *Saint Joachim Reading* (fig.19), *Saint Joseph* (fig.18), the *Triumph of Bacchus* (fig.63) and the *Mystic Marriage of Saint Catherine* (fig.37).[29] The use of this reddish-brown ground may indicate an influence from Italy, where artists traditionally preferred to work on a brown ground. Does this mean that she travelled to Southern Europe, where she became familiar with an alternative composition of the ground layers? This cannot be ruled out. While her technique clearly shows strong Italian influences, however, this in itself is not proof that she actually spent time in Rome. It does make it clear that Wautier was knowledgeable about the Italian tradition and experimented in preparing her canvases. She consciously chose the ground of her paintings in relation to the image and the colours she proposed to use.

The presence of a reddish ground cannot be interpreted exclusively as proof of the painting's place of origin, as has been done for the work of Michael Sweerts (1618–64), a contemporary Brussels painter who lived in Italy for almost ten years. When his paintings are painted on a reddish ground, they are attributed to his Italian period, while the use of a grey ground suggests his years in the Low Countries.[30] In Wautier's case, it is striking that this reddish ground is found in both early paintings and those of her later career. It is therefore difficult to believe that they were all painted in Italy. Although both artists lived in Brussels around the same time, there is little evidence that Sweerts influenced Wautier. Sweerts was first documented as living in Rome in 1646, and

no paintings are known to have been made by him in Brussels before that date. By the time he returned from Italy and established his academy in Brussels around 1655, Wautier had already completed most of her known works.[31] It will become clear later that it was Sweerts who adopted Wautier's innovative approach to depicting lively boys, as seen in *The Five Senses*, and he did not start painting them before his return from Italy.

THE EARLIEST TESTIMONIES: PORTRAITS AS THE STARTING POINT, *c.*1640–49

Wautier's dated paintings are all from the years 1643 to 1659, a period of barely 16 years. It is unlikely that she would only have produced paintings when she was between the ages of about 29 and 45, especially since she lived for about 75 years and we have no reason to assume that she was by then incapable of painting. On 25 April 1682 she still put an elegant signature under a notarial deed.[32] The stylistic evolution of the paintings is difficult to define, which makes it hard to link the undated works to the ten signed and dated paintings.[33] Her paintings will be discussed here in chronological clusters so that we can trace the evolution of her oeuvre as adequately as possible.

The two earliest dated works by her hand are portraits. Of the already mentioned *Portrait of Commander Andrea Cantelmo*, only a copper engraving has been preserved (see fig.8).[34] The date 1643 offers us a *terminus ante quem* for the production of the painted original. It is virtually impossible that the prototype for this engraving was the first work she made. It is simply too balanced and too expressive.

A family portrait in which the parents have been rendered as the Biblical couple Isaac and Rebecca contains many characteristics of Wautier's work in a nutshell (fig.35), and it stands to reason that this painting is one of the artist's earliest existing works. The group portrayed here is arranged horizontally and the composition is dominated by the wide

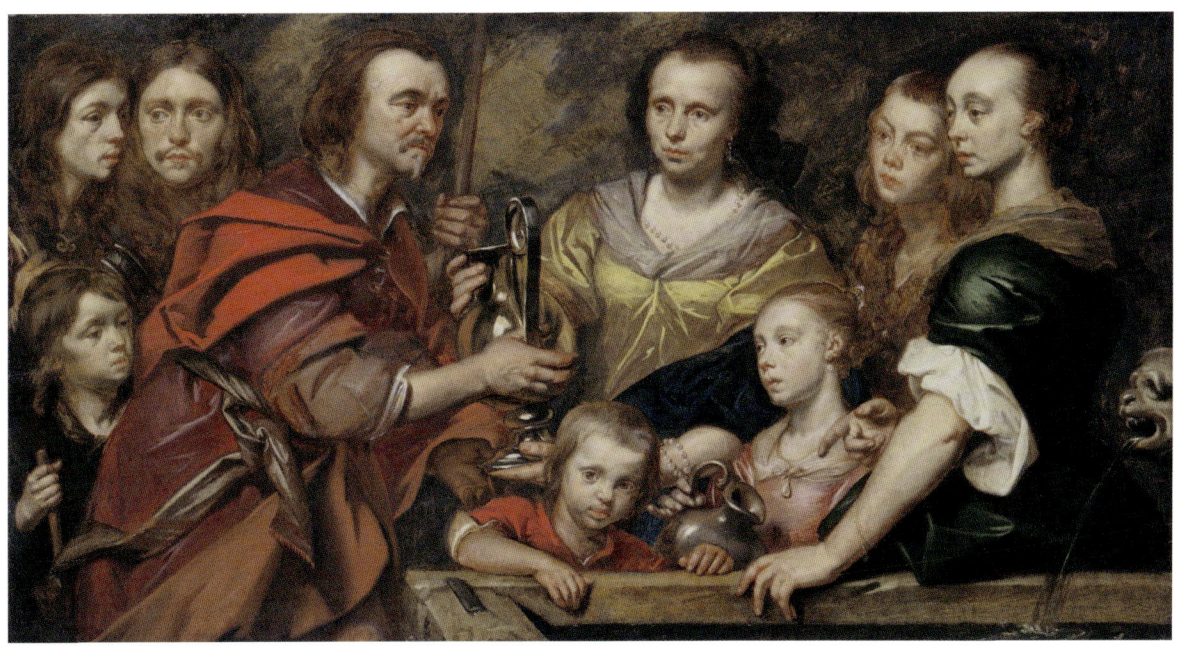

35 Michaelina Wautier, *Portrait Historié of a Family with Parents Posing as Isaac and Rebecca*, c.1640, oil on canvas,
101.6 × 186.1 cm (40 × 73 ¼ in), private collection

spring basin that runs parallel to the edge of the
painting. The parents are placed in the centre and
the children form a circle around them. The quality
of the parents' portraits is disappointing, but the
depiction of the girls in the foreground to the
right and the elder brothers to the left foreshadows
Wautier's mature manner. The girls with their bowed
heads and melancholy expressions will be repeated
in later *portraits historiés*. And with the rigid but
self-confident portrait of the front-facing elder son,
second from left in the background, she anticipates
the impressive men's portraits she would produce later.

This portrait is difficult to date, but the simple
composition with the somewhat awkwardly placed
figures, whose portraits are not always equally
successful, and the dark colour scheme, suggest that
it was painted around 1640 at the latest, several years
before the skilful depiction of Andrea Cantelmo.

The frontal head in the upper left corner of the
family portrait shows similarities to the *Portrait of
a Military Commander in the Spanish Army* (fig.36),
which is fully signed and bears the date 1646. It is
no coincidence that the two earliest dated works by
Wautier are portraits of soldiers. As appears from her
biography, her father had been a page to the Duke of
Fuentes, commander-in-chief of the Spanish troops
in the Southern Netherlands, and Pierre, the brother
three years her senior, also chose a military career.
The artillery general Cantelmo is depicted in armour
with the sash of the Spanish army knotted around
his left arm, while the man in the 1646 portrait wears
an ochre buff coat, with a sash, in the pink hue of
the Spanish king, diagonally across his breast. The
colour scheme is restricted and, apart from the sash,
the portrait has been executed in earth tones against
a dark background. The model is static and placed

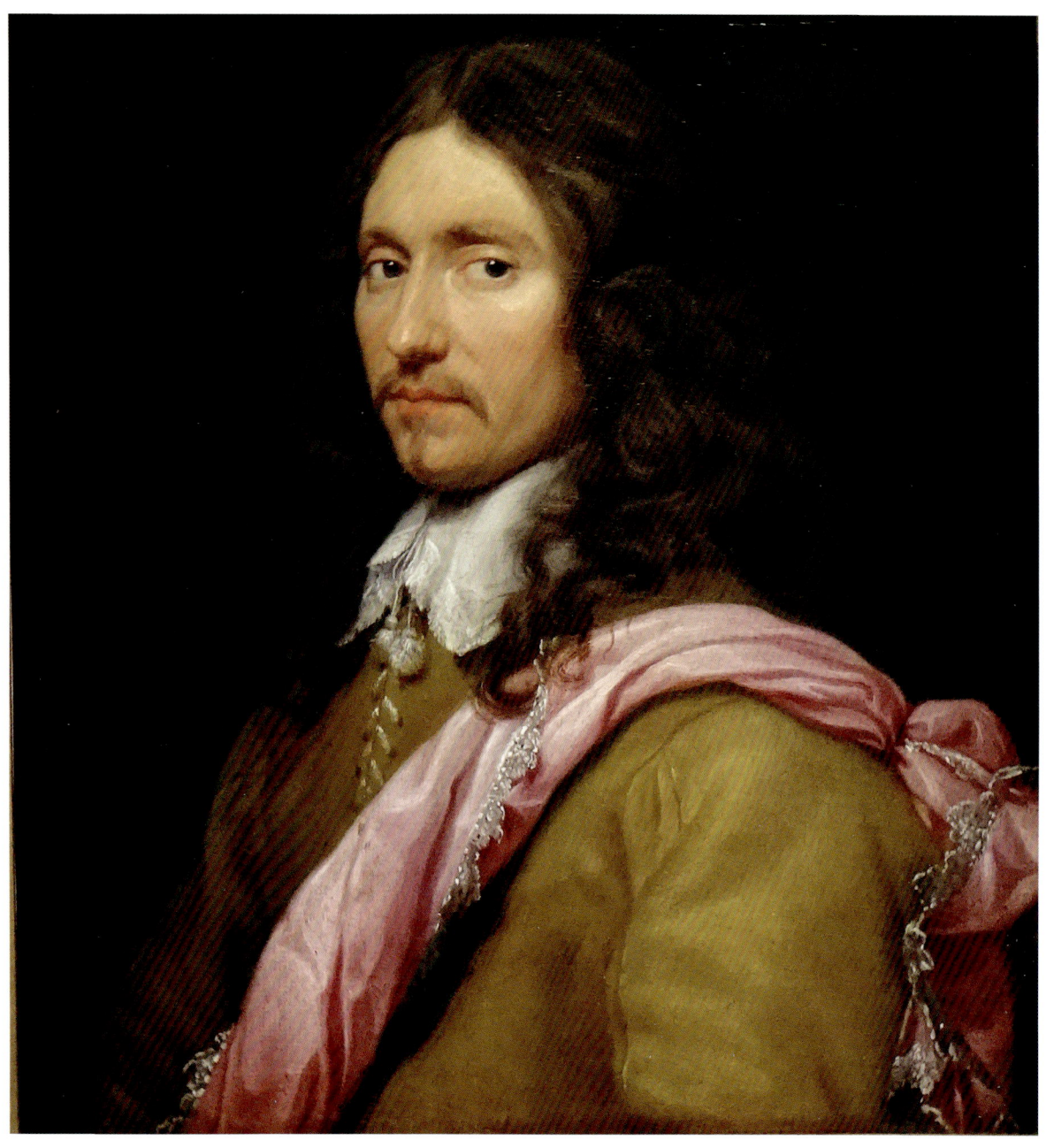

36 Michaelina Wautier, *Portrait of a Military Commander in the Spanish Army*, 1646, oil on canvas, 63 × 56.5 cm (24 ¾ × 22 ¼ in), Royal Museums of Fine Arts of Belgium, Brussels

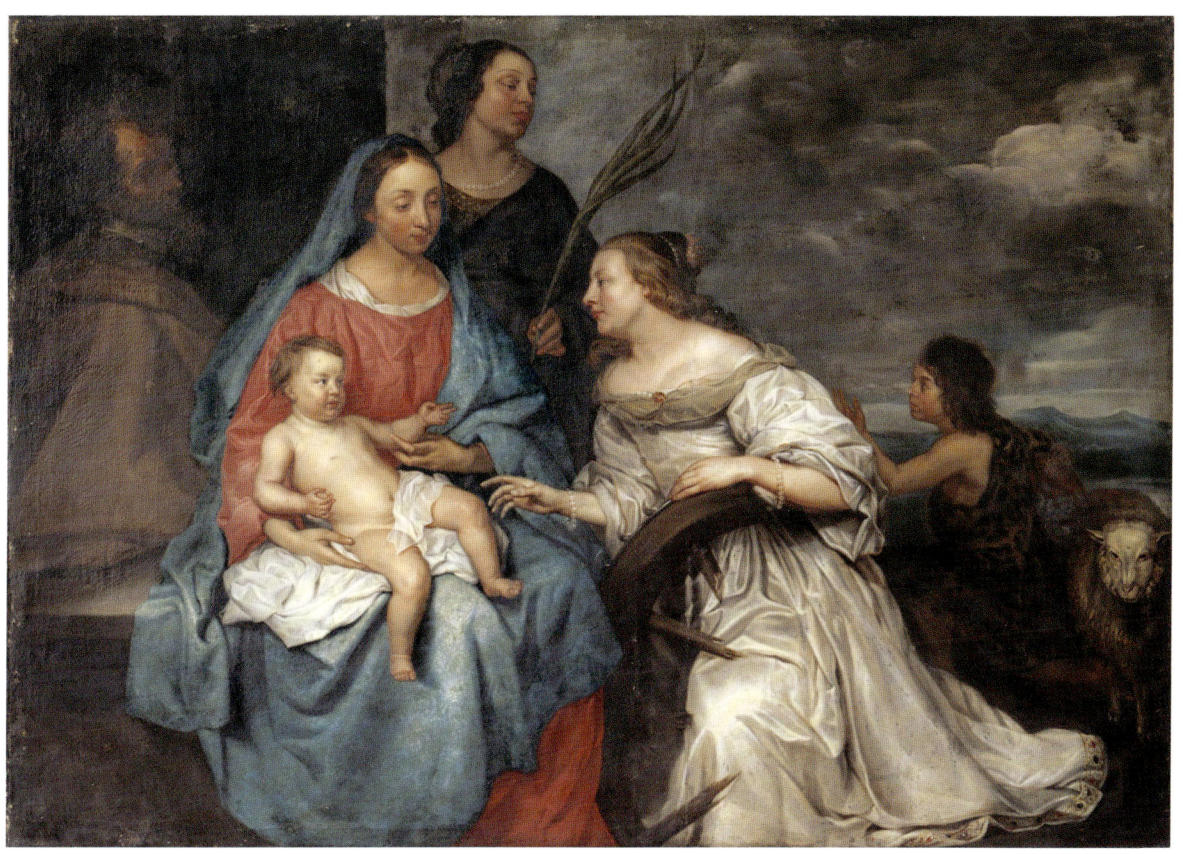

37 Michaelina Wautier, *Mystic Marriage of Saint Catherine*, 1649, oil on canvas, 156.5 × 218 cm (61 ⅝ × 85 ⅞ in),
Séminaire diocésain, Namur

exactly in the centre. This positioning – enhanced by the close framing, a characteristic of her portraits – focuses attention on the face. The elaboration of the hair is typical. It is painted boldly and contains a wide spectrum of colours. As always, she strives to adapt the texture of the hair to the individuality of the model. Some have voluminous, curled locks, some have more finely rendered hair or closely cropped hairstyles. Red hair appears next to brown, and blond next to red; and Wautier seems to take special care with the representation of greying hair, as in the *Portrait of Martino Martini* (see fig.58) or in that of her brother Pierre (fig.10). We see that this fascination not only is evident in her portraits but is a recurring stylistic element. In her genre paintings as

well, the pliable hair attracts attention. The series *The Five Senses* offers the greatest example in this respect. When painting children, she gives the anecdotal impression that someone has just run a comb through their hair one last time. The hair is an extension of the personality. This also applies to her paintings of male saints, where the hair gives them greater expressiveness and adds to their humanity.

A SURPRISING MYSTIC MARRIAGE, 1649

After a few portraits marking the start of her career, suddenly, out of the blue, there is the first history piece. In 1649, Wautier painted the *Mystic Marriage of Saint Catherine* (fig.37), a mature, monumental painting.[35]

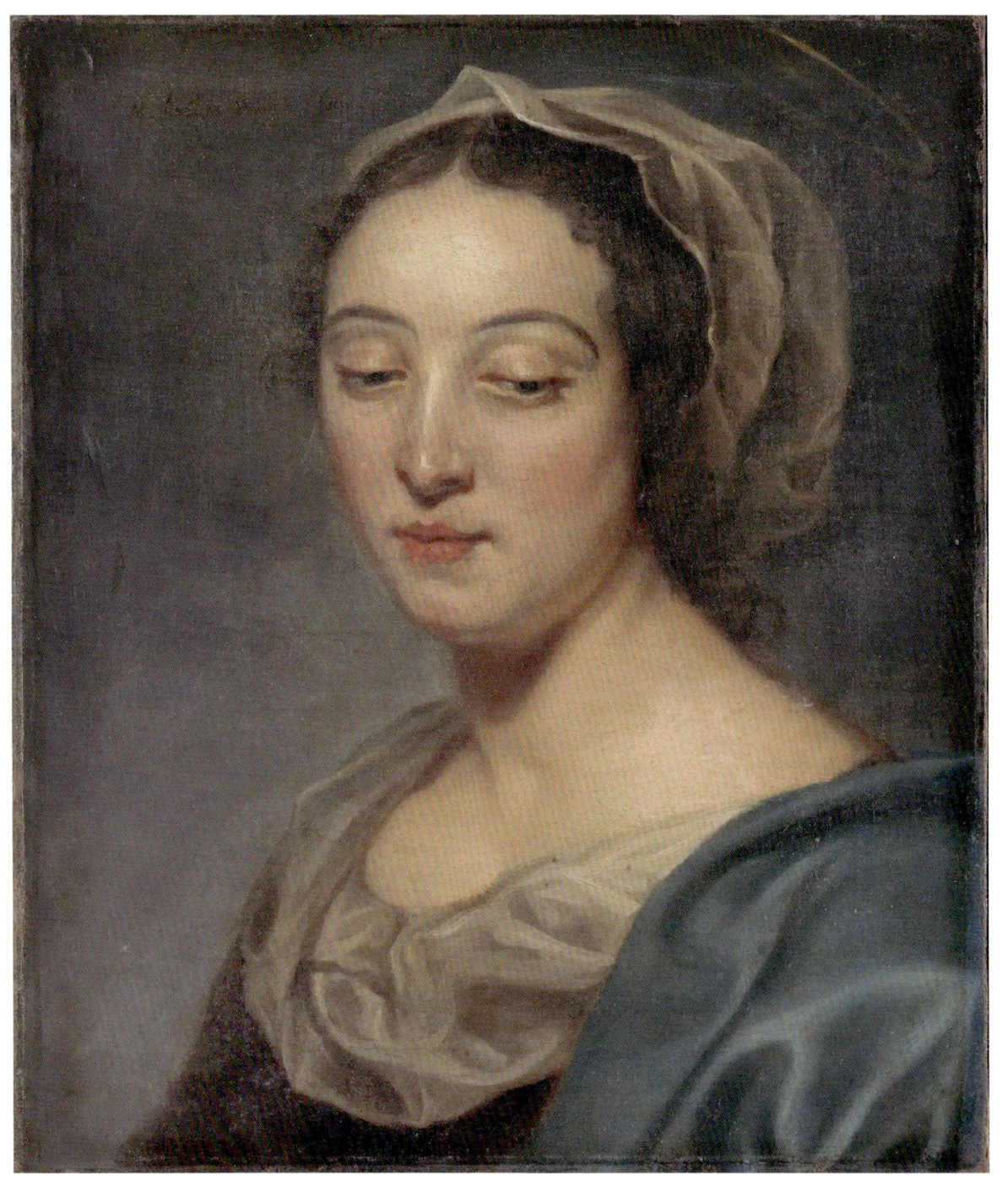

38 Michaelina Wautier, *Bust of a Saint*, c.1645, oil on canvas, 44.6 × 37.2 cm (17 ½ × 14 ⅝ in), The Phoebus Foundation

In the same year, the Italian painter Artemisia Gentileschi wrote in a letter to the Sicilian collector Don Antonio Ruffo (1610–78) that she would show an illustrious client what a woman was capable of.[36] This is a beautiful coincidence, impressing upon us that intelligent female artists were very conscious of the exceptionality of their work and that they expressly strived to foreground themselves. From the period 1643 to 1649, we know of no other work by the artist with a format similar to this religious painting. In it, she displays her ambition to paint life-size protagonists. The canvas is more than two metres wide. Its size suggests that it must have functioned as an altarpiece, which leads us to assume that it was a commission rather than a project that she initiated herself. The positioning of this pyramidal group in an open landscape, the massive bodies, the frail silhouettes and the angular yet decorative folds of their colourful garments – red, blue, white – are already showing signs of refinement and maturity. In terms of its size, stability and harmony, the *Mystic Marriage* can easily be compared to later history paintings, such as the 1656 *Education of the Virgin* (see fig.59) or the 1659 *Annunciation* (fig.34), although the brushstrokes gradually become smoother. Additionally, in the *Annunciation*, her interest in depicting a domestic setting has grown. The hands of the figure of Catherine, half opened, with long, bent fingers – are a style element Wautier would return to. The saints seem to be conversing, and the graceful poses with the stylised profiles remind us of the ethereal religious scenes by Anthony van Dyck, who, especially in his 'Second Antwerp period' (*c*.1627–34), had developed a refined style with contained emotions and a scintillating palette. Wautier undoubtedly prepared this complex composition with partial studies such as the *Bust of a Saint* (fig.38), which is also from this early period, and the *Study of the Head of a Bearded Man* (see fig.61).

That a woman could make a history painting of this quality and size was unprecedented in the Low Countries. Wautier's signature indicates that she was conscious of her exceptional accomplishment here:

'Michaelina Wautier invenit et fecit 1649.' It is thus hard to believe that she would have produced no other history painting before this one. Archival evidence supports this conclusion. In his accounting book, the dance master Adam-Pierre de La Grené noted that in 1650 he had bought a 'Bacchus' de madamoiselle Wautier' which seems not to have been preserved.[37] This source demonstrates that she painted at least several history paintings in this period. The size of the painting of Saint Catherine warrants the assumption that she made the painting on commission. It is too big for a domestic setting and would be better suited for a private chapel. If Wautier, as early in her career as 1649, did indeed receive a commission to make a religious painting of this size, that tells us much about the reputation she enjoyed at the time. Sadly, no information about the provenance of the painting is available.[38] The self-portrait, made around 1650 (fig.1), is also from this phase in her development. This painting shows her posing as a consummate artist, suggesting that in this period she considered herself to have reached an important milestone as a painter, as exemplified in the *Mystic Marriage*.

THE DISCOVERY OF NEW GENRES, 1650–55

Wautier's creativity was never limited to a single genre of painting, and she practised several within the same period. In the years 1650 to 1655, for instance, she painted genre paintings, flower pieces, portraits and history pieces. The series of *The Five Senses* is from 1650 (see figs 39–43); the extremely sophisticated two *Garlands of Flowers* from 1652 (figs 48–9); 1653 is the date of the *Study of a Young Man* (fig.54); and a year later, she produced the breathtaking portrait of Martino Martini (fig.58).

Boys as a Favourite Theme

The importance of *The Five Senses* (figs 39–43) for providing better insight into, and appreciation of, Wautier's oeuvre cannot be understated.[39]

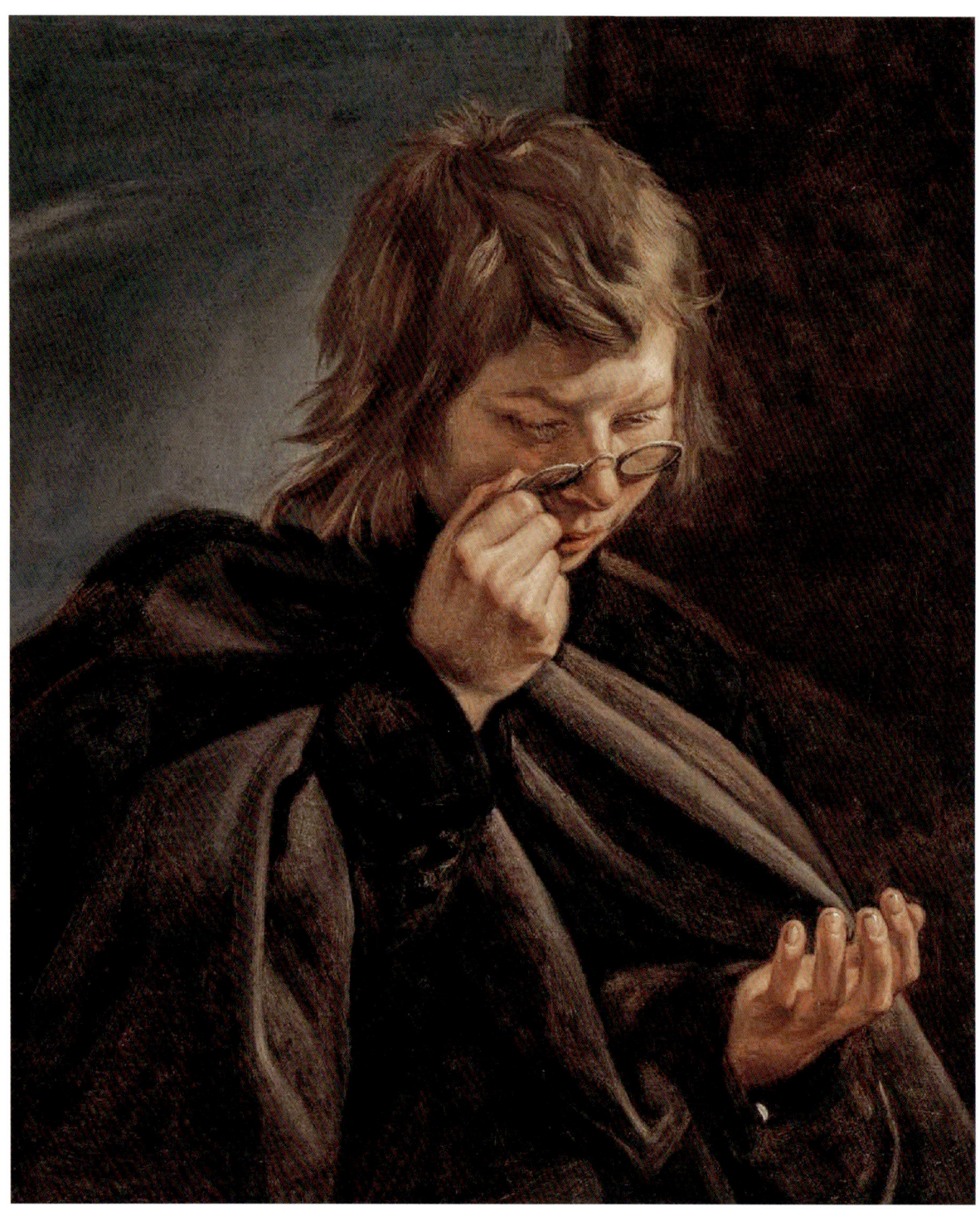

39 Michaelina Wautier, *The Five Senses: Sight*, 1650, oil on canvas, 69.5 × 61 cm (27 ⅜ × 24 in), Museum of Fine Arts, Boston, MA, on loan as a promised gift from Rose-Marie and Eijk van Otterloo

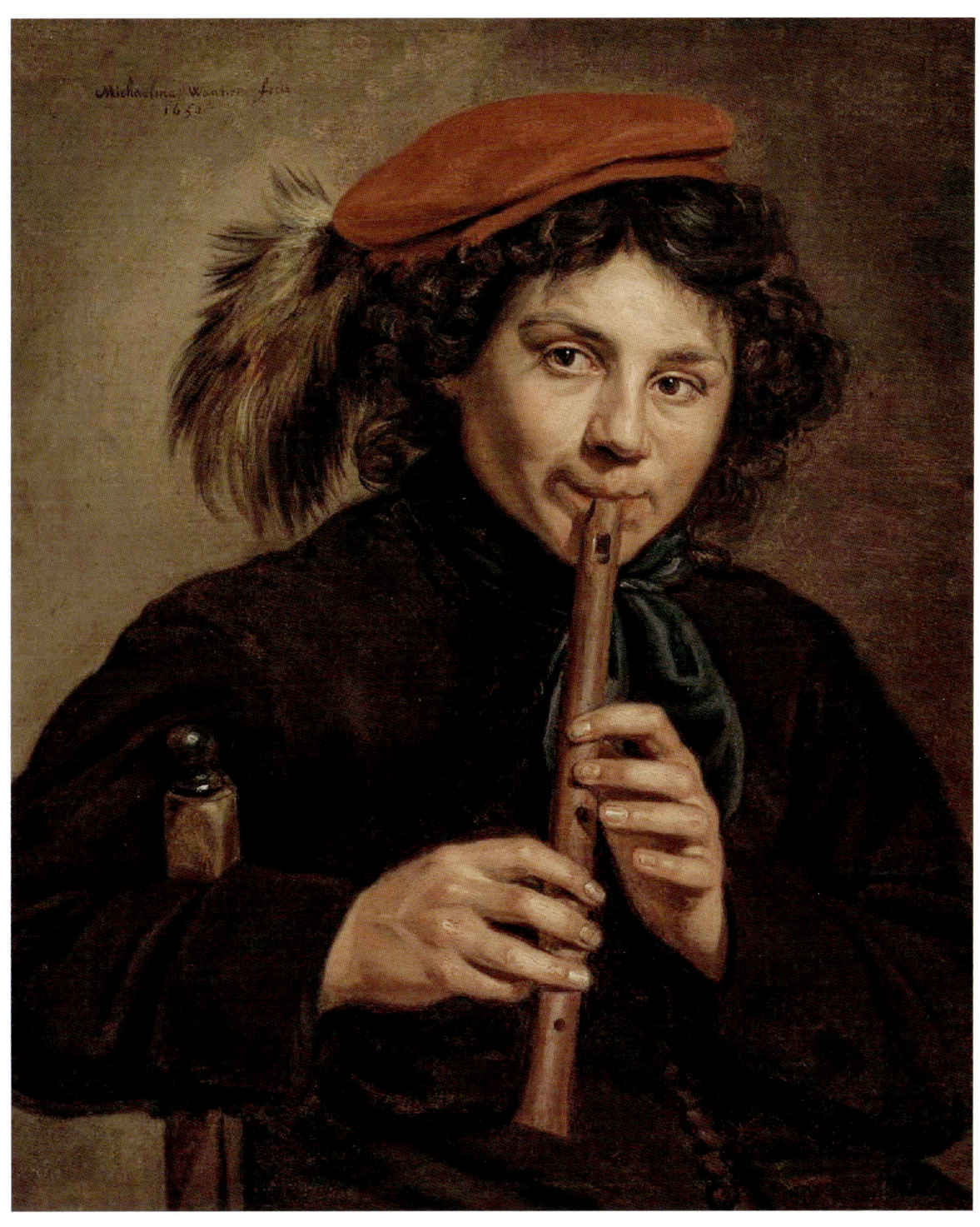

40 Michaelina Wautier, *The Five Senses: Hearing*, 1650, oil on canvas, 69.5 × 61 cm (27 ⅜ × 24 in), Museum of Fine Arts, Boston, MA, on loan as a promised gift from Rose-Marie and Eijk van Otterloo

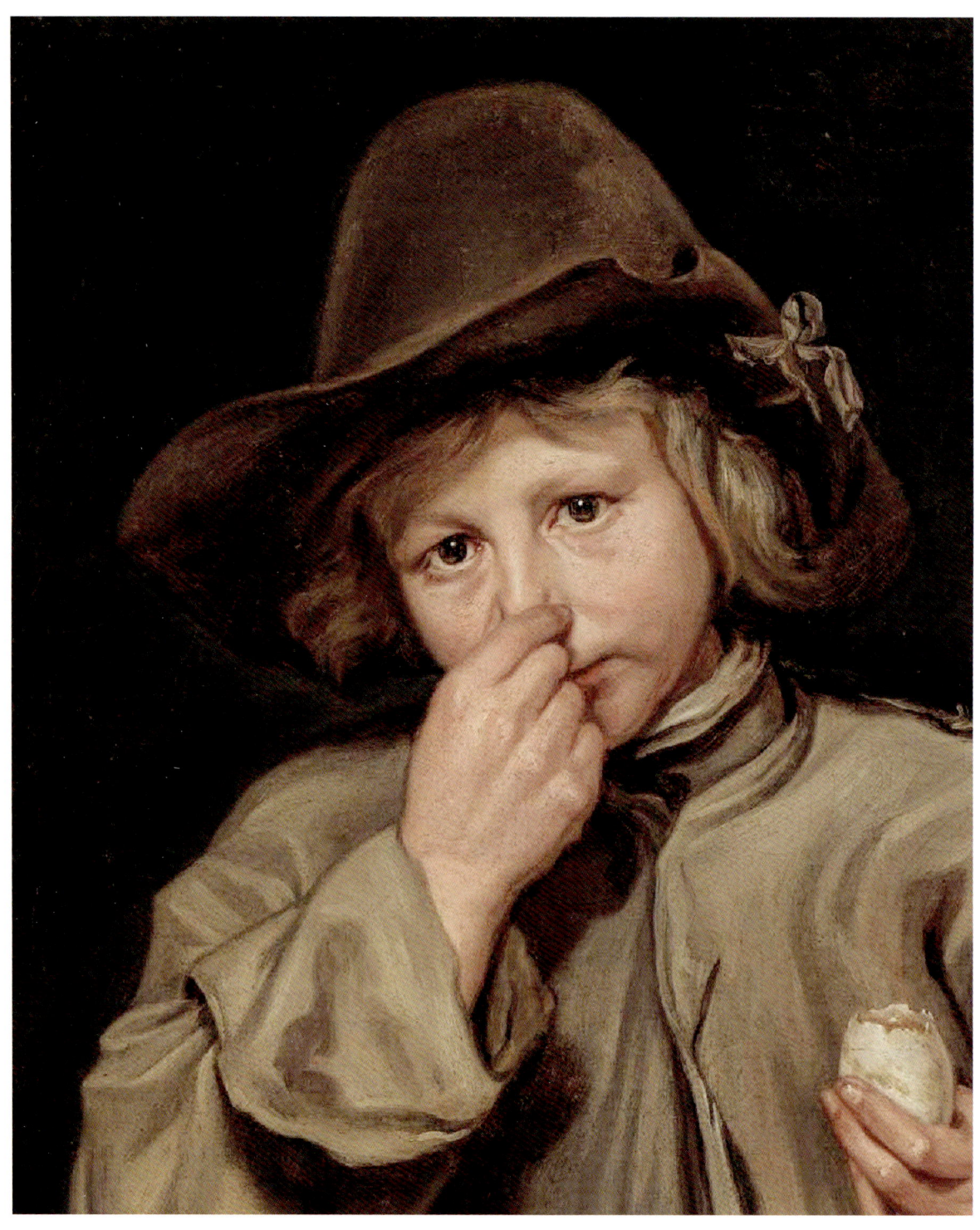

41 Michaelina Wautier, *The Five Senses: Smell*, 1650, oil on canvas, 69.5 × 61 cm (27 ⅜ × 24 in), Museum of Fine Arts, Boston, MA, on loan as a promised gift from Rose-Marie and Eijk van Otterloo

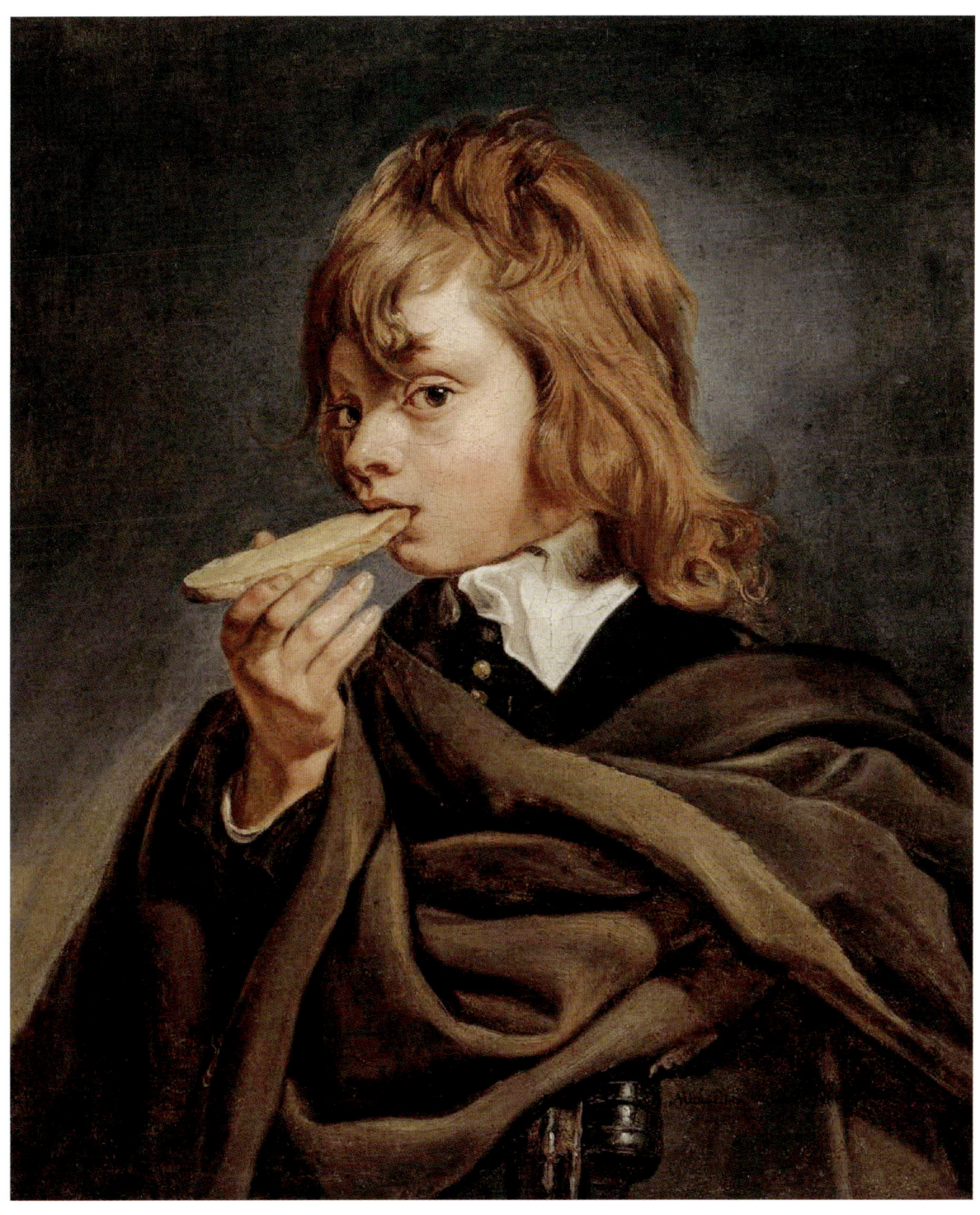

42 Michaelina Wautier, *The Five Senses: Taste*, 1650, oil on canvas, 69.5 × 61 cm (27 ⅜ × 24 in), Museum of Fine Arts, Boston, MA, on loan as a promised gift from Rose-Marie and Eijk van Otterloo

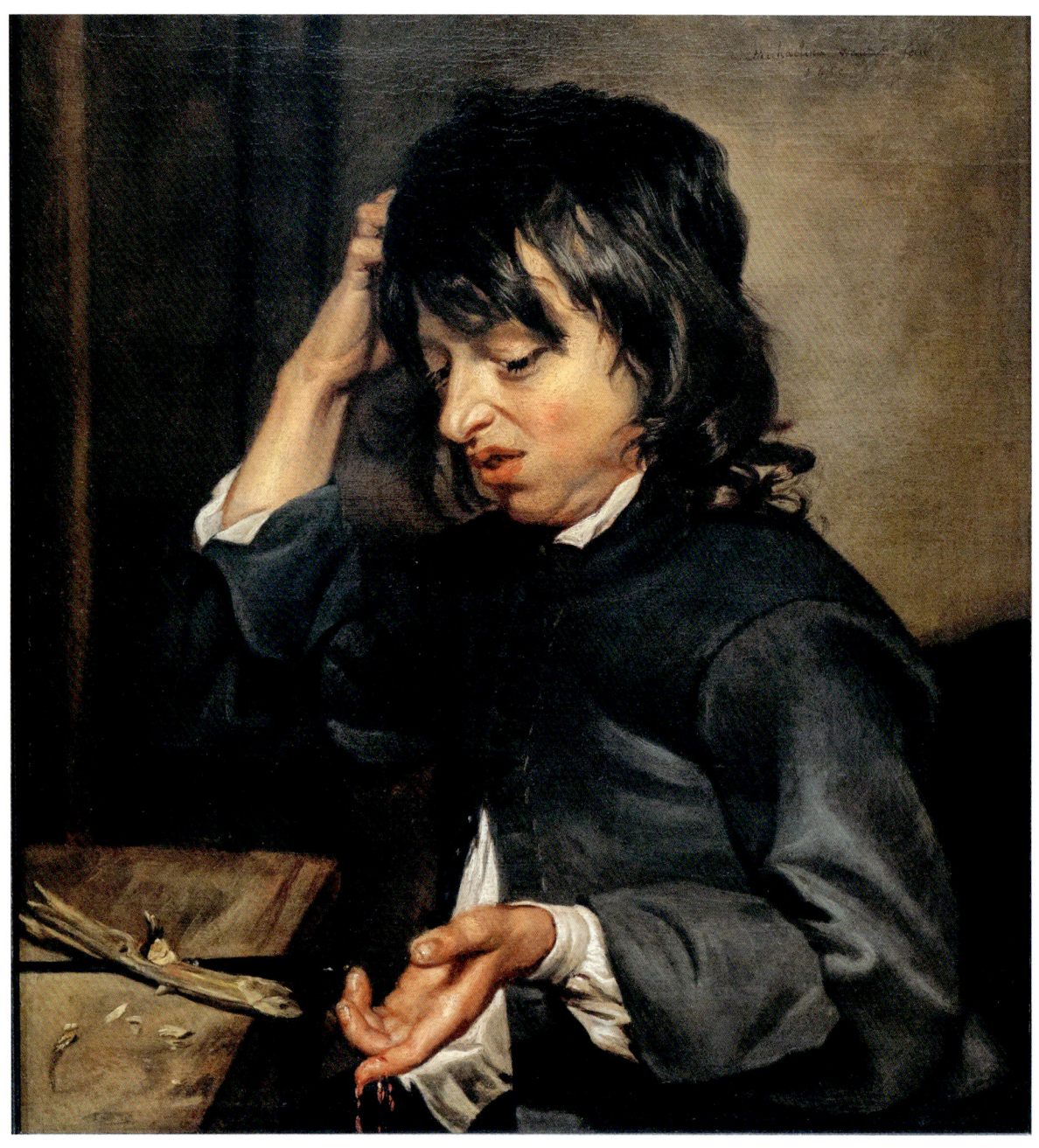

43 Michaelina Wautier, *The Five Senses: Touch*, 1650, oil on canvas, 69.5 × 61 cm (27 ⅜ × 24 in), Museum of Fine Arts, Boston, MA, on loan as a promised gift from Rose-Marie and Eijk van Otterloo

The unexpected discovery of the five paintings and the subsequent transfer by Rose-Marie and Eijk van Otterloo as 'a promised gift' to the Museum of Fine Arts in Boston in 2022, along with an accompanying exhibition, was a significant milestone in the recognition of Wautier since the exhibition in Antwerp in 2018. The series affirms her stunning versatility and illustrates the unique way she conceived genre scenes. Wautier signed and dated the five paintings in full 'Michaelina Wautier 1650', as she regularly did throughout her career. What is remarkable about this series is that she placed her signature in different places in the compositions. For example, in the allegory of *Hearing* it is at the upper left corner, in *Sight* it is on the right at shoulder level, in *Smell* it is to the right of the cap, in *Taste* it is at the lower right of the metal bowl, and in *Touch* it is at the upper right corner.[40]

Traditionally, the senses are almost exclusively personified by adult men. Wautier deviated from this tradition by portraying boys. They are arranged against dark backgrounds, with the light coming from the front. Wautier used the chiaroscuro effects from the Caravaggesque idiom. She achieved optimal variation by depicting five distinct personalities with completely different physiognomies. Moreover, the boys are characterised by different hairstyles and hair colour. Genre scenes populated by children with utterly lively and natural expressions, and colourful incidental details, were a unique Dutch Republic phenomenon. In Haarlem, for example, from the 1620s onwards, representations of the senses were made on individual supports and in larger formats. Iconographically and compositionally, Wautier's flute player, the depiction of *Hearing* within this series, dovetails neatly with this Haarlem type, as can be seen in Judith Leyster's *Boy Playing the Flute* from *c.*1630–33 (fig.44). Consequently, it is no surprise that Wautier, as the author of *The Five Senses*, was described in the auction catalogue of 1883 as an excellent pupil of Adriaen Brouwer (1605/6–38) and Frans Hals (1582/3–1666).[41] Louis Le Nain

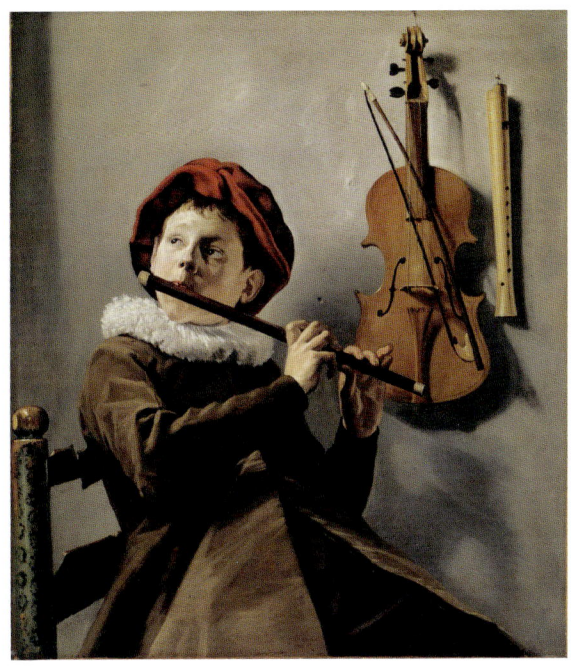

44 Judith Leyster, *Boy Playing the Flute*, *c.*1630–33, oil on canvas, 73 × 62 cm (28 ¾ × 24 ⅜ in), Nationalmuseum, Stockholm

(*c.*1600–48), in line with other Haarlem artists such as Hals and Leyster, also tended to depict youngsters in all kinds of genre scenes. The type of boys is surprisingly similar to the models Wautier used for her *Five Senses*. Le Nain's *The Young Card-Players* from around 1636–40 is a good example (fig.45).[42]

Wautier's innovative approach to representations of boys was admired by at least one painter of her era, who adopted it for his works. Earlier publications on Wautier had assumed that for her half-body, realistic depictions of boys, she was inspired by the examples of the enigmatic Michael Sweerts, also active in Brussels, who was about her age. Little is known about the work he made in Brussels before he was first mentioned in Italy in 1646. Interestingly, however, he did not start to paint attractive representations of young boys before his return from Italy around 1655. For that reason,

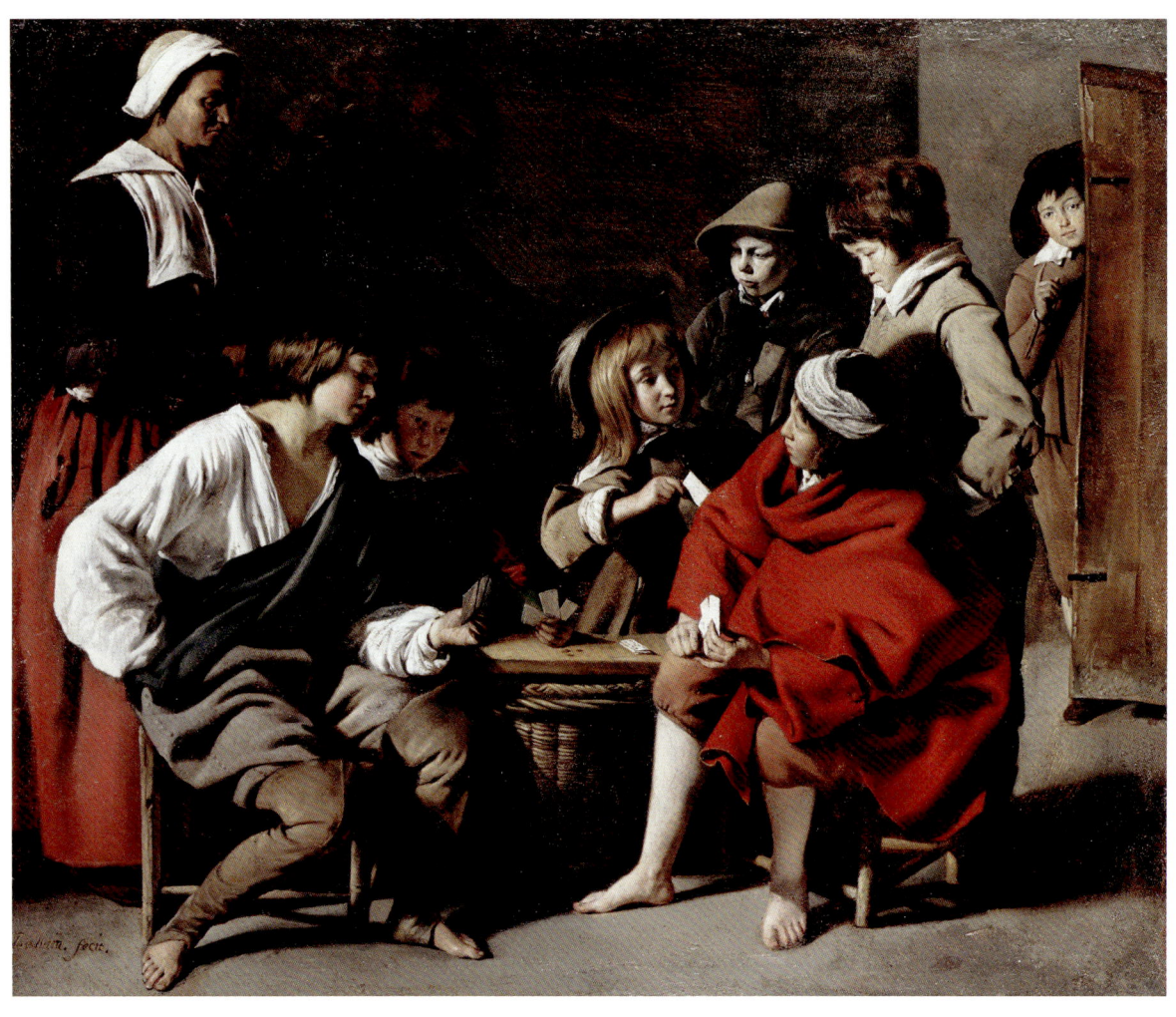

45 Louis Le Nain, *The Young Card-Players*, c.1636–40, oil on canvas, 55 × 64.2 cm (21 ⅝ × 25 ¼ in), Royal Collection Trust

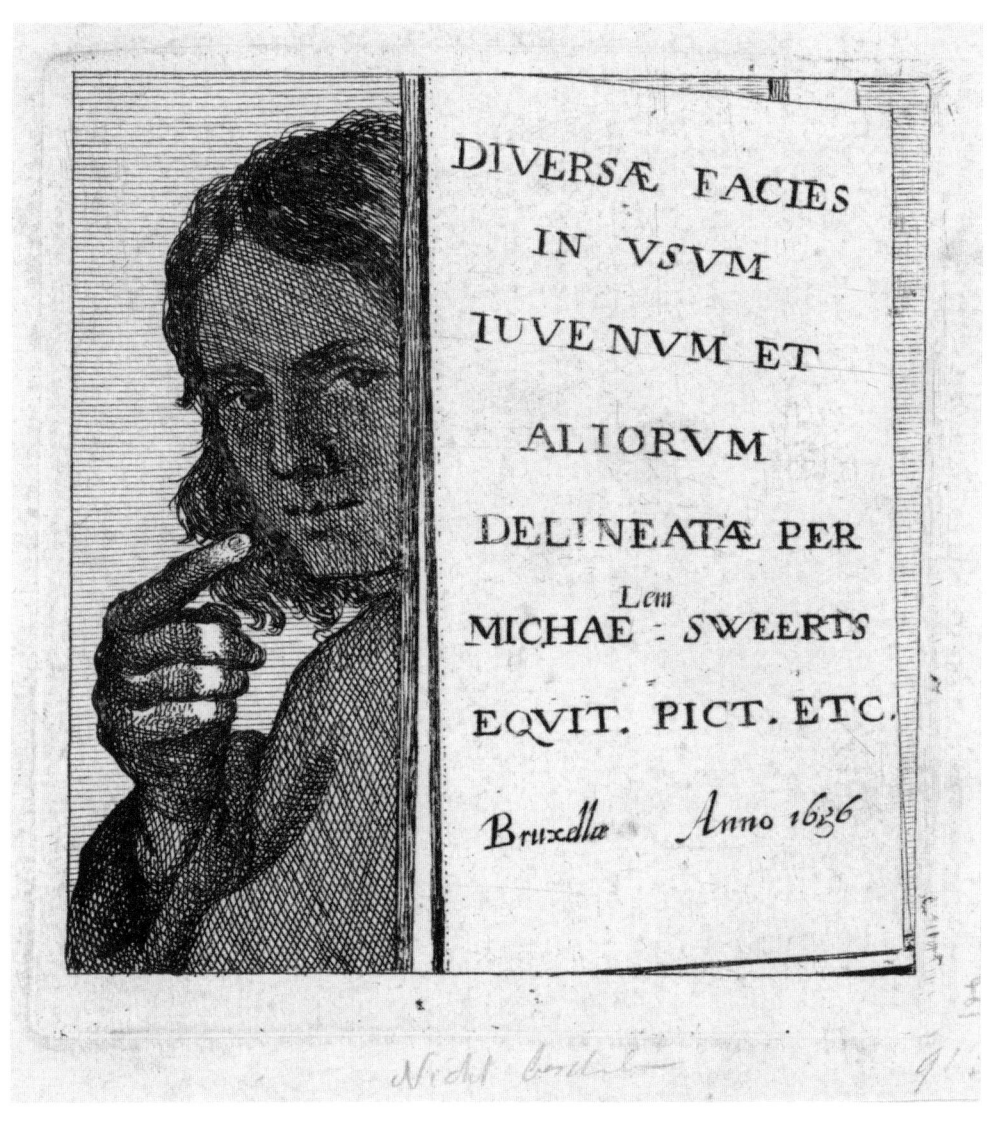

46 Michael Sweerts, *Young Man behind an Easel*, 1656, from *Diversae facies in vsvm iuvenvm et aliorvm delineatae*, etching, 9 × 8.1 cm (3 ½ × 3 ¼ in), Rijksprentenkabinet, Amsterdam

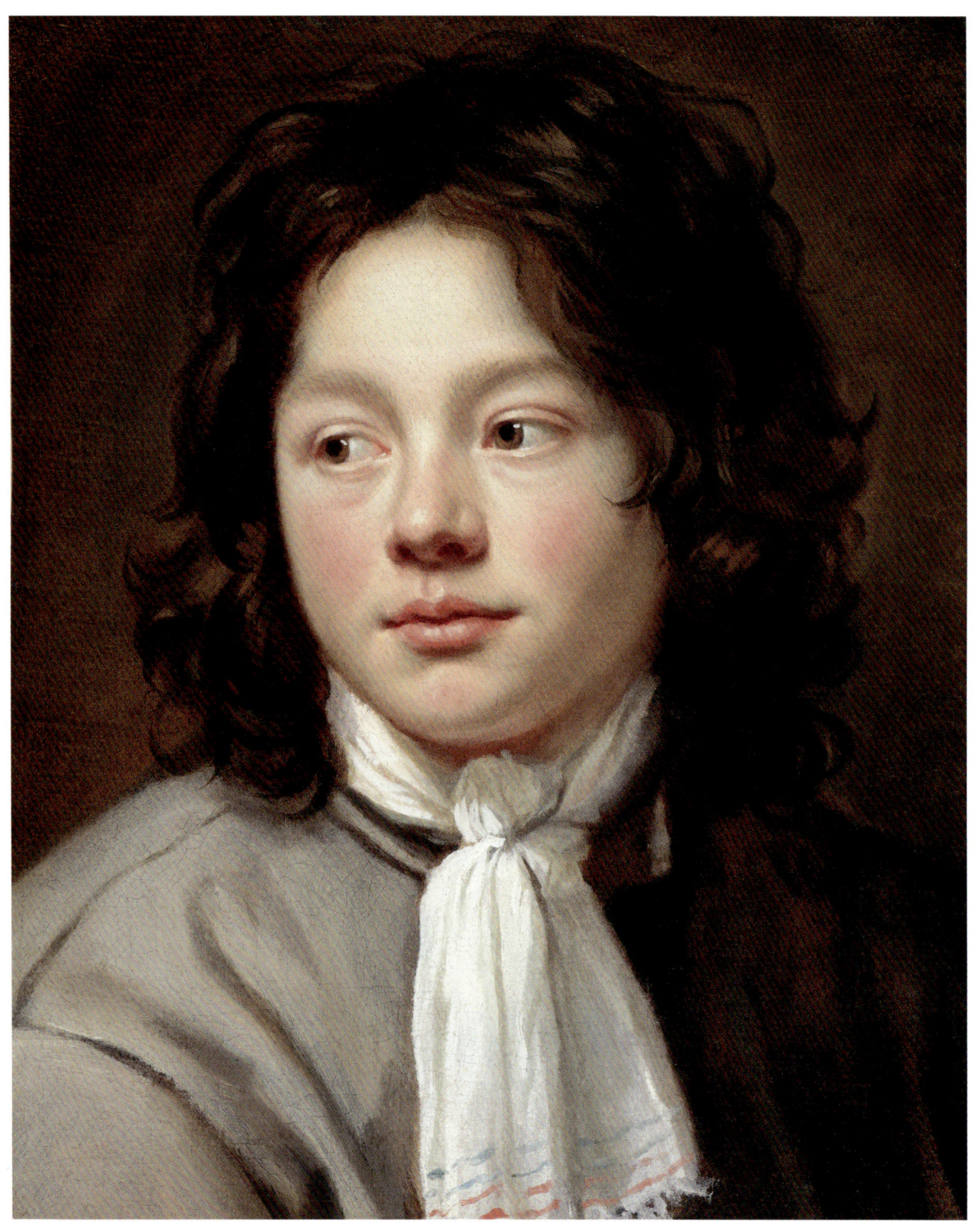

47 Michaelina Wautier, *Boy with a White Cravat*, *c.*1650–55, oil on canvas, 41.7 × 33.6 cm (16 ⅜ × 13 ¼ in), The Kremer Collection

we cannot doubt that Wautier's *Five Senses* inspired Sweerts and that the series of etchings he published in 1656 under the title *Diversae facies in vsvm iuvenvm et aliorvm delieatae* (fig.46) could never have been made without thc innovative typology Wautier introduced.[43] Her appealing *Boy with a White Cravat* of 1650–55 (fig.47) shows how great the affinity in their works is and to what extent Sweerts was inspired by Wautier's new idea of the natural depiction of boys, drawn or painted from life (see fig.66).[44]

Two Garlands of Flowers

The two known surviving paintings by Wautier of garlands of flowers both bear the signature 'Michaelina Wautier fecit. 1652' (figs 48–9).[45] These are Wautier's most atypical creations. Without exaggeration, we can say that no one would have associated these flower pieces with her if they had not been signed.[46] In the first half of the seventeenth-century, in Antwerp – the main production centre for this genre – flower still lifes were considered a distinct specialisation within the range of iconographic themes pursued by artists. Artists such as Daniel Seghers (1590–1661) and Jan Davidsz. de Heem (1606–84) had created a new genre, featuring floral bouquets as the main motif of their compositions. This implied that painters of still lifes in general or flower pieces more specifically were so specialised that they never endeavoured to paint in other genres, such as history pieces or portraits. Even Rubens left the floral elements of his compositions to flower painters such as Osias Beert (*c*.1580–1624), Jan Brueghel the Elder and Frans Snijders (1579–1657).[47] This doubtlessly labour-intensive specialism demanded extensive botanical knowledge, and the talent to execute minute details and to design virtual compositions. Until far into the nineteenth century, flower painting was regarded as gender-specific – well suited for women, who were thought to have little imagination[48] – and some female artists, such as Rachel Ruysch (1664–1750), devoted themselves

exclusively to this genre.[49] For Wautier, the flower still life was only one aspect of her oeuvre. Even so, her lavishly assorted garlands made a groundbreaking contribution. The botanical culture at the Brussels court – in which Leopold Wilhelm was himself a keen participant, for he had gardens constructed near Coudenberg Palace and was a fervent collector of flower still lifes – possibly stimulated her interest in flowers.[50]

Around 1650, flower garlands were a new variation in the development of flower painting as a genre. Wautier's garlands date from 1652, around the time that Seghers made his first independent flower garland as a sub-genre of floral still-life painting. But none of his compositions of garlands suspended from the characteristic blue bows can be dated with certainty before the middle of the century. That leaves open the possibility that Wautier was the first to paint them, although it will remain impossible to prove.[51] In any case, as far as we know, Wautier was the first painter in either Antwerp or Brussels to create flower garlands as companion pieces. In this respect, she followed the Netherlandish tradition of symmetrically displaying paintings alongside fireplaces or wooden cabinets, for example.[52] The panels are in the same format, and their compositions are very similar. While a dragonfly hovers above one of the garlands (fig.48), a butterfly floats above the other (fig.49). The colour palette differs considerably. The colours in the floral arrangement with the butterfly are more traditional, with red and white overtones, but the garland beneath the dragonfly shows a more experimental colour scheme with orange accents. Wautier's selection of flowers is highly varied. For this latter bouquet, she chose a variety of smaller flowers, including carnations, marigolds, cornflowers, African marigolds, daisies, foxgloves, sweet peas and yellow bachelor's buttons. The white, orange and red carnations definitely attract attention and would have done so around 1650, when they were exotic flowers bred for the ornamental garden. Apparently, Wautier placed the most exotic flowers at the centre of the garland, while the more familiar flowers were gathered

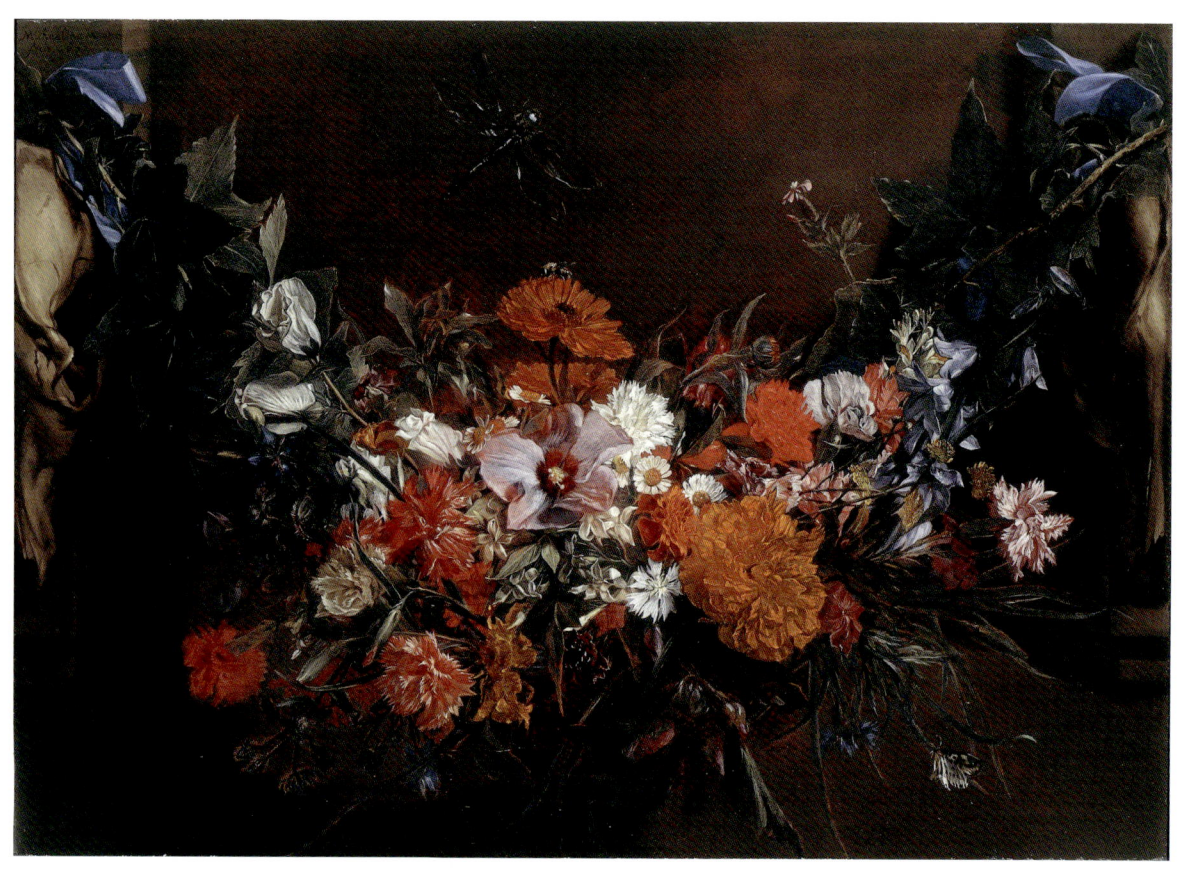

48 Michaelina Wautier, *Garland of Flowers with Dragonfly*, 1652, oil on panel, 41.1 × 57.4 cm (16 ⅛ × 22 ⅝ in), private collection

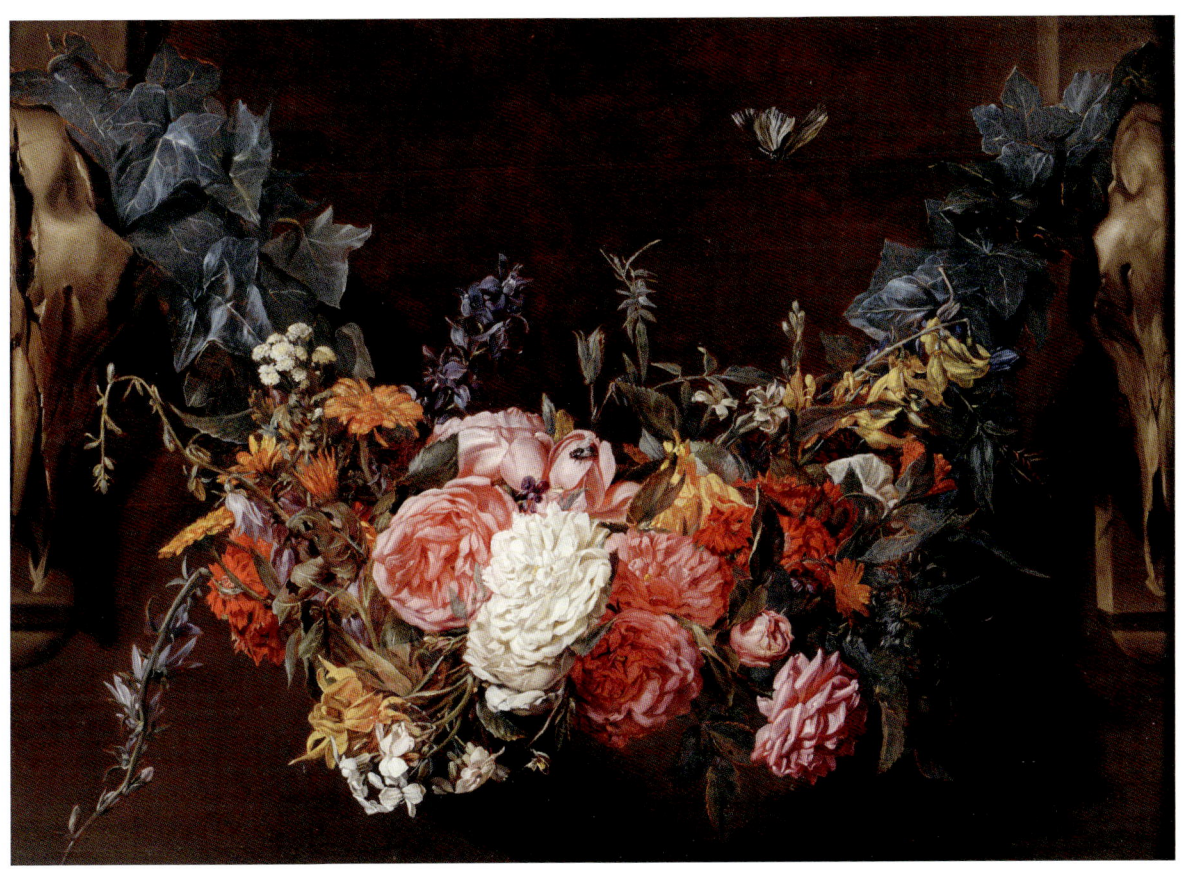

49 Michaelina Wautier, *Garland of Flowers with Butterfly*, 1652, oil on panel, 42 × 57 cm (16 ½ × 22 ½ in), private collection, on loan to the Noordbrabants Museum, 's-Hertogenbosch

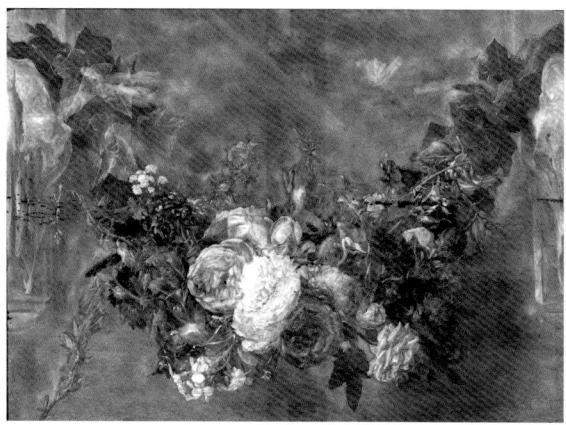

50 Ma-xrf (Pb-L) map of fig. 49.

at the edges.[53] In order to render them so naturally, she must have had access to botanical books or the opportunity to visit exclusive gardens. From a technical point of view, the garlands must have challenged Wautier's artistic imagination. They are painted with a sense of detail and precision that is lacking in her other works. It is clear that she adapted her style to the genre, choosing panels that were better suited to painting in thin layers and achieving a satin-like finish. Wautier could only achieve this range of colours by using expensive blue pigments such as azurite and ultramarine.[54] Her investment in acquiring and learning to apply these pigments may confirm her desire to emulate her male colleagues by becoming equally skilled in the technical aspects of her work.

The most original aspect of these still lifes is how they link the brevity of floral beauty with the antique motif of bucrania, architectural decorations in which flower garlands were suspended from animal skulls, representing transience. It is evident that the skulls added a strong *memento mori* connotation. Both in shape and in content, Wautier's garlands reach back to the Hellenistic-Roman bucrania friezes. The combination of this antique motif with the glory of a colourful painted flower garland is completely

original. Even though some engravings were known of comparable Roman reliefs – for instance of the interior of the Ara Pacis Augustae in Rome – Wautier's composition even more closely corresponds with the motif on the Roman funerary altar dedicated to Genius Decuria (Museo Archeologico Nazionale, Naples), or the funerary urn of Acilia Hygia (Rijksmuseum van Oudheden, Leiden). The fact that these bucrania decorate an urn emphasises their funerary and commemorative character. To see this funerary monument, Wautier did not need to travel to Rome. In 1618, the urn of Acilia Hygia was acquired by Rubens from the collection of antique sculptures of Sir Dudley Carleton (1573–1632), then British ambassador to the States General at The Hague. Rubens sold the urn in 1626 to George Villiers (1592–1628), 1st Duke of Buckingham. The majority of his collection of antiquities was sold in Antwerp, in 1648. Leopold Wilhelm was interested in this collection but we cannot verify whether he actually bought any sculptures.[55] Where and whether Wautier saw the urn is unclear. She cannot have seen it at Rubens's house, since she was much too young, but when it was sold around 1650 in Antwerp, it is possible that this classical object caught her fancy. That could also explain why she integrated the motif in her flower still lifes. And with that, the argument that the composition of her garlands proves that she went to Italy is no longer tenable. She may well have encountered the inspiring motif in Antwerp or Brussels, too.[56]

Some Wautier paintings have been subjected recently to material research, which has revealed new discoveries about her working methods. For instance, MA-XRF scanning, a non-invasive imaging technique based on X-ray fluorescence (XRF), reveals the preparatory stages and pentimenti beneath the surface of the *Garland of Flowers with Butterfly* (fig.50), yielding a better understanding of the genesis of her work. Studied in this way, the garland shows a clear technical influence from the Antwerp flower painters mentioned above, in particular Seghers.[57] Wautier may have prepared several flowers (red or pink) with a vermilion underpainting or dead colour, roughly indicating the final shape and placement of the flower in the early stages of painting. Some of these brightly coloured patches were ultimately discarded, implying that they were intended to be replaced at a later stage of the creative process. This technique of using more or less abstract shapes was first introduced by Seghers. The question, then, is how and where Wautier learned this technique. Charles never painted floral still lifes, so she could not have learned this from him. Since Seghers was one of the most important flower painters working in Antwerp, it seems likely that Wautier was in contact with him in one way or another. Her connection with Antwerp is also evident from the fact that she purchased the panels supporting the garlands there, as they bear the city's hallmarks. Her half-brother Albert, who lived in Antwerp until his death in 1639, may have supplied the connection. Wautier may have kept in touch with his wife, Jeronima Sivori, and their son Charles. Most significantly, the Archduke Leopold Wilhelm may also have played a crucial role. He was a great admirer of Seghers's floral still lifes, of which he collected three. He was in frequent contact with Seghers and visited the artist in his studio in 1648.[58]

Wautier may well have been a pioneer with her flower still lifes. Until now, very little technical research has been carried out on women's paintings, but the great recent interest in women artists in general – and Wautier in particula – has led private collectors and museums such as the Kunsthistorisches Museum in Vienna and the Museum of Fine Arts in Boston to invest in this area. As the analysis of this garland by Wautier shows, in-depth object-based research can contribute to a better understanding of the genesis of artistic practice and the innovations of artists.

Hidden Models and a Jesuit

The series *The Five Senses* (figs 39–43), dated 1650, anticipates other genre scenes throughout Wautier's active period, in which the type of boy represented there plays the leading role. Two horizontal compositions, each depicting two boys interacting, are reminiscent of the boys personifying the senses. In the scene featuring *Two Boys Blowing Bubbles* (fig.51), the boys are entirely focused on their game and do not seem to be aware of the viewer. Two very similar children are seen in the playful *Two Boys Squabbling over an Egg* (fig.52).[59] If we compare the boys in *The Five Senses* to those in the two paintings, it is immediately clear that they are the same models. This raises the probability that the two large genre paintings come from this same period, although Wautier could also have made sketches and studies of the boys and reused these later. Furthermore, it is striking that the pose in which they are depicted is always different. None of these scenes are portraits or *portraits historiés*, where actual people are dressed up and fitted out as historical, mythological or Biblical characters. Rather, they are representations of picturesque models who should be perceived in their totality as an allegory. Through her faithful, frieze-like representations of life-size children, she created a unique, easily accessible metaphorical genre.

The boys blowing bubbles that immediately burst represent Vanitas or the impermanence of existence. Bubbles are the ultimate symbol of transience and an age-old emblem that remained extremely popular in the seventeenth century. As early as the first century BCE, Marcus Terentius Varro wrote that man is like a bubble ('si est homo bulla'). This metaphor was popularised in the Low Countries by Erasmus, who, in his *Adagia* of 1500, proclaimed that 'there is nothing more brittle, fleeting or empty than human life'.[60] What is particularly striking in Wautier's painting is the lack of interaction between the two figures, who are both focused on their personal game and looking in opposite directions. Despite being a similar age, they could not be more different. The boy in red has darker skin and abundant black curls. His fashionable attire, consisting of a jacket fastened with a row of buttons, wide cuffs and a red cloak, captures the viewer's attention. The top of his white undershirt

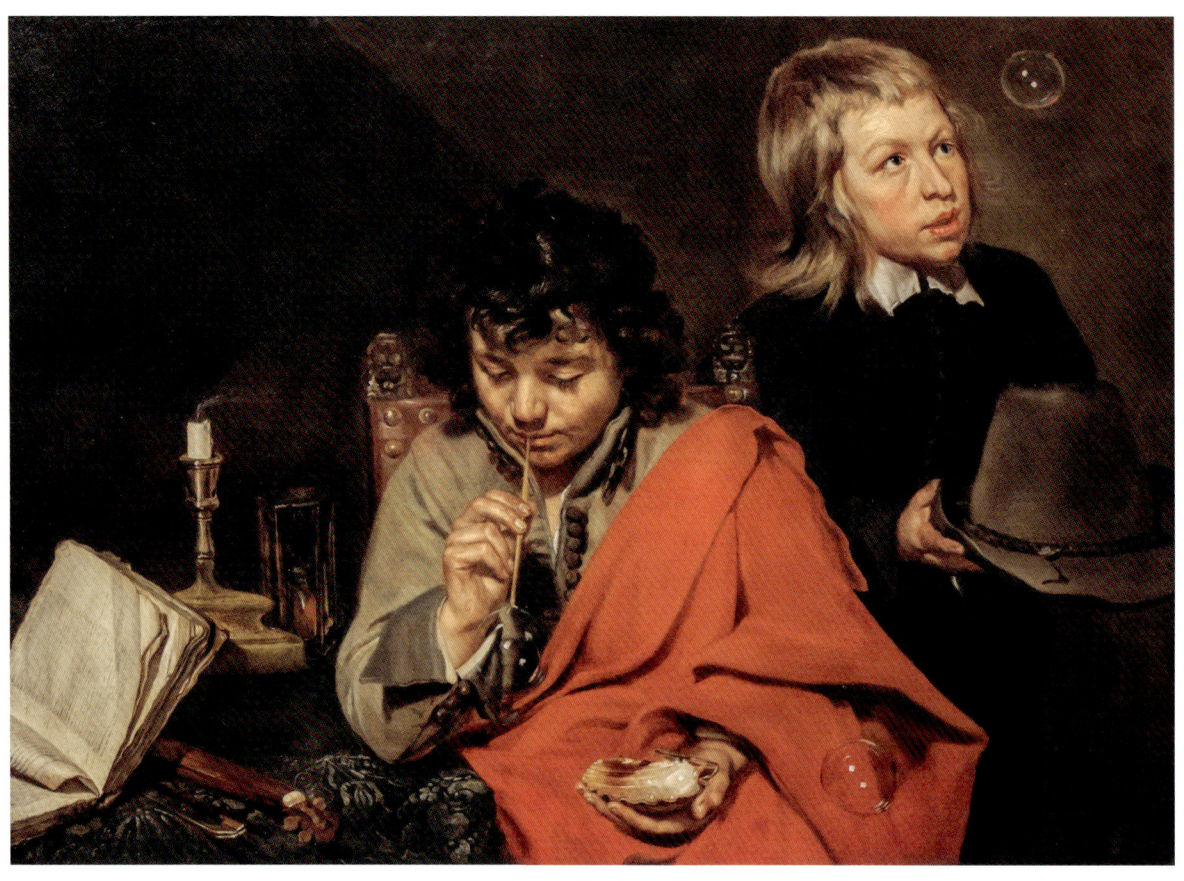

51 Michaelina Wautier, *Two Boys Blowing Bubbles*, *c.*1650–55, oil on canvas, 90.5 × 121.3 cm (35 ⅝ × 47 ¾ in), Seattle Art Museum, Seattle

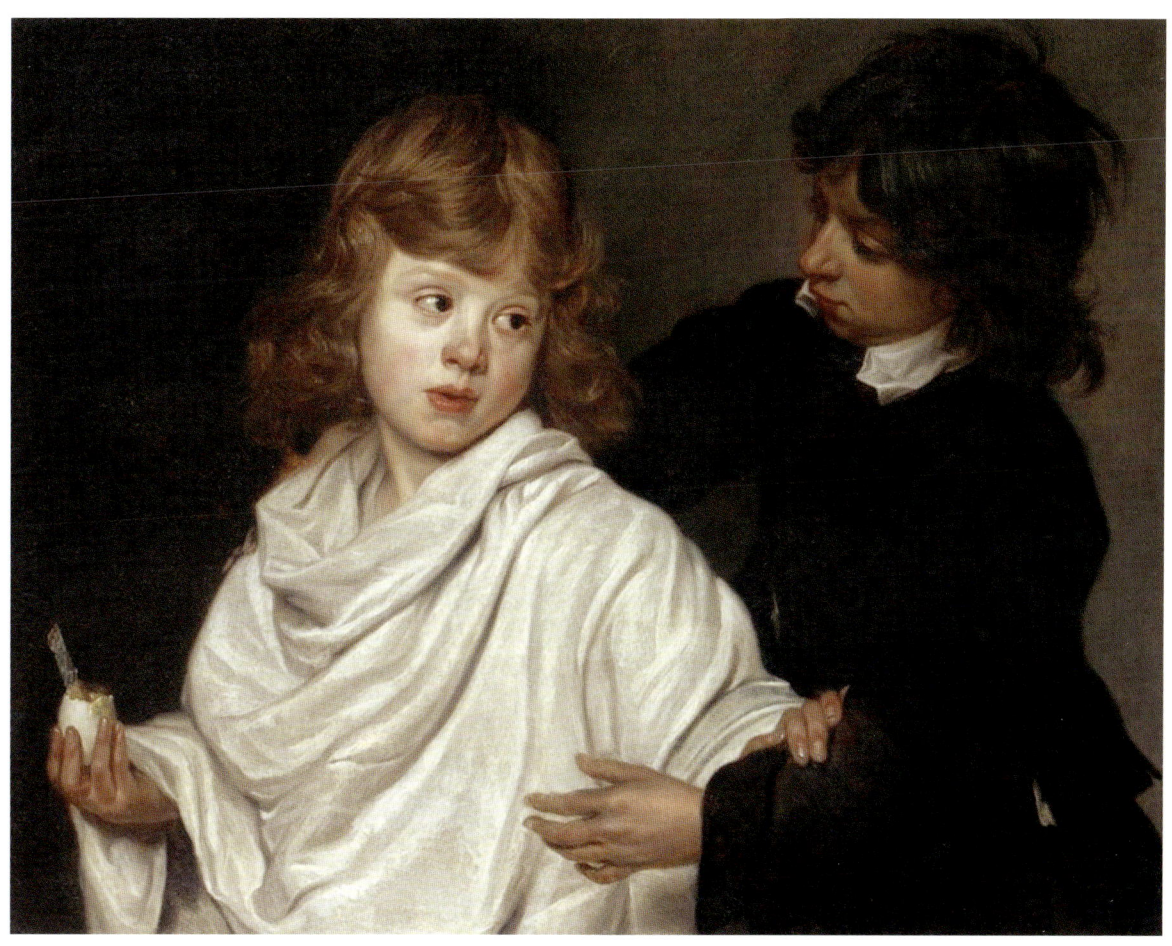

52 Michaelina Wautier, *Two Boys Squabbling over an Egg*, *c.*1650–55, oil on canvas, 66 × 82 cm (26 × 32 ¼ in),
The Phoebus Foundation

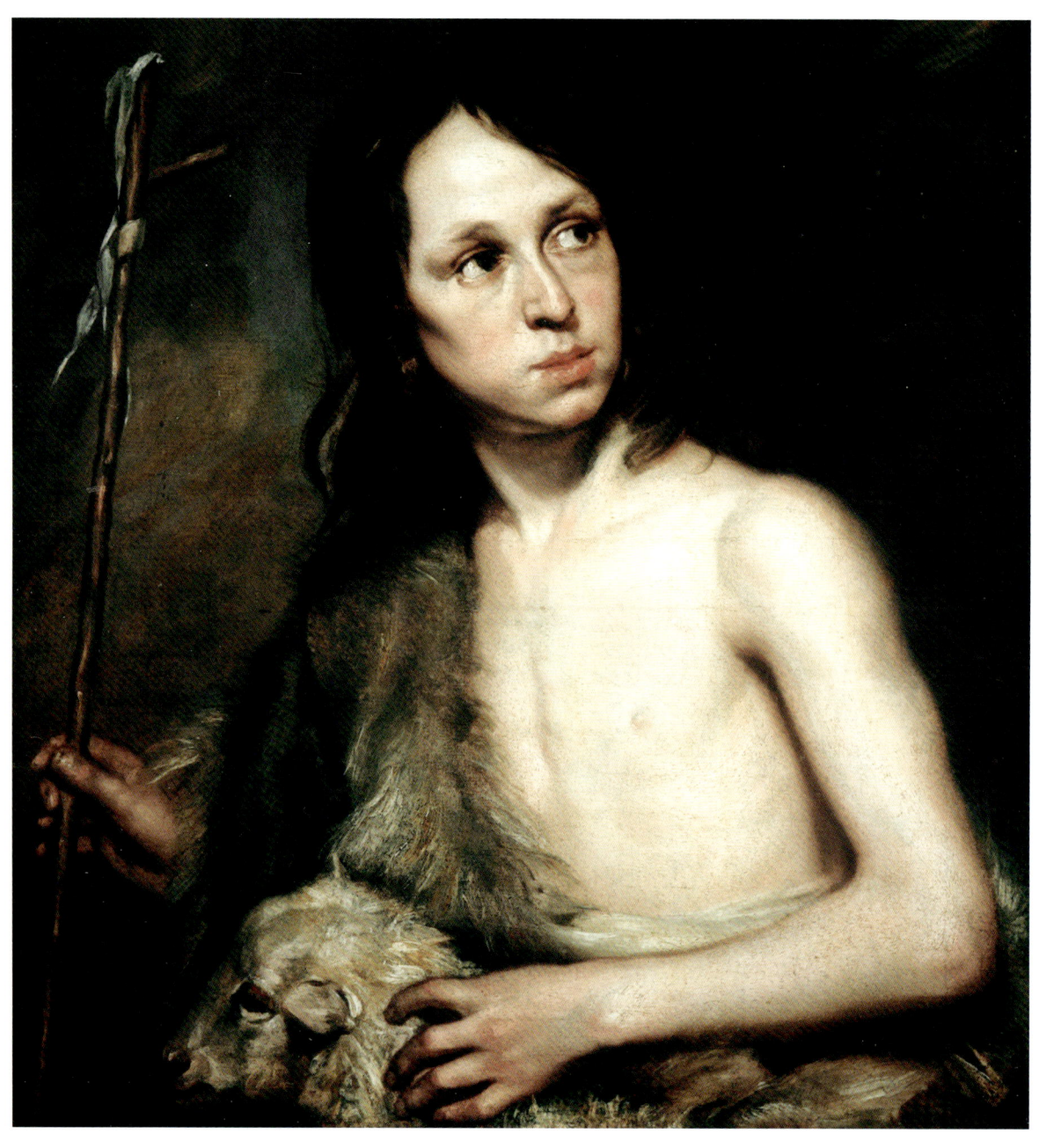

53 Michaelina Wautier, *Saint John the Baptist as a Boy*, *c.*1655, oil on canvas, 68 × 61 cm (26 ¾ × 24 in), Museo Lázaro Galdiano, Madrid

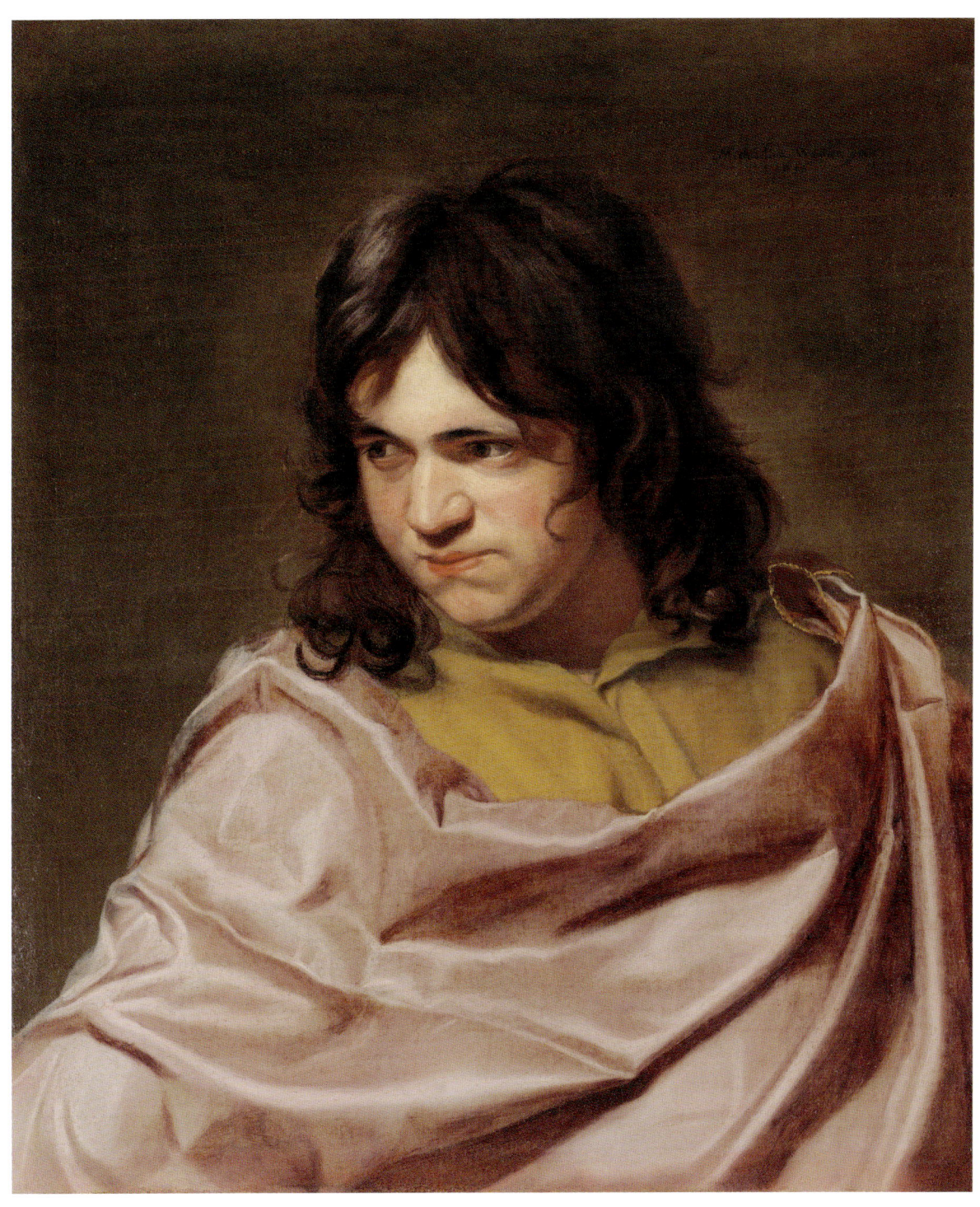

54 Michaelina Wautier, *Study of a Young Man*, 1653, oil on canvas, 69 × 58 cm (27 ⅛ × 22 ⅞ in), Royal Museum of Fine Arts, Antwerp

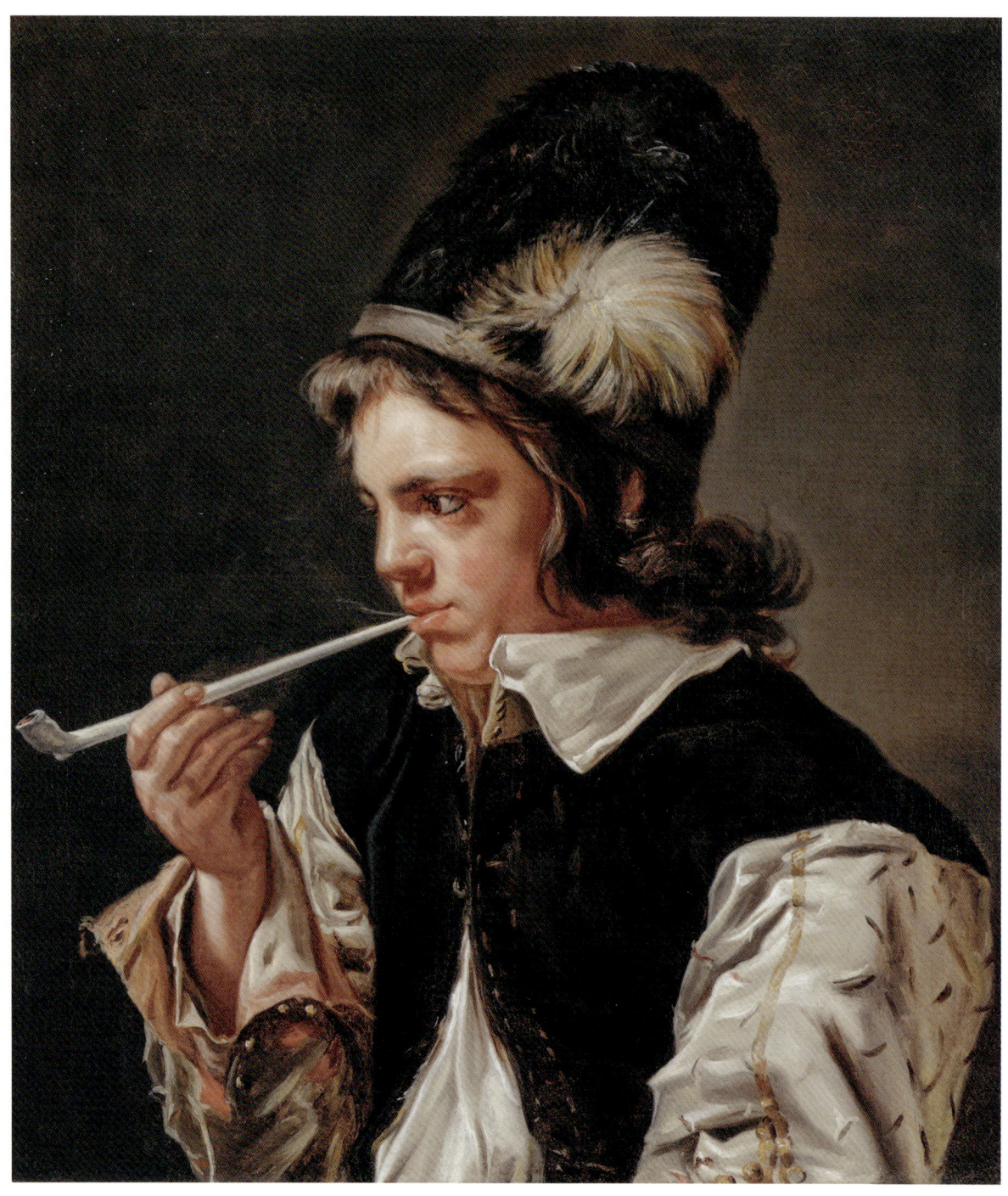

55 Michaelina Wautier, *Young Man Smoking a Pipe*, 16[5]6, oil on canvas, 68.5 × 58.5 cm (27 × 23 in), The Klesch Collection

is visible beneath his open jacket, lending him a more informal look. The boy behind him has medium-length blonde hair and is wearing a plain black suit. The two boys are positioned in a dark space, with the face of the blonde boy catching the light. The dreamy figures are rendered with the magnificent use of a fluid impasto technique, the dark-haired child's face being particularly expressively modelled. He looks as if he has stepped out of one of Caravaggio's early works.

If we compare the physiognomy of the blond boy in *Two Boys Blowing Bubbles* with *Saint John the Baptist as a Boy* (fig.53), we see that the same boy served as the model. The dark skin colour, heavy eyebrows and bent pose of the boy in red are very similar to those of the youth in *Study of a Young Man* (fig.54), whose body is also largely concealed beneath the folds of a mantle. The palette is, however, different. In *Two Boys Blowing Bubbles* the vermilion-like colour of the cloak contrasts vividly with the black clothing of the boy in the background and the overall darkness of the scene.

Wautier's *Young Man Smoking a Pipe* (fig.55) is almost certainly from 1656, although the third digit of the date is difficult to read. The artist's keen observation of the world is evident in this monochromatic work, which builds on the style of her *Five Senses*, created six years earlier. Although it cannot be ruled out that this painting was originally also part of a series depicting the senses (representing 'smell'), it can be enjoyed in its own right. The young man, whose face appears sculpted in wax with red and brown tones on his cheeks, is painted with broad brushstrokes. The free painting technique is clearly visible in the cap, which is decorated with a brilliantly rendered feather, and even more so in the cascade of different textiles, of which his left white sleeve stands out most.

Wautier also painted more explicit 'disguised portraits' or *portraits historiés*, and these are among the most sensitive works in her oeuvre.[61] One could even say that she had a certain preference for this specific type of portrait, which offered her the possibility to transcend the individual image by attaching a moralising message to it. In doing so, she was perfectly in touch with her time. Rubens, Rembrandt (1606–69) and many other seventeenth-century Flemish and Dutch artists enjoyed disguising themselves or their sitters in this manner, too. By doing so, they demonstrated the vanity of earthly life in contrast to everlasting religious or philosophical thoughts. *Two Girls as Saint Agnes and Saint Dorothy* (fig.56) exemplifies all of her superior characteristics.[62] The composition of this scene is similar to that of *Two Boys Squabbling over an Egg* (fig.52), with the pose of Dorothy mimicking that of the blond boy. This is now seen as one of Wautier's most iconic paintings, due to the intimate, melancholy atmosphere and the sophisticated technique. While the faces have been produced with delicate shadings, their garments fall in angular, thickly painted folds. The two girls are depicted as female martyrs. Agnes caresses a lamb, while Dorothy holds a rose in her right hand. Saint Agnes was only 13 years old when she was tortured to death for refusing to marry anyone but 'the Lamb of God', Christ. Saint Dorothy was also a 'bride of Christ'. When she was about to be executed for refusing to renounce her faith, the young lawyer Theophilus mockingly asked her to send him roses and apples from the garden of her heavenly groom. After her death, a boy brought Theophilus a basket filled with the requested flowers and fruit, and he promptly converted. Wautier indeed depicts the young saint with roses and shiny red apples in a wicker basket. The fate of the young martyrs is reflected in their poses and expressions. They do not talk to each other but are connected by their willingness to die for Christ.[63] Their age difference and the staging of the portrait suggest that the models are sisters. They are in an undefined space containing only a table in the foreground to the left. In the bottom right corner, Agnes caresses the lamb with her left hand and points at it with her right. Not only does Wautier use the lamb as an attribute of Saint Agnes, she also makes it part of the story, in

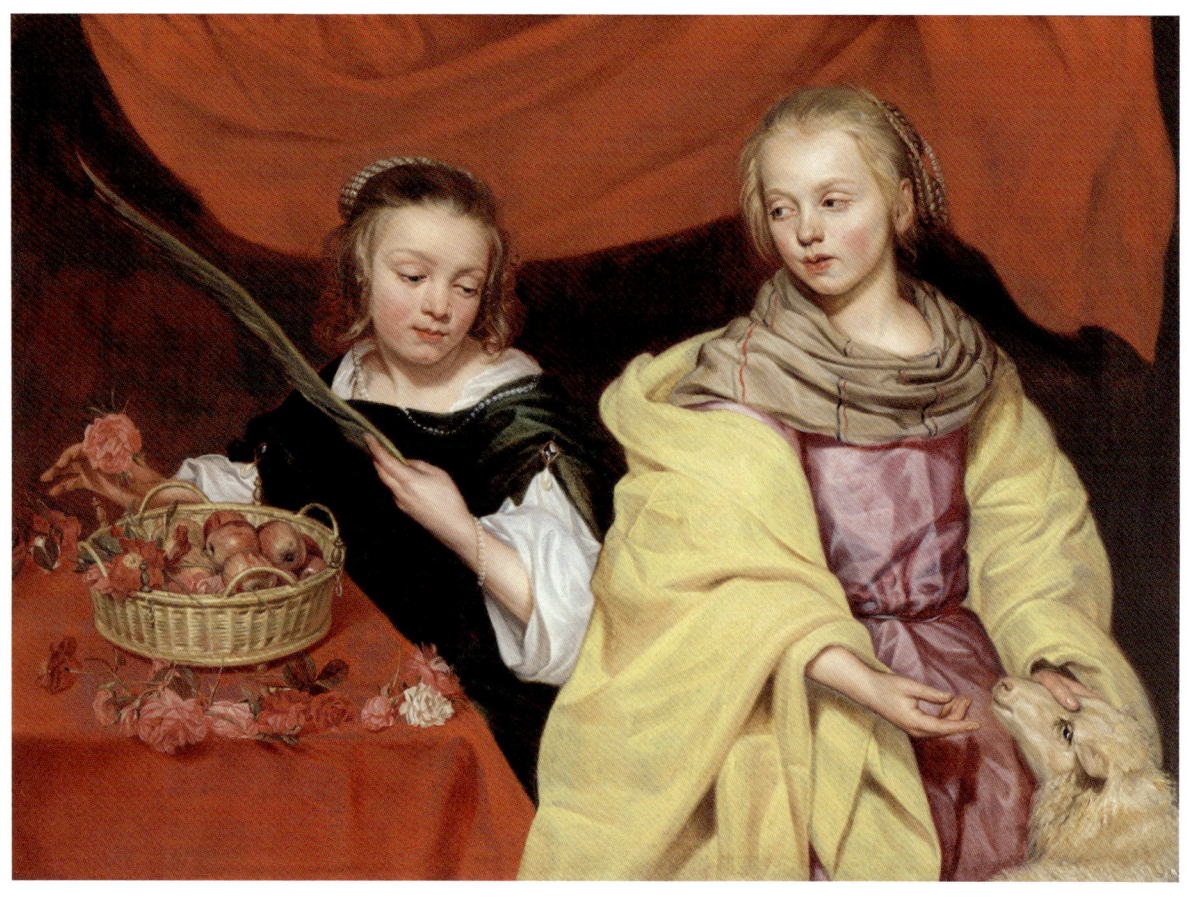

56 Michaelina Wautier, *Two Girls as Saint Agnes and Saint Dorothy*, *c.*1650–55, oil on canvas, 89.7 × 122 cm (35 ⅜ × 48 in), Royal Museum of Fine Arts, Antwerp

which the girls communicate without words. Agnes shows the lamb to Dorothy, who looks at the animal with pity in turn. The blush on their cheeks shows how vulnerable they are. The virgins' costumes once again showcase Wautier's originality. A cord holds Agnes's dress at the waist. Her wide, yellow mantle is made of heavy fabric and falls in broad pleats. She has draped an Eastern-looking shawl around her shoulders, and her hair is styled in braids. Her clothing is timeless, and it is noticeable that, unlike Dorothy, she does not wear any jewellery. Dorothy, on the other hand, is dressed in a more contemporary style. The dress has a square neckline, and the loose-fitting white blouse with wide sleeves underneath corresponds to the fashion of the late 1650s. The upper garment's sleeves are adorned with precious brooches. She wears a pearl necklace, which is partly hidden under her dress, a bracelet made of pearls on her left wrist and her cap is embellished with rows of pearls. By wearing more contemporary clothing, Dorothy's message was adapted to the modern era, and her example undoubtedly had a more direct impact. The figures are modelled with assured touches, and Agnes's face is characterised in a manner very similar to Mary's in the 1659 *Annunciation* (fig.34), Wautier's latest dated work. The palette offers a sample of the artist's favourite colours, dominated by the sandy yellow and the vieux rose. The painting is dominated by the colour red, which is clearly a reference to the blood that the young saints were willing to shed for their faith.[64]

The earliest known work by Wautier, also a disguised portrait, brought to life the story of Isaac and Rebecca at the source via a family portrait (fig.35). She also used this strategy in individual portraits, for instance, an experimental portrait of a man, represented in the guise of the Biblical shepherd Jacob, Isaac and Rebecca's son (fig.57). The man, with lusciously falling grey locks, looks over his shoulder and makes a rhetorical hand gesture. The key to the identification is engraved in the rock face in the upper right corner: 'RACHEL.VAUT. BIEN LA PEINE.' After

seven years of service, Jacob had to wait another seven years before Laban, Jacob's uncle, would allow him to marry his daughter Rachel (Genesis 29:1–30). The inscription no doubt refers to the personal situation of a man who identified with Jacob, because he too had to wait a long time for the woman 'who was more than worth it'. This portrait demonstrates that Wautier was exceptionally gifted in conveying her male models' powerful personalities. She emphatically favoured half-length poses, positioning her subjects diagonally in the picture plane.

Another example of this novel approach to portraiture is the nearly monochrome but vigorous *Portrait of a Military Commander*, almost certainly a portrait of Wautier's brother Pierre (see fig.10). Here, we see a break with the tradition of depicting the model from three-quarters to the left or right: the figure is positioned perpendicular to the picture plane with his left shoulder towards the viewer.[65] This turned torso and outward-pointing elbow lend the figure greater dynamism and enhance the sense of direct confrontation. It seems as if he has just stood up and is looking over his shoulder for a moment. The probing gaze and somewhat haughty expression appear very lifelike. Shades of grey, brown and a touch of yellow emerge in the man's flowing hair, which extends far down his back. The transparent, milk-white fabric of the cuffs and collar harmonises with the ochre of the leather and the metallic grey armour. Against this muted colour scheme, the piercing blue eyes stand out even more. Wautier combined the bold pose with exceptionally free brushstrokes. Of all of her portraits, this is technically the most experimental. Just as the *portrait historié* of a man in the guise of Jacob (fig.57), it is unsigned and undated. The almost expressionist brushwork suggests we should situate it rather late than early in her career. In 1654, her brother was appointed *capitaine de cavalerie*, and he died in 1664. This portrait should be dated within this period and there are no arguments against a production date after 1659, the year of the latest known dated painting by Wautier.

In 1654, Wautier also painted the portrait of

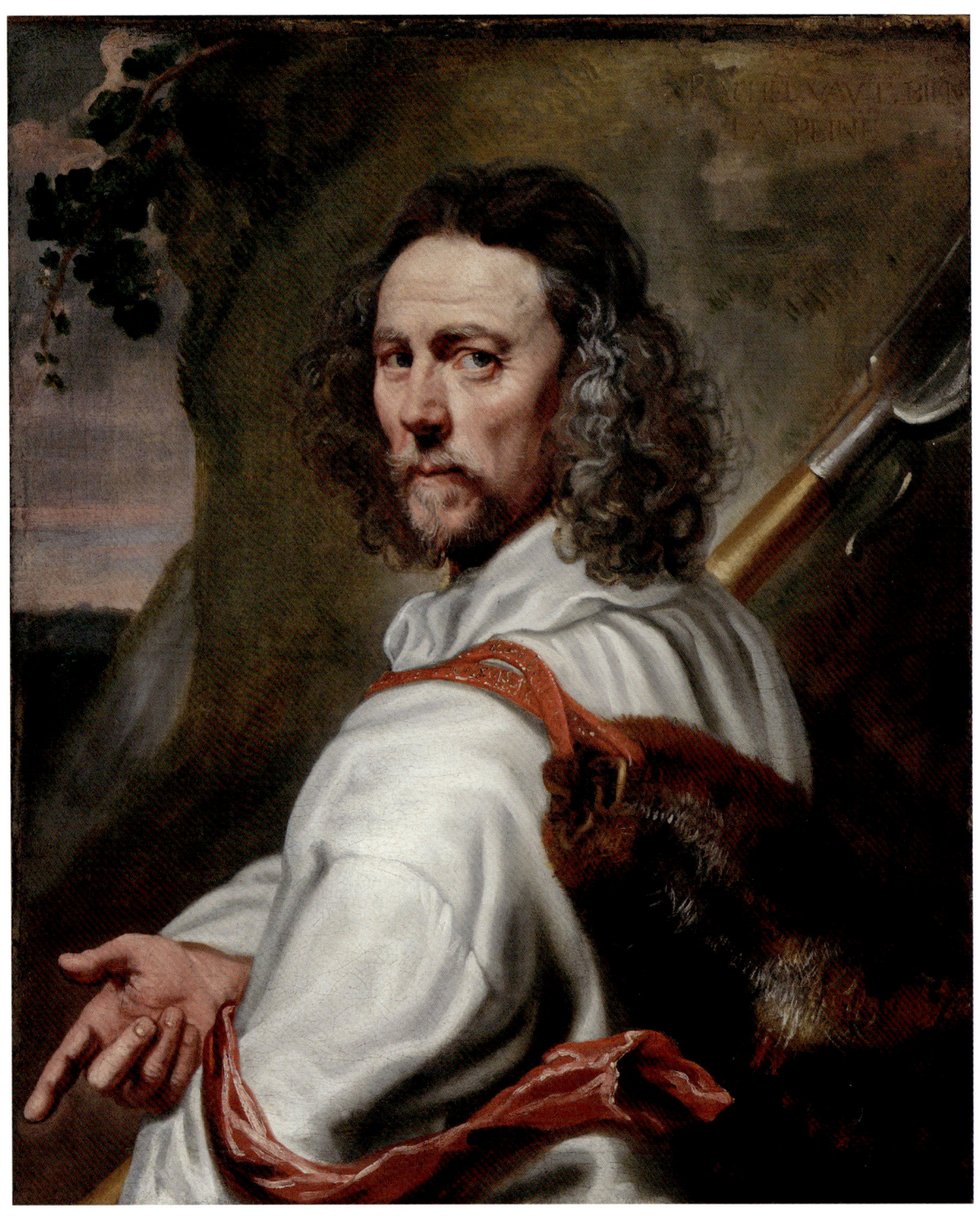

57 Michaelina Wautier, *Portrait Historié of a Man with a Shepherd's Crook and a Water Bag as Jacob, Husband of Rachel, Daughter of Laban*, c.1655–60, oil on canvas, 76.5 × 62 cm, (30 ⅛ × 24 ⅜ in) private collection

the Italian Jesuit Martino Martini (fig.58). It is the most traditional and, simultaneously, the most impressive portrait she ever made.[66] It is signed in full and dated 1654. A Chinese legend that has also been transcribed in Latin script as 'Wei Kuangguo', to be translated as 'he who protects and serves the land [China]', specifies the identity of this missionary dressed in Chinese garb.[67] During the sixteenth and seventeenth centuries, the missionary efforts of the Jesuits contributed not only to the transmission of Christianity, but also of science and culture between China and the West. The Jesuits approached China as an equally civilised nation, an ethos that Martini appears to have embodied. He was a brilliant theologian and philosopher who possessed the gift of the written and spoken word. He corresponded in multiple languages, was a masterful fundraiser and travel organiser, built churches and was a brilliant strategist. In 1640, he travelled to China for the first time, where he applied himself to the study of the Chinese language and of China's history and geography. At the end of 1653, he returned to Europe. With the book he had composed, the *Novus Atlas Sinensis*, the first atlas ever to be made of China, he travelled to Antwerp and subsequently to Amsterdam to find a publisher for this groundbreaking work. Balthasar II Moretus of the Officina Plantiniana shrank back from the risk but, in 1655, the atlas came off the presses of the famous printer Joan Willemsz Blaeu (1596–1673).[68] In 1654, Martini travelled on to Brussels, where he stayed at the Jesuit house in the Ruisbroekstraat, near the archducal court. The reputable fundraiser had an appointment with Leopold Wilhelm, who was willing to support his missionary activities. In gratitude, Martini dedicated the atlas to him. Since the portrait is from 1654, he must have made time to pose for Wautier in these busy four months. A recent finding of a lease contract between Léon Wautier, Michaelina's youngest brother, and the Brussels Jesuits revealed that there had been contact between them and the Wautier family since the

end of 1642.[69] This creates the possibility that the Jesuits commissioned Wautier to portray Martini, while it is still more likely that the collector Leopold Wilhelm, who probably already owned works by her hand, commissioned it or played a mediating role. The dimensions of the painting are similar to those of Wautier's other portraits and the model has also been placed high on the plane; his upper body takes up the whole canvas. This gives the impression that Martini was quite heavyset and creates the image of an extraordinarily imposing figure. The intense blue of the broadly draped *changshan* contrasts with the milky white of the *hanfu*'s lining. Wautier often emphasised the texture of the fabrics; the way light reflects off the undergarment and coat creates the effect of silk. The smooth fabric of the costume contrasts with the fur hat, which has a velvet or wool core adorned with a wide black fur band. Martini is posed against a uniform, dark brown background, with the light-coloured lining wrapping around his shoulders like a silhouette. The breathtaking power of the portrait lies in the way Wautier depicted Martini's physiognomy. The light coming from the left illuminates primarily his right cheek and his forehead and creates highlights in his eyes. Martini's penetrating gaze, which stares into the distance while simultaneously absorbing the surroundings, immediately captures the viewer's attention. The face has been modelled with broad, virtuoso touches. The freshness of the brushwork and the well-aimed highlights are also seen in the elaboration of Martini's beard and moustache. It cannot be emphasised enough that Wautier was a master of painting hair. Whether she was painting portraits or saints, the hairstyles always had the same level of realism. Through precise highlights she achieved the utmost touchability and subtlety. The layout of the portrait suggests sixteenth-century Venetian examples such as Titian's portrait of the art critic Pietro Aretino (Palazzo Pitti, Florence).[70]

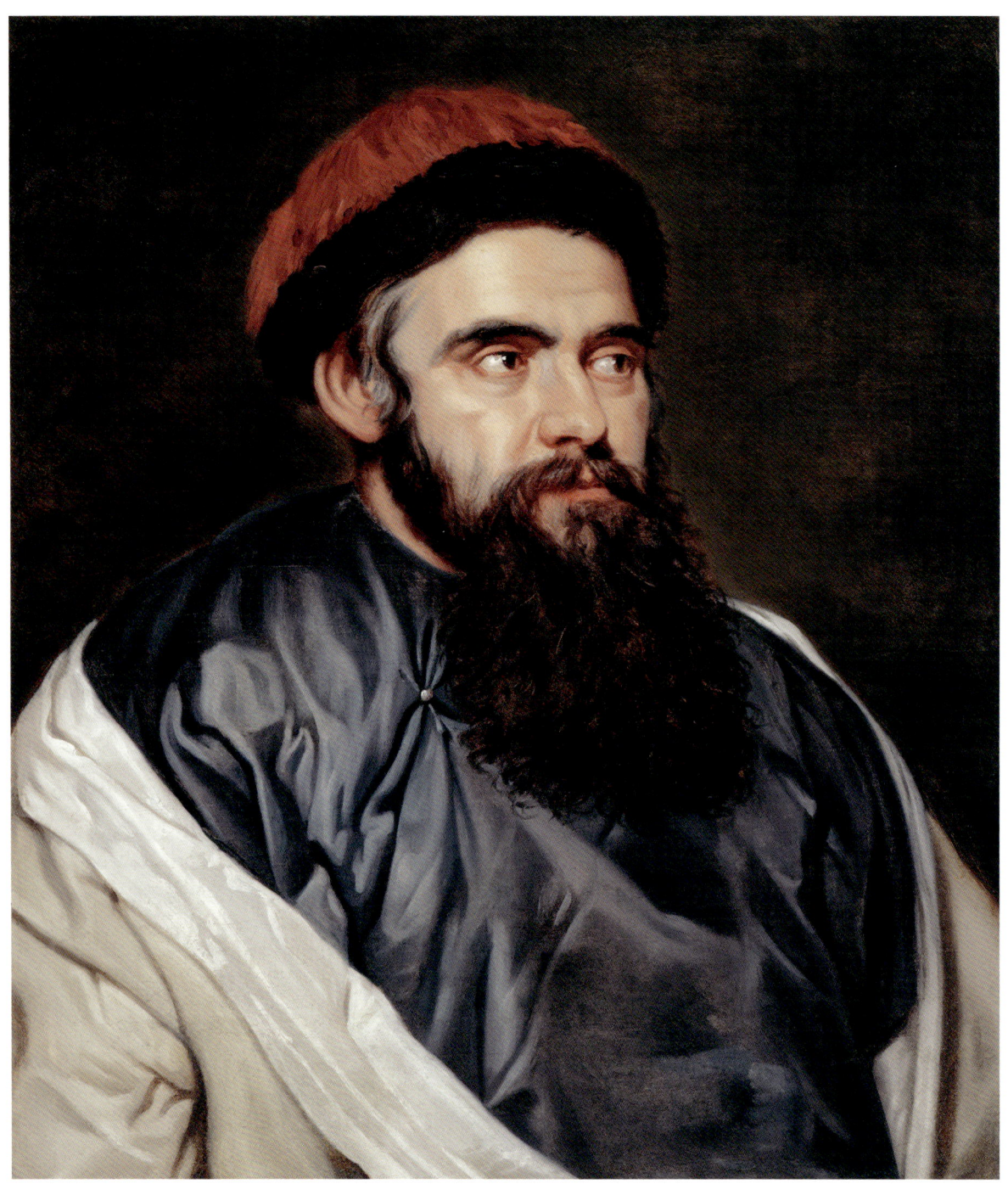

58 Michaelina Wautier, *Portrait of Martino Martini*, 1654, oil on canvas, 69.5 × 59 cm (27 ⅜ × 23 ⅛ in), The Klesch Collection

Prestigious Altarpieces

From the mid-1650s, history paintings of religious themes became more important in Wautier's oeuvre. In 1656, she painted the *Education of the Virgin* (fig.59) and three years after that the magisterial *Annunciation* (see fig.34), produced exactly ten years after the *Mystic Marriage of Saint Catherine* of 1649 (see fig.37). It seems that Wautier employed a more restrained style for these large-scale history pieces. Possibly, this had to do with the expectations of the client and the position the painting was to occupy. By 1686, the *Annunciation*, for instance, hung in the chapel of the Château de Marly near Paris. This does not constitute proof that the painting was intended for that location but at least it tells us something about the distribution of her work and the extent to which it was appreciated.[71]

Wautier's self-confidence as an artist is revealed in the *Education of the Virgin*, one of her most intimate and colourful paintings. The signature reads: 'Michaelina Wautier, inuenit, et fecit 1656.' Just as in the *Mystic Marriage of Saint Catherine*, she distinguishes between the 'conception' of the composition and its 'execution'. This indicates her knowledge of the pictorial tradition in which artists from the Southern Netherlands, as far back as Jan van Eyck (c.1390–1441) and Frans Floris (1519–70), applied this intellectual distinction. Stylistically, this is a very interesting work by Wautier, because it shows different brushwork in a single painting. Jeffrey Muller rightly wrote: 'She seems as well to have modulated her touch to fit the subject.'[72] Mary's head has been painted in a polished and controlled manner, while the face of Saint Anne and, even more so that of Saint Joachim, are composed of bold, thickly painted planes, made even more pronounced by the play of the chiaroscuro, which we can see systematically in Theodoor van Loon's oeuvre.[73] Exceptional also is the presence of the emerald-green cape of Saint Anne, as a striking colour field in the foreground of the painting, in the colour traditionally connected to this saint, and representing the love spanning various generations. The green cape is usually combined with a red undergarment, which is a symbol of rebirth. However, Wautier preferred the ochre that was so characteristic of her palette.[74] The occurrence of different pictorial approaches in a single painting makes it very hard to draw inferences from the style to apply to her undated works. The complexity of the brushwork is less pronounced in the balanced *Annunciation* (see fig.34). Here also, Wautier has wrapped a saint in a loose cape that is draped across her left arm and falls in a cascade of folds. The rendering of the texture of fabric always fascinated her, as was already evident in the way the folds of Saint Catherine's white garment are shaped (see fig.37), but over time, her technique became ever more refined, as appears from the religious paintings from 1656 and 1659. In the *Annunciation* the two figures are life-size. The light enters from the left to illuminate Mary's womb, the place of conception, and the sky above her head breaks open, letting the light of the Holy Spirit pass through. The representation of Mary fits stylistically in Wautier's oeuvre. The angled position of the head that thus catches the light, with the closed eyes and the pouting mouth, occurs in many variations. The androgynous angel appears more earthly than Mary, with facial features that align more closely with those of the realistically depicted boys in *The Five Senses* (see figs 39–43) and genre scenes such as *Two Boys Blowing Bubbles* (see fig.51) and *Two Boys Squabbling over an Egg* (see fig.52). The angel's tresses, a rich brown hue with a reddish tint, cascade luxuriantly over his shoulders. The artist also pays more attention to a suggestive rendering of the elements of the interior, such as the Eastern tapestry on the table, the wooden bench on which Mary kneels and the wooden boards fastened with nails. We can also see how Wautier gradually paid more attention to hands with spread fingers, which dominate the image and enhance emotional expression. While Mary's right hand indicates

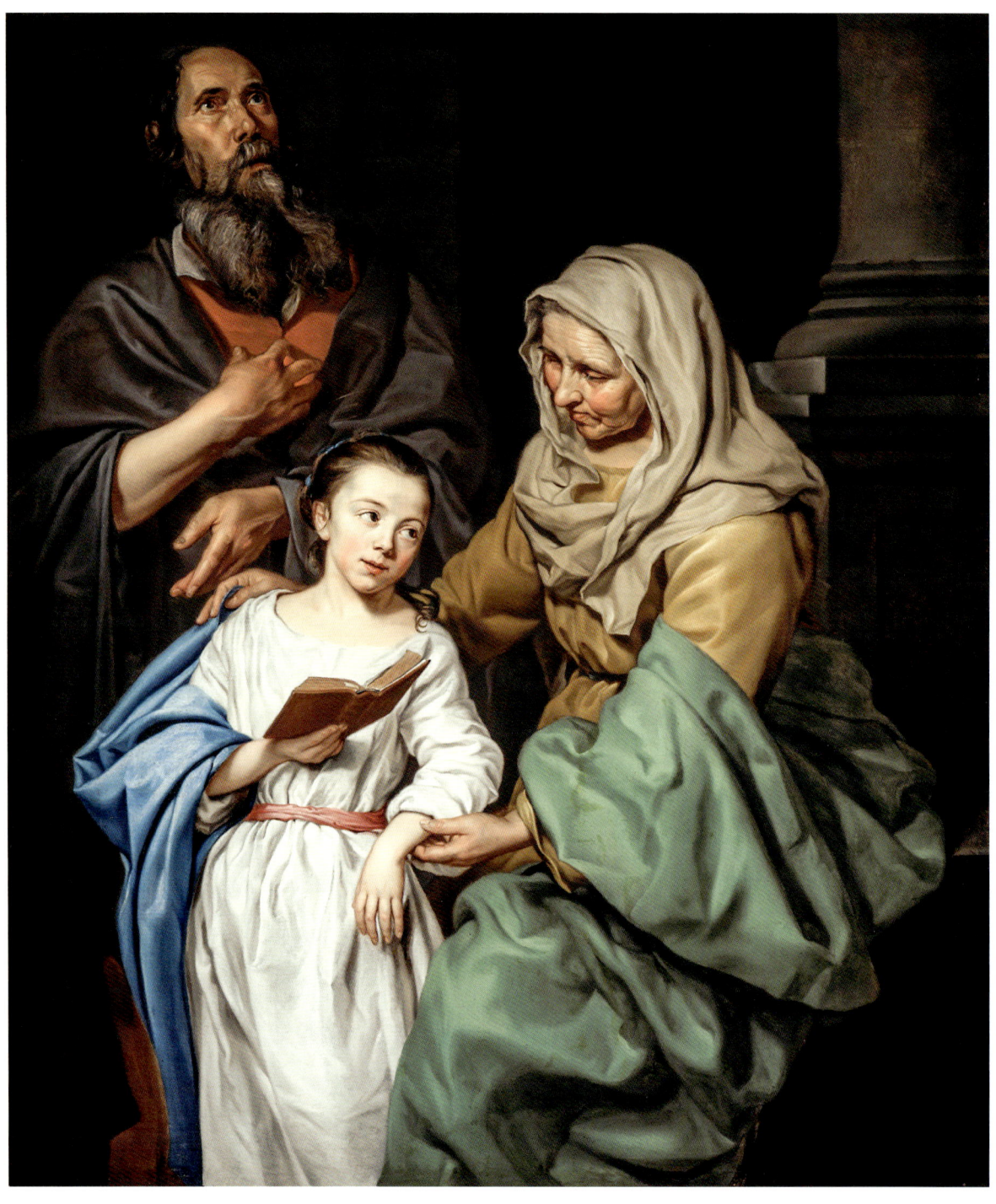

59 Michaelina Wautier, *Education of the Virgin*, 1656, oil on canvas, 147 × 124 cm (57 ⅞ × 48 ⅞ in), Mauritshuis, The Hague, on loan from a private collection

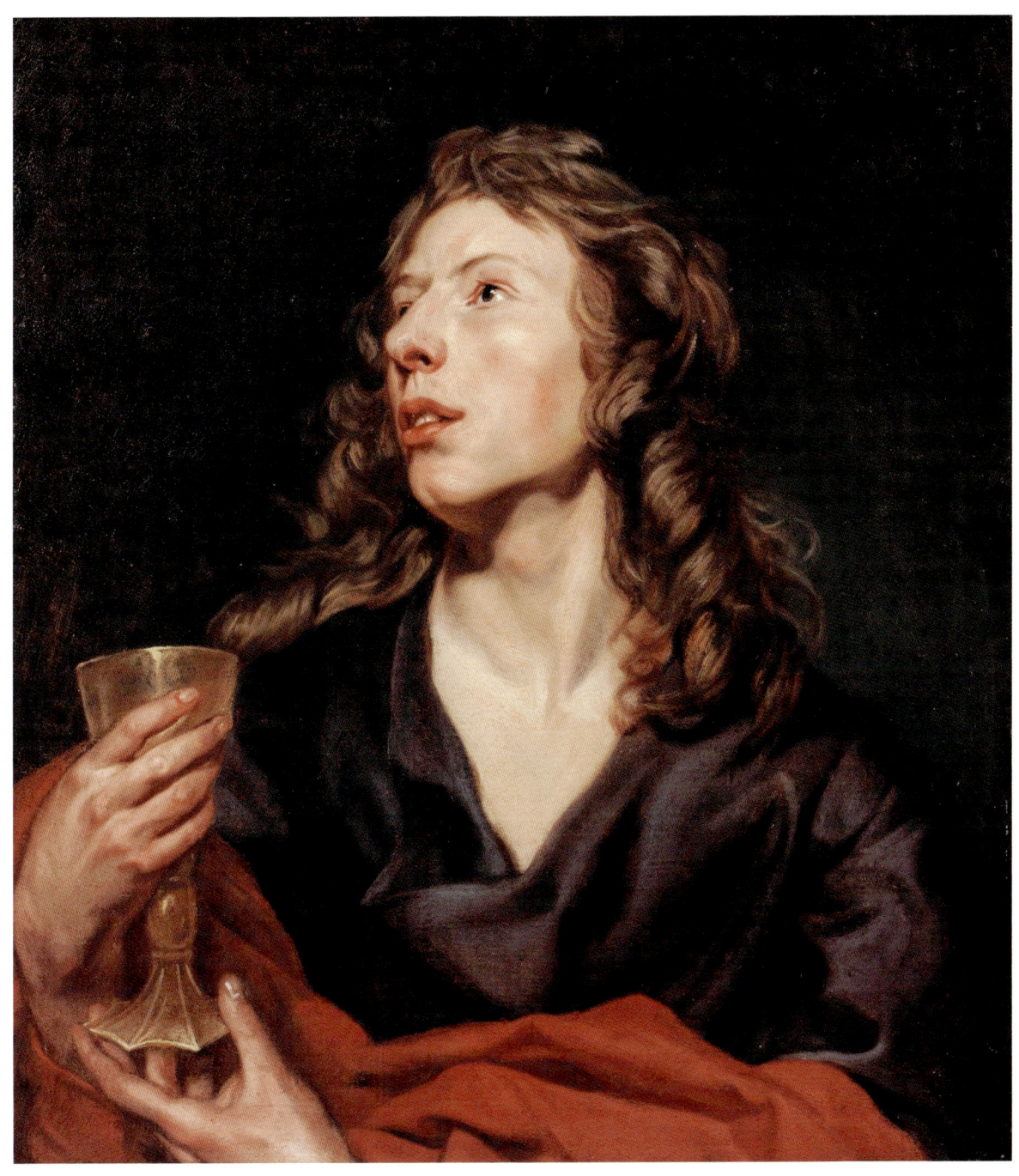

60 Michaelina Wautier, *Saint John the Evangelist*, c.1655, oil on canvas, 69 × 60.5 cm (27 ⅛ × 23 ⅞ in), private collection

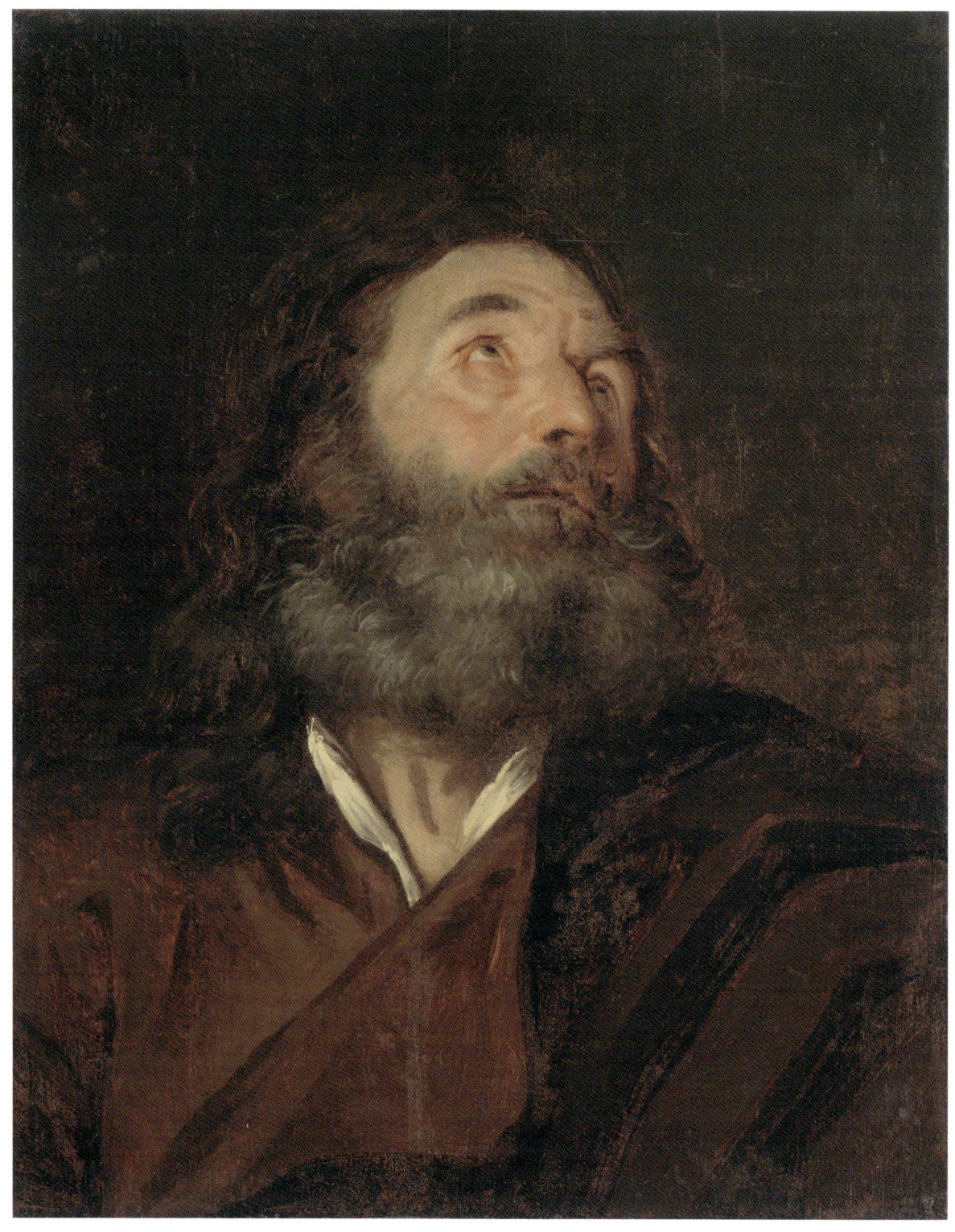

61 Michaelina Wautier, *Study of the Head of a Bearded Man*, *c.*1655, oil on panel, 64.9 × 50 cm (25 ½ × 19 ⅝ in), Museum M, Leuven

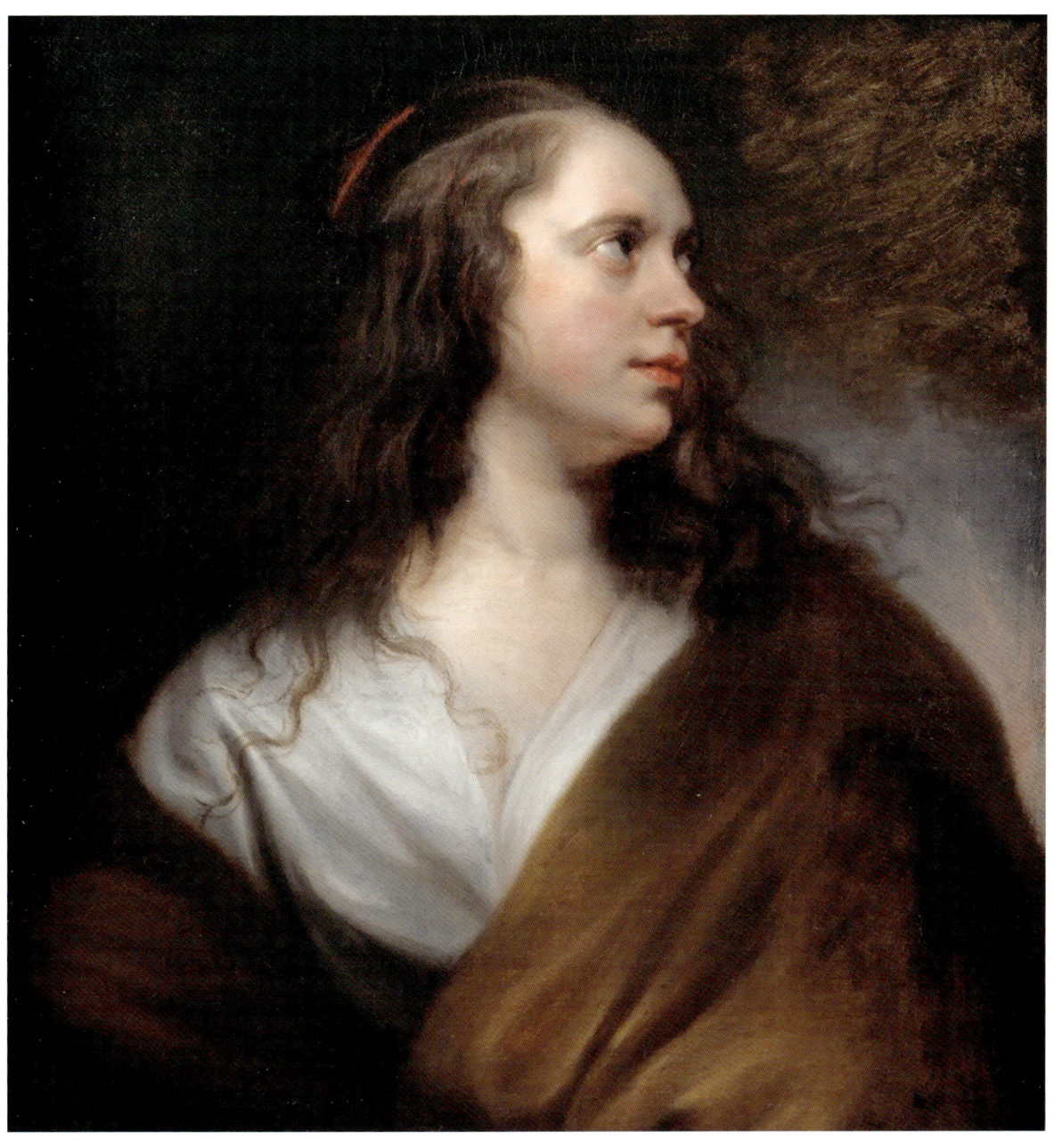

62 Michaelina Wautier, *Study of a Young Woman*, c.1650, oil on canvas, 62.5 × 57.5 cm (24 ⅝ × 22 ⅝ in), The Phoebus Foundation

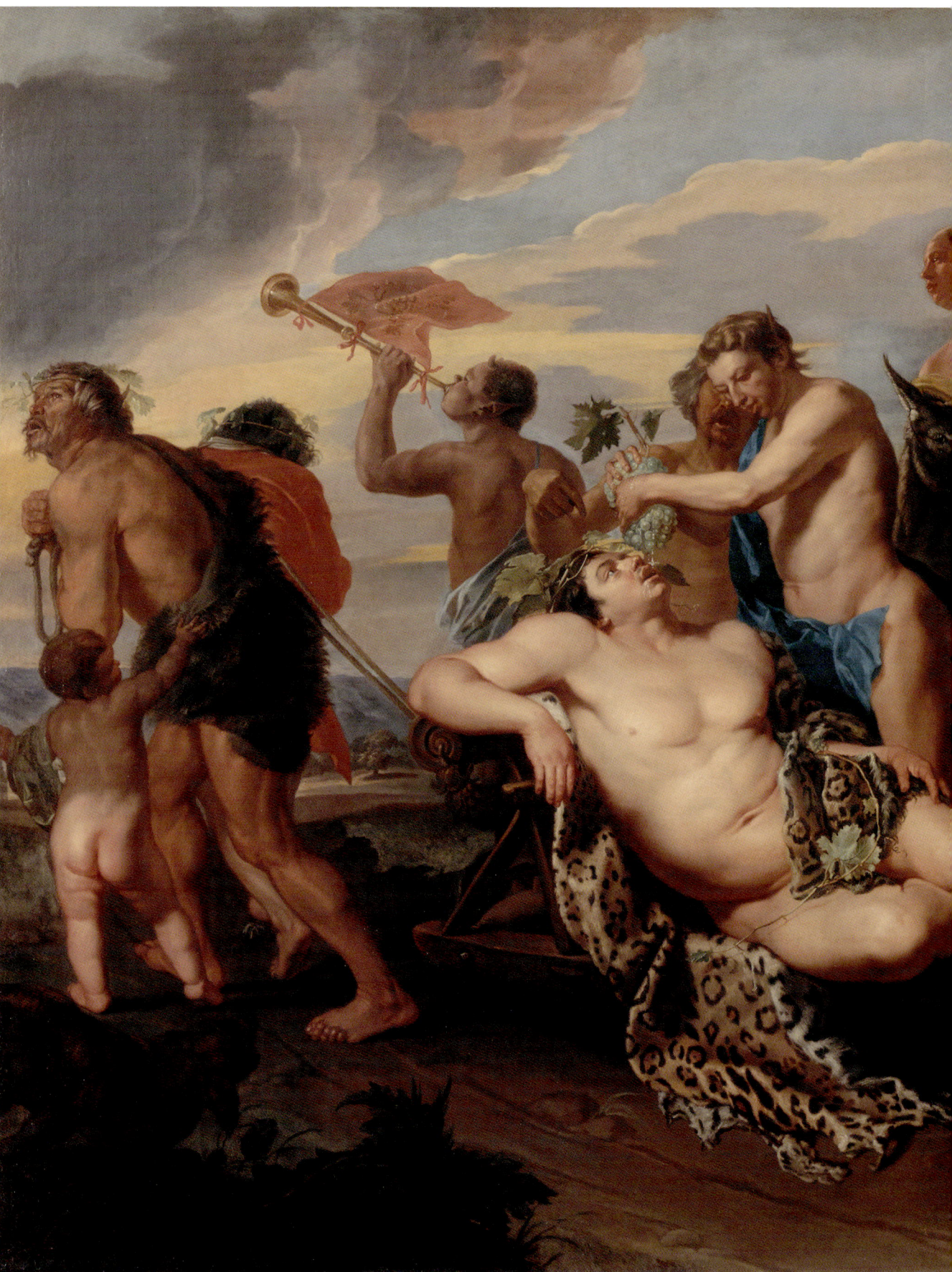

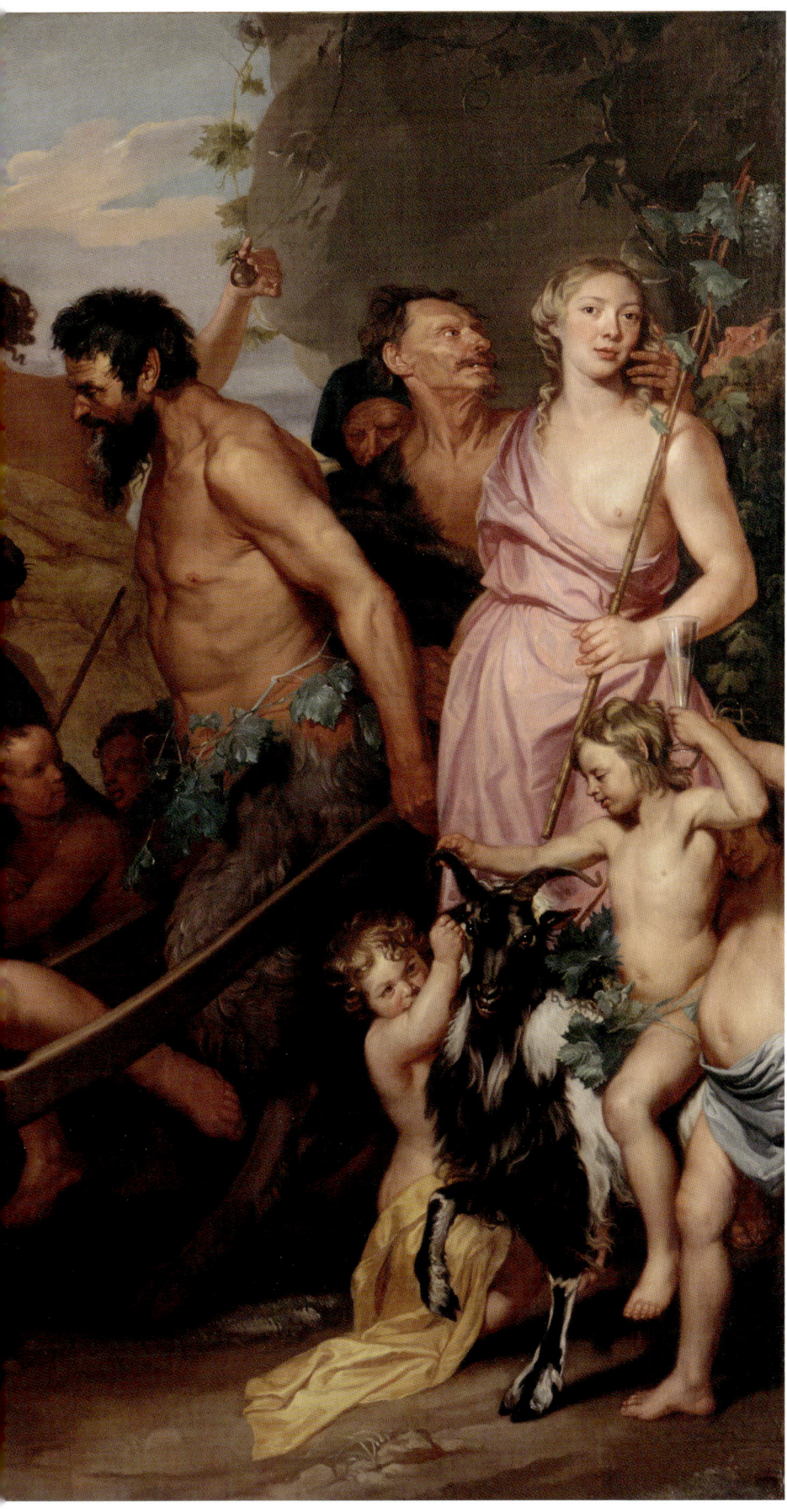

63 Michaelina Wautier, *Triumph of Bacchus*, c.1655–9, oil on canvas, 270 × 354 cm , (106 ¼ × 139 ⅜ in) Kunsthistorisches Museum, Vienna

receptivity and compliance, the position of the left seems to suggest a startled reaction to the sudden appearance of the angel. These characteristics are also present in her *Saint John the Evangelist* (fig.60), who raises his eyes to heaven and holds a chalice in his nervously tense hands with full devotion.[75]

Saints and Bacchants

The narrative style with measured colour accents is missing from Wautier's three half-body representations of saints. These paintings are well documented because they are described in the Archduke's 1659 inventory; two have been identified as Saint Joachim and one as Saint Joseph (see figs 17–19). These are semi-monochrome canvases that appear to be studies of character heads. The rough physiognomy of the saints is varied and each has his unique pose: one bends his head, another raises it and the third looks at the viewer. Their hair and beards stress their individuality. The hands of both depictions of Saint Joachim disappear in the dark beneath the book they are holding, while Saint Joseph's right hand holds a lily as a symbol of purity.[76] The viewer's attention is drawn to their expressions, which are emphasised by the Caravaggesque play of the light. *Saint Joachim Reading* and *Saint Joseph* are turned towards each other and the palette is uniform. Stylistically, they have been executed with exuberant skill. The broad touches on the forehead and in the hair are extraordinarily free. They are composed of several overlapping layers, which here and there are transparent. The dating of these paintings is very complex. Their description in the 1659 inventory supplies us with a *terminus ante quem*, since it is not entirely clear whether Leopold Wilhelm imported paintings from Brussels after he had left the city in 1656. They can best be considered as studies which were probably made in preparation of later compositions, such as the *Study of the Head of a Bearded Man*, rendered in broad brushstrokes (fig.61) or the *Study of a Young Woman* (fig.62), in which the face has been executed in a much thinner layer of paint.

The fourth painting mentioned in the Leopold Wilhelm inventory is the *Triumph of Bacchus*, a masterly painting of commanding dimensions (fig.63). While for the three saints, it is expressly stated that they are by the hand of 'Magdalena', this work is described as 'A large piece, oil on canvas, on which the Triumph of Bacchus can be seen . . . An original by N. Woutiers.'[77] The initial 'N' is difficult to interpret. It may refer to 'Nomen Nescio', a statement meaning that the name is unknown to the writer of the document.[78] It could also refer to Charles, whose name does not occur in the inventory since the Archduke did not own any work by him. The most convincing arguments come from an analysis of the style. Günther Heinz, curator of the Gemäldegalerie of the Kunsthistorisches Museum, Vienna, wrote in 1967: 'die charakteristische Handschrift [ist] ein so deutlich Gemeinsames, dass diese Werke . . . als Schöpfungen einer Hand erkannt werden können' ('The characteristic handwriting is so clearly the same, that these works should be recognised as creations by one and the same hand').[79] With this assessment of the same stylistic idiom, he contradicted the eminent Rubens connoisseur Gustav Glück, who in 1933 had deemed an attribution to Michaelina Wautier impossible because he was of the opinion that such a large painting could never be a woman's work.[80]

Wautier derived the narrative of the *Triumph of Bacchus* from the writings of the ancient Roman author Virgil. Traditionally in paintings representing this popular theme, Bacchus is surrounded by rowdy bacchants and maenads who seek his company. They can be recognised by their *chiton* and their *thyrsus*, a staff wound with vines. Compared to previous examples, however, Wautier's painting is breathtakingly original, both in the way she reinterprets characters and motives. Instead of the usual triumphal chariot on which Bacchus reclines, she uses a common wheelbarrow. A leopard's skin is draped over it and covers his genitals. The

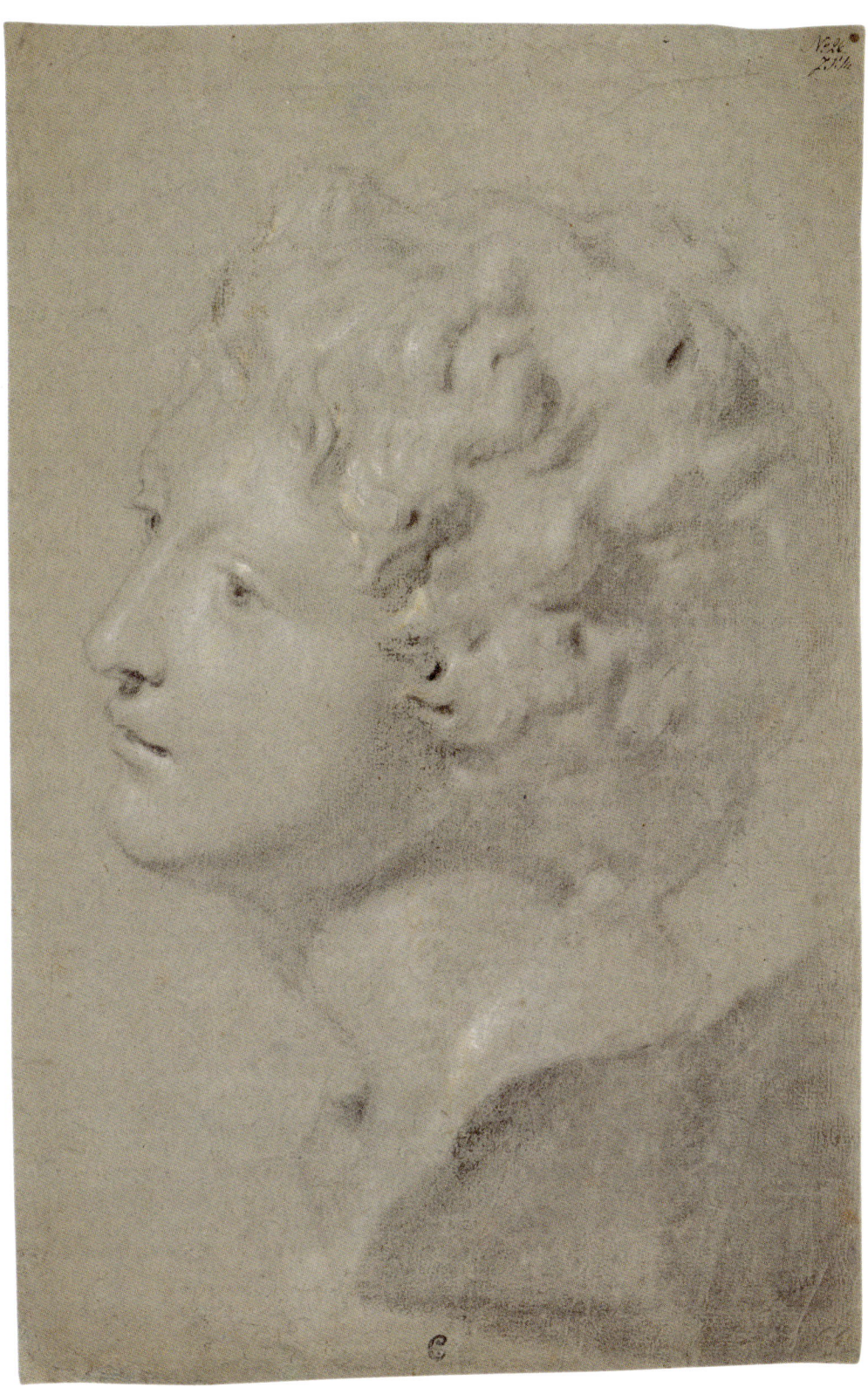

64 Michaelina Wautier, *Study after an Antique Head of Ganymede*, c.1640–50, black and white chalk on paper, 43 × 28.3 cm (16 ⅞ × 11 ⅛ in), private collection

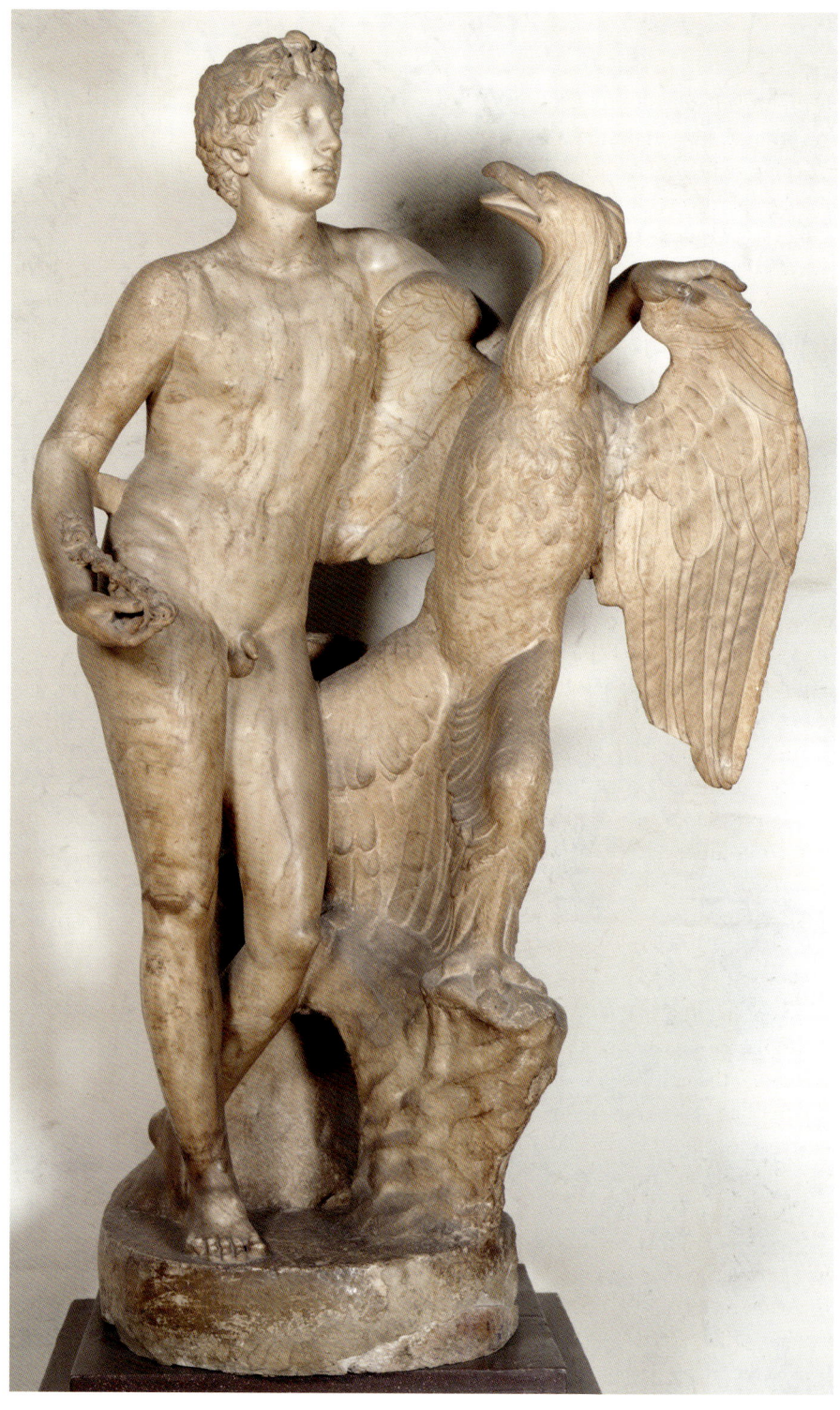

65 *Ganymede with the Eagle*, Roman, first century CE, Italian marble, height 142 cm
(55 ⅞ in), Galleria degli Uffizi, Florence

composition is dominated by more than a dozen life-size figures who walk from right to left through a landscape in evening twilight. Centre stage, a satyr pushes the wheelbarrow with the intoxicated young Bacchus. The satyr is depicted as a tormented grey-haired man, closely related to the paintings of three saints by Wautier that were also in Leopold Wilhelm's collection (see figs 17–19). None of the figures in the *Triumph* looks at the viewer, except the woman at the extreme right. No doubt, this is a historicised self-portrait in which Wautier depicts herself as part of the procession but not part of the bacchanal. She keeps to herself and ignores the pushy lecher beside her. For this avant-garde manner of self-fashioning, she must have sought inspiration in classical sculptures of bacchantes and Amazons. Wautier often looked at classical prototypes, as appears from the only drawing by her hand that has been preserved (fig.64). Drawing from plaster sculptures and busts was part of a young artist's training, and Wautier had apparently also honed her skills in this way. *The Artist's Studio* by Jacob van Oost gives an impression of the way boys drew from classical busts.[81] Wautier's drawing *Study after an Antique Head of Ganymede* references the head of *Ganymede with the Eagle* (fig.65), dating from the first century CE but restored in the sixteenth century. In the middle of the seventeenth century, this sculpture was kept in the Villa Medici in Rome. Since no marble or plaster copies were made before the end of the seventeenth century,[82] this might indicate that Wautier had seen the bust herself or that another artist, for instance her brother Charles, made a drawing of it in Rome and took it home for Michaelina to copy. No drawings by Charles are extant, but that does not mean he did not make any. Michaelina in her turn left only one drawing.

Drawing from classical prototypes was an ideal start for an artist, but sufficient familiarisation with the anatomy of the human body can only be accomplished by drawing from a live model. Wautier must surely have had the chance to do this together with her brother Charles. Nowhere is her expertise better expressed than in the *Triumph of Bacchus*, where she depicts an array of naked bodies. Although we know little about their collaboration, we may assume they worked in the same studio or at least had a studio in the same house, as discussed in Chapter 3. Only in such a private context would it have been possible for a woman to draw from a live model. The Brussels fascination with the study from life as the foundation of an artist's training also appears from the request Michael Sweerts sent to the Brussels magistrate in 1655. He desired a tax exemption because he wanted to spare no expense towards the 'Academy' he had founded, where many 'youths' were practising daily to learn to draw from life.[83] In his painting *The Drawing School*, a man poses in the midst of a group of boys and youths busily drawing. The painting gives an impression of 'drawing from a live model' as it was practiced *c.*1655 in Brussels (fig.66).[84] Wautier had already practised it in the privacy of their studio. Otherwise, she could never have been able to realise the *Triumph of Bacchus* in that same period.

In early modern north-western Europe, no other female artist is known who had the opportunity to study and represent male anatomy in this way. Even in Italy, paintings or drawings by women based on life studies of the male nude are rare. An exceptional example is a compositional drawing attributed to Marietta Robusti (1550–90), also known as Tintoretta, the *Study of a Bishop Baptising Plague Victims*. However, given the small size of the blue paper (19.5 × 27 cm), it cannot be ruled out that this is a copy of another work.[85] It seems at least some of Wautier's motivation for executing the Bacchus painting was that she wanted to demonstrate her exceptional ability. For the procession, she emphatically selected men of various ages, skin colours and body types. Small boys also enliven the composition with their expressive gestures. They play with a billy goat, an animal traditionally seen as a symbol of lasciviousness. In Cesare Ripa's *Iconologia* of 1604, an allegory of Luxuria (Lust) is depicted

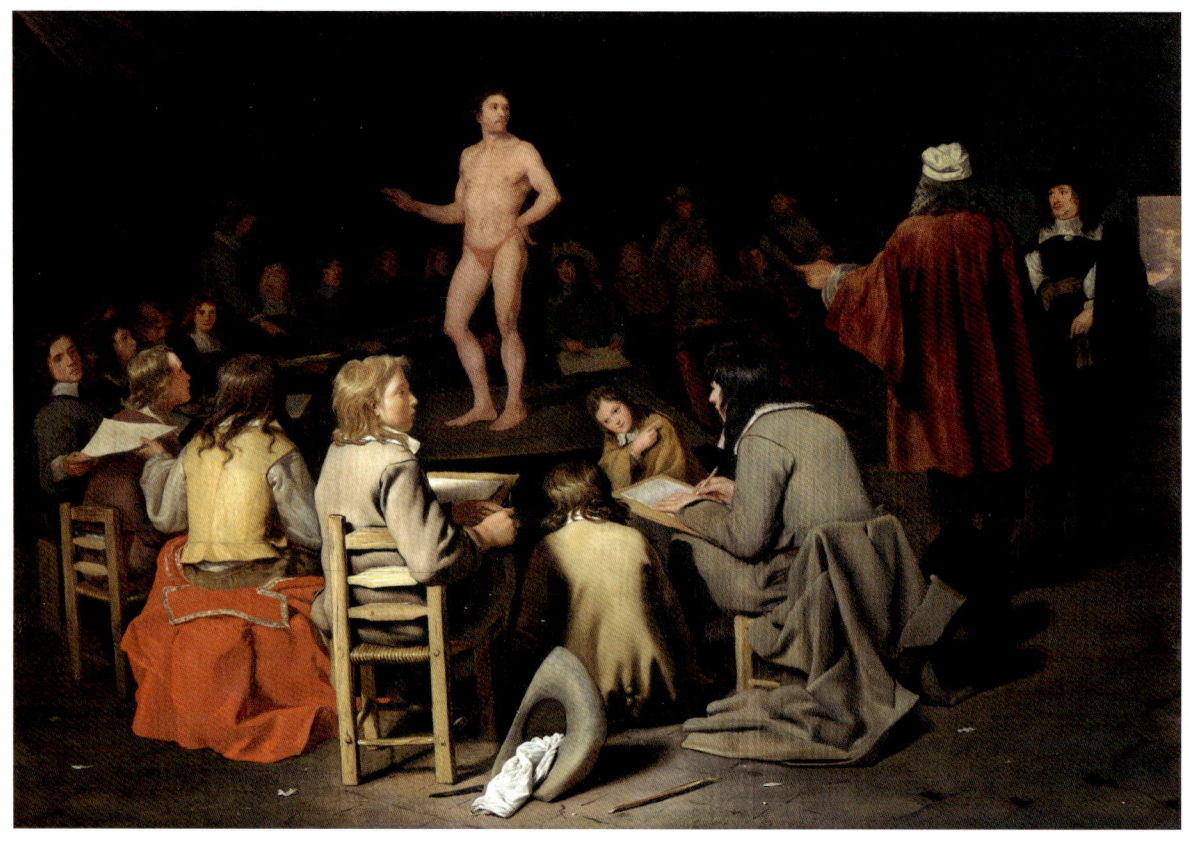

66 Michael Sweerts, *The Drawing School*, c.1655, oil on canvas, 103.4 × 136.5 cm (40 ¾ × 53 ¾ in), Frans Halsmuseum, Haarlem

as a woman sitting under vines with a scorpion in one hand and a male goat by her side.[86] Wautier's alter ego is a multi-layered character, making her personality more enigmatic than ever. From contemporary sources, it appears that Bacchus, the god of wine, was not solely interpreted as a symbol of lust and excess but could also refer to an 'Apollonian' form of creative power. That is doubtlessly a reason why eighteenth-century women liked to depict themselves as bacchantes.[87] Not only Wautier, but also Anna Dorothea Lisiewska (1721–82; State Hermitage Museum, Saint Petersburg) and Angelika Kauffman (1741–1807; Staatliche Museen, Berlin) made a self-portrait where they appear as bacchantes, and Elisabeth Vigée-Le Brun (1755–1842) made a portrait of a woman who poses as a half-naked bacchante.[88]

The style of the whole work is not exactly homogeneous, but all parts have the same impressive quality. The variation shows itself just as convincingly in the expressions. The young satyr on the billy goat pleasantly raises his glass, Wautier herself fixes her uncertain smile on the viewer, while the satyr in the foreground pushes the wheelbarrow with effort and the man who pulls it looks exaltedly towards the heavens. There is a similar variety in the skin colour of the protagonists, from white, as for instance Wautier herself, to swarthy. A dark-skinned man plays a trumpet and a dark-curled boy accompanies the satyr. Parts of the composition correspond to the figures and motifs in Wautier's other paintings. There is, for instance, a likeness between the playing children on the extreme right to figures in her genre paintings, and the profile of the woman in the background, in yellow, with castanets, is identical to that of the kneeling Saint Catherine (fig.37).

The flexibility with which Wautier adapted her style to each situation makes it difficult to grasp the development of her oeuvre. The chronological survey has already shown us that her work did not evolve in a straight line. Even her earliest known paintings testify to an all-round education and, in the long run, she focused on experimenting with subject matter

and style, as she had always done. Her approach is free of monotony, even within a single painting. The *Education of the Virgin* (fig.59), discussed above, is a characteristic example. A contrast in style is apparent within a single composition and also between her paintings, which complicates the attributions. The Van Dyck-inspired *Mystic Marriage of Saint Catherine* from 1649 (see fig.37) and the series of *The Five Senses* (figs 39–43), which are far more creative and innovative, were painted within an interval of one year. And if we compare *The Five Senses* from 1650 with the flower still lifes dated 1652, we see worlds of difference. Wautier's scope as an artist is exceptionally broad. She effortlessly combined the Italian Caravaggesque style and French-inclined classicism, to which she adds a touch of Dutch realism. She developed her own aesthetics of daily life, as expressed in the boy eating a breadcrust (see fig.42), the shell with soap suds in the hand of one of the boys blowing bubbles (fig.51), Saint Dorothy's wicker basket with roses and apples (fig.56), and the twisted ribbon around the Virgin's waist in the *Annunciation* (fig.34). She is witness to the poignant ecstasy of Saint John the Evangelist (fig.60) and the young Saint John the Baptist (fig.53). She is the engineer of innovation when she suspends flower garlands from bucrania. She is the psychologist of her male models, whom she allows to express confidence in their own power through their commanding faces and their body language. All of this makes Michaelina Wautier a unique interpreter of the Flemish Baroque, in whose work the undertone of transience is always present, like the ticking of the precious watch on her easel.

Epilogue

Michaelina Wautier's *Triumph of Bacchus* was part of Leopold Wilhelm's collection in 1659. There are various reasons to assume that the Governor commissioned the painting. When the inventory was drawn up in Vienna, the person responsible must have been aware that it had been made by the hand of a woman and, for him also, it must surely have made a difference that it was 'Madamoiselle Wautier' who had painted this exciting scene. Nonetheless, his successors quickly forgot her name. The *Triumph of Bacchus* became attributed instead to male artists such as Cornelis Wautier [Cornelis Vandrier], Cornelis Schut and Frans Wouters, or it was linked to Peter Paul Rubens's entourage as 'School of Rubens' or 'Copy after Rubens'. Not before 1967 was the painting attributed to 'Micheline Woutiers'. It wound up in the Kunsthistorisches Museum's 'Secondary Gallery' and was shown for the first time in 2009, within the context of the exhibition *Rubens and His Circle's Images of Women*. Finally, in 2014, after a restoration and the relentless efforts of Gerlinde Gruber, the painting was awarded a place on the *belle étage* of the Kunsthistorisches Museum among the paintings by Rubens and Anthony van Dyck.[1] What happened to Wautier's most triumphant painting is a metaphor for what happened to her oeuvre as a whole and to her as an artist. For nearly four centuries, it was as if she had never existed.

The recovery has gained momentum. The world premier exhibition at MAS in 2018, *Baroque's Leading Lady*,[2] has given the impetus and yielded an unexpected spinoff when, on 18 June 2019, the Google banner contained a drawing of her self-portrait at the easel with the caption: 'Today's Doodle celebrates the Belgian artist Michaelina Wautier, born 415 years ago. Michaelina Wautier: entering the limelight after 300 years: Giving a Lost Baroque Master Her Due.' In that same year, on 30 January 2019, *Garland of Flowers with Dragonfly* (fig.48), was sold at Sotheby's New York for US$471,000. On 16 November 1993, this same flower still life had been acquired by a Dutch art dealer for the sum of €14,193 at Sotheby's Amsterdam. *Boy with a White Cravat* (fig.47) was auctioned at Christie's London on 8 July 2021 (under the title *Head of a Boy*), with an estimated value of £40,000–£60,000, and sold for £400,000. As ever, the market price follows the canon, and the re-evaluation of Wautier's canon encourages museums to collect paintings by her, as evidenced by the Museum M in Leuven's acquisition of the *Study of the Head of a Bearded Man* (fig.61) in 2023.[3] The boom in prices for her work since 2018 confirms that she has entered the highest echelon of Western European art.

The exhibition – a first-ever Wautier show in the United States – of no fewer than six paintings at the Museum of Fine Arts in Boston in 2022–3, the rediscovered series of *The Five Senses* and her self-portrait, has unleashed a torrent of interest. Talk of 'historical amnesia' gained traction, and the *Boston Globe* of 10 November 2022 carried the headline: 'The best female Old Master you've never heard of. Until now.' In the weekend edition of 3–4 December 2022, Wautier's self-portrait appeared on the cover of *The New York Times* (international edition) with the caption, 'Her art was overlooked for centuries. No more.' In 2025 and 2026, monographic exhibitions of her work are being held at the Kunsthistorisches Museum in Vienna and the Royal Academy in London.[4] Michaelina Wautier had, in the words of Virginia Woolf, 'A Room of Her Own', and made it into 'A World of Her Own'.

Overlooked? No more.

Notes

ACKNOWLEDGEMENTS

1   Dirk Pültau, 'De affirmatieve vrouw in de kunst: Over Gynaika en "Inside the Visible"', *De witte raaf*, vol.63, 1996.

2   Katlijne Van der Stighelen, '"Une robustesse extraordinaire chez une femme": de schilderijen van Michaelina Woutiers', in Leen Huet and Wim Neetens (eds), *An Unexpected Journey: Vrouw en kunst – Woman and Art*, Gynaika, Antwerp, 1996, pp 286–94.

3   Katlijne Van der Stighelen and Mirjam Westen (eds), *Elck Zijn Waerom: Vrouwelijke Kunstenaars in België en Nederland, 1500–1950*, exh.cat., Koninklijk Museum voor Schone Kunsten, Antwerp, and Museum voor Moderne Kunst, Arnhem, Ludion, Ghent and Amsterdam, 1999.

4   Katlijne Van der Stighelen, '"Prima inter pares": Over de voorkeur van aartshertog Leopold-Wilhelm voor Michaelina Woutiers (ca.1620–na 1682)', in Hans Vlieghe and Katlijne Van der Stighelen (eds), *Sponsors of the Past: Flemish Art and Patronage, 1550–1700*, Brepols, Turnhout, 2005, pp 91–116.

5   Katlijne Van der Stighelen (ed.), *Michaelina Wautier 1604–1689: Glorifying a Forgotten Talent*, BAI, Antwerp, 2018, p.7.

INTRODUCTION

1   For the family context for female artists in general and especially for Michaelina Wautier, see: Katrin Dyballa and Sabine Engel, 'Michaelina Wautier (1604–1689)', in Katrin Dyballa, Bodo Brinkmann and Ariane Mensger (eds), *Geniale Frauen: Künstlerinnen und ihre Weggefährten*, exh.cat., Bucerius Kunst Forum, Hamburg, and Kunstmuseum, Basel, 2024, pp 98–105. See also: León Krempel, *Family Affairs: Broers en zusters in de kunst. Frères et soeurs dans l'art*, exh.cat., Bozar, Brussels, 2006.

2   See: Aaron M. Hyman, *Rubens in Repeat: The Logic of the Copy in Colonial Latin America*, Getty Publications, Los Angeles, CA, 2021.

3   Virginia Woolf, *A Room of One's Own*, ed. David Bradshaw and Stuart N. Clark, Wiley-Blackwell, Oxford, 2015, pp 35–6.

4   See: Adam Eaker, *Gesina ter Borch*, Illuminating Women Artists, Lund Humphries, London, 2024, p.14.

I THE TRUE STORY BEHIND THE ARTIST

1   In the United Kingdom, this process of recuperation is impressively practised by Philippa Gregory, *Normal Women: 900 Years of Making History*, William Collins, London and Dublin, 2023.

2   Biographical and genealogical information has increased enormously due to Jean Bastiaensen's research since the Michaelina Wautier exhibition at the MAS (Museum aan de Stroom) in Antwerp in 2018. See references throughout this chapter.

3 See: Kirsten Derks, 'Leaving Her Mark: Michaelina Wautier's Signing Practice', in Lieke van Deinsen, Bert Schepers, Marjan Sterckx, Hans Vlieghe and Bert Watteeuw (eds), *Campaspe Talks Back: Women Who Made a Difference in Early Modern Art. Essays in Honour of Katlijne Van der Stighelen*, Brepols, Turnhout, 2024, pp 167–72.

4 The *portrait historié* will be analysed in Chapter 5.

5 Gina Strumwasser, *Politically Incorrect: Women Artists and Female Imagery in Early Modern Europe*, Cognella, San Diego, CA, 2012, pp 5–10, 113.

6 We are not sure that the portrait of a woman sitting at a richly laid table is a self-portrait of Clara Peeters. In at least eight paintings, the miniscule reflection of the artist can be seen, a sophisticated way of making herself present in her work. See: Alejandro Vergara (ed.), *The Art of Clara Peeters*, exh.cat., Museum Snijders and Rockoxhuis, Antwerp, and Museo Nacional del Prado, Madrid, 2016, pp 17, 64, fig.33.

7 See: James A. Welu and Pieter Biesboer, *Judith Leyster: Schilderes in een mannenwereld*, exh.cat., Frans Halsmuseum, Haarlem, Zwolle, 1993, pp 162–7, cat.no.7.

8 See: Keith Christiansen and Judith W. Mann, *Orazio and Artemisia Gentileschi*, exh.cat., The Metropolitan Museum, New York, 2001, pp 417–21; Nicole Birnfeld, 'Ein Leben für die Kunst? – Anmerkungen zu Pictura-Darstellungen nördlich der Alpen', in Simone Roggendorf and Sigrid Ruby (eds), *(En)gendered: Frühneuzeitlicher Kunstdiskurs und weibliche Porträtkultur nördlich der Alpen*, Jonas Verlag, Marburg, 2004, pp 111–22, on pp 116–18; Sheila Barker, *Artemisia Gentileschi*, Illuminating Women Artists, Lund Humphries, London, 2022, pp 101–3.

9 This aspect will be treated in relation to Wautier in Chapter 4.

10 Artcurial auction, Paris, 23 March 2022, lot 101. Hitherto attributed to Sébastien Bourdon, it was recently acquired by the Château de Versailles (canvas, 130 × 96 cm), inv.no.V.2022.7. See: 'Acquisition du portrait de Catherine Duchemin', Château de Versailles, at https://www.chateauversailles.fr/actualites/vie-domaine/acquisition-portrait-catherine-duchemin (accessed 3 January 2025).

11 Kirsten Derks and Alice Limb are preparing a contribution on Wautier's self-portrait, in which this aspect will be analysed in detail. I am very grateful to the authors for sharing the results of their research with me. The moles are part of the original paint layer and were planned from the outset.

12 See: n.11.

13 The author is grateful to Marieke de Winkel for this information. The fabric of the black mantle Wautier wears over her informal gown could be silk or velvet. According to De Winkel, it is a fantasy garment, the colour of which emphasises the sitter's prestige. I am equally grateful to Bianca du Mortier who agrees with De Winkel that Wautier wears a fantasy garment and suggests that the collar might be a so-called 'kamdoeck'. See: C.J. Platteschorre-Weurman, 'De peignoir', in *Kostuum: Jaarboek van de Nederlandse Vereniging voor Kostuum*, 2008, pp 17–29.

14 As is the case with the *Self-Portrait by Maria Schalcken*, c.1680, panel, 44.1 × 34.3 cm, Museum of Fine Arts, Boston, MA, promised gift of Rose-Marie and Eijk van Otterloo, in support of the Center for Netherlandish Art.

15 Hans Vlieghe, *Rubens. Portraits of Identified Sitters Painted in Antwerp*, Corpus Rubenianum Ludwig Burchard, vol.XIX.2, Harvey Miller, London, 1987, pp 159–60.

16 See: n.11.

17 Katlijne Van der Stighelen, 'Het sleuteltje van het "sackhorologie" van Michaelina Wautier (1614–1689): Een detail van een detail', *Verslagen en Mededelingen van de Koninklijke Academie voor Nederlandse Taal en Letteren*, vol.134, 2024, pp 65–72.

18 The question is whether her self-portrait was still part of Charles Wautier's collection when his belongings were sold shortly before he died. The auction is discussed further below: see p.26.

19 For a detailed provenance, see: Jahel Sanzsalazar, 'Michaelina Wautier y la incomparable Anna Maria van Schurman: feminismo, arte y erudición en los Países Bajos en el siglo XVII', *Tendencias del Mercado del Arte*, vol.113, May 2018, pp 86–91; see: Katlijne Van der Stighelen (ed.), *Michaelina Wautier 1604–1689: Glorifying a Forgotten Talent*, BAI, Antwerp, 2018, pp 18–20; the same author assumes that it was already acquired by Robert Spencer, 2nd Earl of Sunderland (1640–1702).

20 New York, *Old Master Paintings*, 12 January 1989, lot 116. Later on, the painting was acquired by the present owners; Jahel Sanzsalazar identified the 'self-portrait' of Michaelina Wautier as a portrait of Anna Maria van Schurman: 'Michaelina Wautier y la incomparable Anna Maria van Schurman', p.90, nn 13–14. This seems unlikely since the likeness of the model to Van Schurman is limited and the two artists never met. Moreover, there is no known life-size portrait or history piece by Van Schurman, which would make it strange that she is here depicted as the maker of a monumental painting.

21 See: Jean Bastiaensen, 'A Revised Biography of Michaelina Wautier', in Gerlinde Gruber, Katlijne Van der Stighelen and Julien Domerque (eds), *Michaelina Wautier: Painter*, exh.cat., Kunsthistorisches Museum, Vienna, and The Royal Academy, London, 2025, pp 107–21.

22 See: Jean-Marie Cauchies, Virginien Horge, Corentin Rousman and Sophie Simon, *Histoire de la ville de Mons: Politique, militaire, aménagement du territoire*, Racine, Brussels, 2024.

23 Jean-Louis Van Belle and Pierre-Jean Niebes (eds), *Vivre à Mons aux XVIIe et XVIIIe siècles: Le témoignage des chroniques*, Collection Témoins d'Histoire, no.8, Éditions Safran, Brussels, 2021, pp 83–5; Laurent Honnoré, René Plisnier, Caroline Pousseur and Pierre Tilly (eds), *1000 Personnalités de Mons & de la Région: Dictionnaire Biographique*, Avant-Propos, Waterloo, 2015, pp 208–10, 211–13, 324, 580–81; F. De Vriendt, 'Le père Charles Malapert S.J. (1581–1630), un savant montois au temps de l'apogée des Jesuites', in J. Lory, A. Minette and J. Walravens (eds), *Les Jesuites à Mons: Liber memorialis*, Association Royale des anciens élèves du Collège Saint-Stanislas, Mons, 1999, pp 107–35.

24 See: Van der Stighelen (ed.), *Michaelina Wautier*, pp 18–20.

25 ibid., pp 16–17.

26 The castle that belonged to the De Merode family still exists in Ham-sur-Heure but is now the property of the municipality of Ham-sur-Heure-Nalinnes.

27 See: Bastiaensen, 'A Revised Biography of Michaelina Wautier', p.107.

28 ibid., p.109.

29 See: Van der Stighelen (ed.), *Michaelina Wautier*, p.17, n.20.

30 See: https://www.ursulines-mons.be/organisation/historique (accessed 5 March 2025).

31 Anna Maria van Schurman, *Eucleria, of uitkiezing van Het Beste Deel*, facsimile edn, intro. S. van der Linde, De Tille, Leeuwarden, 1978; Mirjam de Baar, 'Now as for the Faint Rumours of Fame Attached to my Name . . . The Eukleria as Autobiography', in: Mirjam de Baar, Machteld Löwensteyn, Marit Monteiro and A. Agnes Sneller (eds), *Choosing the Better Part: Anna Maria van Schurman (1607–1678)*, International Archives of the History of Ideas, no.146, Kluwer Academic, Dordrecht, Boston, MA and London, 1996, pp 87–102.

32 See below: p.25.

33 Interestingly, the funeral register of the Church of Our Lady of the Chapel in Brussels mentions: 'Miss Michael [*sic*] Wautier', a reference that closely corresponds to the signature on her paintings. See further below: p.26.

34 See: Gerlinde Gruber, 'Michaelina Wautier's Paintings in the Habsburg Collections', in Gruber et al. (eds), *Michaelina Wautier*, pp 123–33, on p.127.

35 I first suggested this in the exhibition catalogue of 2018, and this led to the erroneous conclusion that Michaelina was the same as Marie Magdelaine Wautier, and that Michaelina Wautier, therefore, was born in 1604, according to the baptismal certificate. About the complexity of the identification, see: Van der Stighelen (ed.), *Michaelina Wautier*, p.16.

36 See: Bastiaensen, 'A Revised Biography of Michaelina Wautier', pp 115–16.

37 Private archive Diego de Wautier, Brussels, Genealogical Material. For the context of the 'devotaire', see: Maurits de Vroede, *'Kwezels' en 'zusters': De geestelijke dochters in de Zuidelijke Nederlanden*, AWLSK, Brussels, 1994; Sarah Moran, 'Resurrecting the "Spiritual Daughters": The Houtappel Chapel and Women's Patronage of Jesuit Building Programs in the Spanish Netherlands', in Sarah Moran and Amanda Pipkin (eds), *Women and Gender in the Early Modern Low Countries 1500–1750*, Brill, Leiden, 2019, pp 266–322.

38 To keep this biography consistent, this edition

chooses to situate her date of birth 'around 1614', and employs this date as a reference point.

39   Archives de l'Ètat, Mons, Manuscrits 370, 11, 3120, no.980. See: [A.D.], 'Le Mémorial d'une famille montoise 1587–1716', *Bulletin du bibliophile et du bibliothécaire*, 1866, pp 295–6. See also: Van der Stighelen (ed.), *Michaelina Wautier*, p.18; and Bastiaensen, 'A Revised Biography of Michaelina Wautier', nn 3, 8–9, 16.

40   See: Bastiaensen, 'A Revised Biography of Michaelina Wautier', p.109.

41   See: Van der Stighelen (ed.), *Michaelina Wautier*, p.37, n.44 (with ref. to archival source).

42   See: Honnoré et al. (eds), *1000 Personnalités de Mons*, p.62.

43   See: Armand Louant (ed.), *Le Livre de ballades de Jehan et Charles Bocquet, bourgeois de Mons au XVIe siecle*, Palais des Académies, Brussels 1954, p.59: Ballade XVII, fol.13ᵛ, Ballade XIX, fol.14. About the Bosquet family, see also: 'Histoire généalogique de la famille Boussu, de Mons', at http://www.genealexis.fr/pdf/histoire-famille-de-boussu.pdf (accessed 5 March 2025).

44   See: Bastiaensen, 'A Revised Biography of Michaelina Wautier', p.109.

45   ibid., p.121.

46   ibid., p.112.

47   ibid., pp 112–14.

48   See: Van der Stighelen (ed.), *Michaelina Wautier*, pp 22, 38.

49   See: Jahel Sanzsalazar, 'Michaelina Wautier y la boda de su hermano: historia de un retrato identificado', *Tendencias del Mercado del Arte*, vol.69, January 2014, pp 90–94, on p.94; Van der Stighelen (ed.), *Michaelina Wautier*, pp 182–5. In terms of style and empathy, this portrait is very similar to the *Portrait of a Gentleman*, which is attributed to Michael Sweerts and dates from around 1655–9. If it is indeed by Sweerts, it clearly shows the profound influence that Wautier's portraits had on him. See: Lara Yeager-Crasselt, *Portrait of a Gentleman: Michael Sweerts (1618–1664) and the Elegance of Brussels Portraiture*, Phoebus Focus, no.21, Hannibal Books, Veurne, 2021, pp 6–9, 65–71. See also: Van der Stighelen (ed.), *Michaelina Wautier*, p.182, fig.C.

50   See: Bastiaensen, 'A Revised Biography of Michaelina Wautier', p.112.

51   ibid.

52   ibid.

53   ibid., p.116. The discoverer of this archival document states that the sequence may have to do with the fact that the older Marie Magdelaine had not been present on the occasion and was mentioned last for that reason.

54   See: Bastiaensen, 'A Revised Biography of Michaelina Wautier', p.114.

55   Van der Stighelen (ed.), *Michaelina Wautier*, pp 29–30.

56   ibid., pp 30–32 for a survey of the houses in their ownership.

57   ibid., p.34.

58   Bastiaensen, 'A Revised Biography of Michaelina Wautier', p.120.

59   See: n.37.

60   See: Bastiaensen, 'A Revised Biography of Michaelina Wautier', p.120.

61   The reason that her name was registered in the parish registers in the male form, 'Michael', and not 'Michaelina' is unknown. It is probably because the name was abbreviated carelessly, without the use of a contraction sign. Names are indeed abbreviated systematically in parish registers.

62   See: Bastiaensen, 'A Revised Biography of Michaelina Wautier', p.121.

2 PATRONS, PATRONAGE AND ART CONNOISSEURS

1   See: Robert Tittler, 'The "Feminine Dynamic" in Tudor Art: A Reassessment', *British Art Journal*, vol.17, no.1, 2016, pp 123–30, on pp 125, 128, 130, who also references the painter Margaret Holsewyther, the wife of Susanna's brother Lucas Horenbout and the daughter of another immigrant painter. She possibly took over Lucas's studio after his death; about the contacts between Teerlinck and Anguissola, see: Annemie Leemans, 'Tra storia e legenda. Indigani sul network artístico tra Sofonisba Anguissola, Giulio Clovio e Levina Teerlinc', *INTRECCI d'arte*, vol.3, 2014, pp 35–55, https://doi.org/10.6092/issn.2240-7251/4580. On Teerlinck, see also: Louisa Woodville,

'Levina Teerlinc, Illuminator at the Tudor Court', *Art Herstory*, 12 May 2020, at https://artherstory.net/levina-teerlinc/.

2   See: S.E. James, 'The Horenbout Family Workshop at the Tudor Court, 1522–1541: Collaboration, Patronage and Production', *Cogent Arts & Humanities*, vol.8, no.1, 2021, pp 3–5, 21–2, https://doi.org/10.1080/233119 83.2021.1915933.

3   Jennifer Courts, 'Caterina van Hemessen in the Habsburg Court of Mary of Hungary', in Tanja L. Jones (ed.), *Women Artists in the Early Modern Courts of Europe, c.1450–1700*, Visual and Material Culture, 1300–1700, Amsterdam University Press, Amsterdam, 2021, pp 71–89; E. Sutton (ed.), *Women Artists and Patrons in the Netherlands, 1500–1700*, Amsterdam University Press, Amsterdam, 2019.

4   Katlijne Van der Stighelen, 'Anna Francisca de Bruyns (1604/5–1656), Artist, Wife and Mother: A Contextual Approach to Her Forgotten Artistic Career', in Sarah Moran and Amanda Pipkin (eds), *Women and Gender in the Early Modern Low Countries 1500–1750*, Brill, Leiden, 2019, pp 192–228.

5   Leticia Ruiz Gómez (ed.), *A Tale of Two Women Painters: Sofonisba Anguissola and Lavinia Fontana*, exh.cat., Museo Nacional del Prado, Madrid, 2019, pp 156–7; Cecilia Gamberini, *Sofonisba Anguissola*, Illuminating Women Artists, Lund Humphries, London, 2024, pp 94–100, figs 44–5.

6   See: Jean Bastiaensen, '"Finding Clara": Establishing the Biographical Details of Clara Peeters (ca.1587–after 1636)', *Boletin del Museo del Prado*, vol.34, 2016, pp 17–31.

7   See: Alejandro Vergara (ed.), *The Art of Clara Peeters*, exh.cat., Museum Snijders and Rockoxhuis, Antwerp, and Museo Nacional del Prado, Madrid, 2016, p.17; Alejandro Vergara Sharp, *Clara Peeters*, Illuminating Women Artists, Lund Humphries, London, 2025, pp 51–2.

8   See: Vergara (ed.), *The Art of Clara Peeters*, pp 68, 72, 76, 80, 84, 88, 92, 96, 103, 106, 110, 113, 116, 120.

9   See: Bastiaensen, '"Finding Clara"', p.25; Vergara Sharp, *Clara Peeters*, p.28.

10 See: Bastiaensen, '"Finding Clara"', pp 22–3 for a family tree; Vergara Sharp, *Clara Peeters*, pp 11–12.

11 See: Jean-Marie Cauchies, Virginien Horge, Corentin Rousman and Sophie Simon, *Histoire de la ville de Mons: Politique, militaire, aménagement du territoire*, Racine, Brussels, 2024.

12 Alexandre Henne and Alphonse Wauters, *Histoire de la ville de Bruxelles*, 5 vols, Librairie Encyclopédique de Perichon, Brussels, 1845, vol.II, p.53; Veerle De Laet, 'At Home in Seventeenth-Century Brussels: Patterns of Art and Luxury in Private Households', in Katlijne Van der Stighelen, Leen Kelchtermans and Koenraad Brosens (eds), *Embracing Brussels: Art and Culture in the Court City, 1600–1800*, Brepols, Turnhout, 2013, pp 11–19, on pp 12–13.

13 Herbert Haupt, 'Kultur und kulturgeschichtliche Nachricht vom Wiener Hofe: Erzherzog Leopold Wilhelm in den Jahren 1646–1654', *Mitteilungen des Österreichischen Staats Archivs*, vol.33, 1980, pp 346–55; Jozef Mertens and Frans Aumann (eds), *Krijg en kunst: Leopold-Willem (1614–1662), Habsburger, landvoogd en kunstverzamelaar*, exh.cat., Landcommanderij Alden Biesen, Bilzen-Rijkhoven, 2003, pp 48–9; Veerle De Laet, *Brussel binnenskamers: Kunst-en luxebezit in het spanningsveld tussen hof en stad, 1600–1735*, Studies Stadsgeschiedenis, Amsterdam University Press, Amsterdam, 2011, pp 145–6; Katlijne Van der Stighelen, '"Prima inter pares": Over de voorkeur van aartshertog Leopold-Wilhelm voor Michaelina Woutiers (ca.1620–na 1682)', in Hans Vlieghe and Katlijne Van der Stighelen (eds), *Sponsors of the Past: Flemish Art and Patronage, 1550–1700*, Brepols, Turnhout, 2005, pp 91–116; Hans Vlieghe, '"Frayicheyt ende kunst daer syne inclinatie toe stryckt": beschouwingen over het mecenaat van aartshertog Leopold-Wilhelm tijdens zijn landvoogdij over de Zuidelijke Nederlanden (1647–1656)', in Vlieghe and Van der Stighelen (eds), *Sponsors of the Past*, pp 61–90.

14 De Laet, *Brussel binnenskamers*, pp 76–89. This division should not be taken too strictly, because some of the nobles and soldiers were billeted with private citizens, which led to a more diverse residency pattern.

15 De Laet, 'At Home in Seventeenth-Century Brussels', pp 12–13.

16 Katlijne Van der Stighelen (ed.), *Michaelina Wautier 1604–1689: Glorifying a Forgotten Talent*, BAI, Antwerp, 2018, pp 30–31.

17 See: Karel Porteman, 'Het Spaanse Spook', *Spiegel der Letteren*, vol.47, 2005, pp 206–10, on pp 206–9. The author translates 'Courtois' as 'hoffelijk' and 'ontzichtelijk' as 'ontzaglijk'.

18 See: Van der Stighelen (ed.), *Michaelina Wautier*, pp 156–9.

19 ibid., p.158, fig.B. See: *The Battle of Kallo* (1638), Royal Museums of Fine Arts of Belgium, Brussels, inv. no.1477.

20 For this portrait, see Cornelis Schut's tapestry cartoon from *c.*1640–42, just predating Wautier's engraved portrait (Rubenshuis, Antwerp). The design of this cartoon depicts Astrologia as a young woman wielding a sceptre. In the foreground a child points to Apollo as protector of the arts driving his sun chariot through the heavens. Kneeling at Astrologia's feet is a young man in armour. Already in 1996 he was identified as the putative patron of the series, Andrea Cantelmo. Comparison of the kneeling commander with Wautier's portrait corroborates that. See: Van der Stighelen (ed.), *Michaelina Wautier*, p.159.

21 Leen Kelchtermans, 'Portret van een zeventiende-eeuwse schildersvrouw: Anna Schut, huisvrouw en weduwe van Peter Snayers', *Oud Holland*, vol.126, 2013, pp 178–97.

22 The only portrait that stylistically can be dated around 1640 is the *Portrait Historié of a Family with Parents Posing as Isaac and Rebecca*, auctioned at Christie's London on 6 December 2018, lot 13A (see fig.35). This will be discussed below.

23 Carolyn James, 'Margherita Cantelmo and the Worth of Women in Renaissance Italy', in Karen Green and Constant J. Mews (eds), *Virtue Ethics for Women, 1250–1500*, Springer, Dordrecht, New York, 2011, pp 145–58.

24 Van der Stighelen (ed.), *Michaelina Wautier*, pp 158–60.

25 We cannot exclude the possibility that Michaelina herself offered to paint his portrait. This is not likely, but even in that case, the commander accepted her proposal, which, in view of his position as a soldier and an art connoisseur, was more than unusual. The rarity of the engraving from the portrait can also be linked to the print run in which it was printed, about

26 See: Mertens and Aumann (eds), *Krijg en kunst*, pp 126–7; Piet Stryckers, 'Music and Music Production in Seventeenth-Century Brussels', in Van der Stighelen et al. (eds), *Embracing Brussels*, pp 59–79.

27 Van der Stighelen (ed.), *Michaelina Wautier*, p.32.

28 ibid., pp 296–7.

29 Owners of portraits such as her brother Pierre Wautier (see fig.10) are not considered as patrons, in view of the personal connection.

30 See: Jean Bastiaensen, 'A Revised Biography of Michaelina Wautier', in Gerlinde Gruber, Katlijne Van der Stighelen and Julien Domerque (eds), *Michaelina Wautier: Painter*, exh.cat., Kunsthistorisches Museum, Vienna, and The Royal Academy, London, 2025, pp 107–21, on pp 114–15.

31 Brussels, State Archives, Manuscript Collection, 1088; See: Van der Stighelen (ed.), *Michaelina Wautier*, pp 296–7. With gratitude to Hannelore Magnus who discovered this source and made it known. The subject of Nicodemus is rather rare in Christian tradition. No painting by Charles Wautier is known depicting the converted Pharisee. For the reference to the Baron of Breda, see: fol.58. For this Mademoiselle 'Ovinne', see: fol.25. See also: Van der Stighelen (ed.), *Michaelina Wautier*, p.32.

32 1 patagon or patacon, a silver coin in Flanders, also called 'Albertusdaalder', is equal to 58 stivers. Since 1 guilder was worth 20 stivers, this would mean that a sum of 30 patacons was equal to 1740 stivers or 87 guilders. See: *Verklaring van allerhande zo goude als zilvere en andere geld-specien*, 2nd edn, Pieter Koumans, Leeuwarden, 1746, pp 64, 189.

33 Wautier made a painting called *Triumph of Bacchus* (see fig.63) but that must be a different painting from the one described here, as will become clear later on.

34 In the same year of 1647, Leopold Wilhelm made his entry into Mons, Wautier's own city, in a procession with among others a dwarf, and which was illuminated by torches; see: Jean-Louis Van Belle and Pierre-Jean Niebes (eds), *Vivre à Mons aux XVIIe et XVIIIe siècles: Le témoignage des chroniques*, Collection Témoins d'Histoire, no.8, Éditions Safran, Brussels, 2021, pp 25–8, 82. The description is by the sexton of

the Church of Saint-Germain in Mons: 'Mémoire d'avoir veu faire l'archiduc Léopold, frère de L'empereur, son entrée à Mons vers le soire. Il estoit à cheval, il y avoit plus[ieu]rs flambeaux avec un beau train, il avoit un nain avec luy bien fait et bien jolly.'

35 See: Hans Vlieghe, 'The Decorations for Archduke Leopold William's State Entry into Antwerp', *Journal of the Warburg and Courtauld Institutes*, vol.39, 1976, pp 190–98.

36 Mertens and Aumann (eds), *Krijg en kunst*, p.89.

37 Francesca del Torre Scheuch and Gerlinde Gruber, 'L'abondance & la diversité: The Gallery of Archduke Leopold Wilhelm', in Van der Stighelen (ed.), *Michaelina Wautier*, pp 53–65, on p.54.

38 Jan Denucé, *Ná Peter Pauwel Rubens: Documenten uit den kunsthandel te Antwerpen in de XVIIe eeuw*, De Sikkel, Antwerp, 1949, p.67; Vlieghe, '"Frayicheyt ende kunst daer syne inclinatie toe stryckt"', p.64.

39 Renate Schreiber, *'Ein Galeria nach meinem Humor': Erzherzog Leopold Wilhelm*, Schriftenreihe des Kunsthistorischen Museums, no.8, Kunsthistorisches Museum, Vienna, 2004, pp 89–129; Vlieghe, '"Frayicheyt ende kunst daer syne inclinatie toe stryckt"'; Gudrun Swoboda, *Die Wege der Bilder: Eine Geschichte der Kaiserlichen Gemäldesammlungen von 1600 bis 1800*, Kunsthistorisches Museum, Vienna, 2008, pp 40–71; Del Torre Scheuch and Gruber, 'L'abondance & la diversité'.

40 See: Sabine van Sprang and Lara de Merode, 'Michaelina Wautier and Artistic Brussels', in Gruber et al. (eds), *Michaelina Wautier*, pp 89–105; Gerlinde Gruber and Julien Domerque, 'The Challenges of Reconstruction', in Gruber et al. (eds), *Michaelina Wautier*, pp 11–16, on p.12; Gerlinde Gruber, 'Michaelina Wautier's Paintings in the Habsburg Collections', in Gruber et al. (eds), *Michaelina Wautier*, pp 123–33, on p.127.

41 See: Adolph Berger, 'Inventar der Kunstsammlung des Erzherzogs Leopold Wilhelm von Österreich. Nach der originalhandschrift im fürstlich Schwarzenberg'schen centralarchive herausgegeben', *Jahrbuch der Kunsthistorischen Sammlungen des Allerhöchsten Kaiserhauses*, vol.1, 1883, pp LXXIX–CXCI, on p.XCIX, nos 87, 88, 75; Gruber, 'Michaelina Wautier's Paintings', pp 127–8.

42 ibid., p.CXXXIV, no.365; Gruber, 'Michaelina Wautier's Paintings', pp 128–31.

43 The description 'Jungfraw' does not refer to a noble title but to her unmarried state. For further information on the different meanings (and the complexity) of the term, see: Martha Schad, *Die Frauen des Hauses Fugger von der Lilie (15.–17. Jahrhundert): Augsburg-Ortenburg-Trient*, Mohr, Tübingen, 1989, pp 17, 52, 67–8, 128, 178; Wolfgang Reinhard, *Lebensformen Europas: Eine historische Kulturanthologie*, Beck, Munich, 2004, pp 76, 314.

44 Gerlinde Gruber has convincingly argued that the neatly calligraphed register in Vienna must be based on an older inventory drawn up previously in Brussels. The existence of such an inventory is supported by the numbers on the picture frames in David Teniers's painting of the picture gallery in Brussels (see fig.15), which match those in the Vienna inventory and are also found on the original backs of the pictures. This was noted by Glück, who suggested Teniers as the author of this earlier, lost inventory. See: Gustav Glück, 'Aus Rubens' Zeit und Schule: Bemerkungen zu einigen Gemälden der Kaiserlichen Galerie in Wien', *Jahrbuch der Kunsthistorischen Sammlungen des Allerhöchsten Kaiserhauses*, vol.24, 1903, pp 1–48, on p.2; Gustav Glück, *Rubens, Van Dyck und ihr Kreis*, A. Schroll, Vienna, 1933, p.210; Klara Garas, 'Die Entstehung der Galerie des Erzherzogs Leopold Wilhelm', *Jahrbuch der Kunsthistorischen Sammlungen in Wien*, vol.27, no.63, new series, 1967, pp 39–80, on p.42; Gruber, 'Michaelina Wautier's Paintings', pp 127–30.

45 See: Gruber, 'Michaelina Wautier's Paintings', pp 124–7.

46 See: Van der Stighelen (ed.), *Michaelina Wautier*, pp 29, 32; Bastiaensen, 'A Revised Biography of Michaelina Wautier', p.108. For a reproduction of the inscription, see: Gruber, 'Michaelina Wautier's Paintings', p.124, fig.102.

47 This happened at the earliest after 1660, which was the date of the publication of the *Theatrum Pictorium* by David Teniers II, the first illustrated and printed catalogue of a major collection of paintings. See: Gruber, 'Michaelina Wautier's Paintings', p.127.

48 See: Gruber and Julien Domerque, 'The Challenges

of Reconstruction', p.13. Some variants only occur in the eighteenth and the nineteenth centuries but have led to some errors in the historiography.

49 Margret Klinge, 'David Teniers d. J. – Theatrum Pictorium', in Jozef Mertens and Frans Aumann (eds), *Krijg en kunst:Leopold-Willem (1614–1662), Habsburger, landvoogd en kunstverzamelaar*, exh.cat., Landcommanderij Alden Biesen, Bilzen-Rijkhoven, 2003, pp 101–8.

50 See: Jahel Sanzsalazar, 'The Influence of Others: The Wautiers, David Teniers and Archduke Leopold Wilhelm's Theatrum Pictorium', in Van der Stighelen (ed.), *Michaelina Wautier*, pp 67–83, on pp 67–8, fig.2.

51 Gruber, 'Michaelina Wautier's Paintings', p.130.

52 Glück, 'Aus Rubens' Zeit und Schule', p.16, Abb.48; Glück, *Rubens, Van Dyck*, p.230: 'Trotzdem wird man selbst in unserem Zeitalter der Frauenemanzipation dieses Bild, das eine sehr kräftige, ja fast derbe Auffassung zeigt, schwerlich einer weiblichen Hand zumuten wollen'; Günther Heinz, 'Studien über Jan van den Hoecke und die Malerei der Niederländer in Wien', in *Jahrbuch der Kunsthistorischen Sammlungen in Wien*, vol.63, 1967, pp 19–164, on p.152. See: Van der Stighelen (ed.), *Michaelina Wautier*, p.45; Gruber, 'Michaelina Wautier's Paintings', p.133.

53 See: Gruber, 'Michaelina Wautier's Paintings', p.123; Bastiaensen, 'A Revised Biography of Michaelina Wautier', p.114. Regarding the portrait, see: Sanzsalazar, 'The Influence of Others', pp 68–71.

54 See: Van der Stighelen (ed.), *Michaelina Wautier*, pp 268–77. Some portraits and the corresponding engravings date from the late 1650s and the early 1660s; Anne Delvingt and Pierre-Yves Kairis, 'Charles Wautier: Status Quaestionis', in Gruber et al. (eds), *Michaelina Wautier*, pp 71–87, on p.81.

55 See: Florent du Rieu, *Les tableaux parlans du peintre namurois*, P. Gérard, Namur, 1658, p.15; Pierre-Yves Kairis, 'Foisonnement et diversité: les peintres du XVII siècle', in *Un double regard sur 2000 ans d'art wallon*, La Renaissance du Livre, Tournai, 2000, pp 321–41; Van der Stighelen, '"Prima inter pares"', p.112; Sanzsalazar, 'The Influence of Others', pp 71–3; Delvingt and Kairis, 'Charles Wautier', p.71.

56 See: Bastiaensen, 'A Revised Biography of Michaelina Wautier', pp 114–15.

57 Nicolas Avancini, *Le prince dévôt et guerrier ou les vertus héroiques de Leopold Guillaume Archiduc d'Autriche*, 1667, trans. H. Bex, Hachett BnF, Paris, 2017. Goran Proot, 'Leopold Willem en het Jezuïetentoneel in de "Provincia Flandro-Belgica"', in Mertens and Aumann (eds), *Krijg en kunst*, pp 65–70. See also: Vlieghe, '"Frayicheyt ende kunst daer syne inclinatie toe stryckt"', p.61.

58 Sandrine Thieffry, 'L'Archiduc Leopold-Guillaume a Bruxelles (1647–1656): le bon usage du mecenat musical et temps de guerre', *Revue belge de Musicologie / Belgisch Tijdschrift voor Muziekwetenschap*, vol.56, 2002, pp 159–75.

59 See: *Ballet du Roy aux festes de Bacchus, dansé par sa Majesté au Palais Royal, le 2ième jour de May 1651*, R. Ballard, Paris, 1651, at https://gallica.bnf.fr/ark:/12148/btv1b105446557/f133.item; Bibliothèque nationale de France Catalogue général, Notice bibliographique, at https://catalogue.bnf.fr/ark:/12148/cb43891704p (accessed 11 March 2025).

60 Diederik Lanoye, 'Het verblijf van Koningin Christina van Zweden in de Nederlanden (1654–1655)', in Mertens and Aumann (eds), *Krijg en kunst*, pp 53–64.

61 About the composition of Adam-Pierre de La Grené's clientele, see: Comte d'Arschot and Joseph Cuvelier, 'La Clientele d'un Maître a danser a Bruxelles, au XVIIe siecle: Adam-Pierre de la Grené', *Revue belge de philologie et d'histoire*, 15, December 1924, pp 3–15; Bastiaensen, 'A Revised Biography of Michaelina Wautier', pp 114–15. On Lozano, see: Dries Raeymaekers, 'Review of José Eloy Hortal Muñoz, Pierre-François Pirlet and África Espíldora García (eds), *El ceremonial en la Corte de Bruselas del siglo XVII: Los manuscritos de Francisco Alonso Lozano*', *Early Modern Low Countries*, vol.3, no.2, 2019, pp 306–7, https://doi.org/10.18352/emlc.121.

62 Jean-Philippe Van Aelbrouck, *Dictionnaire des danseurs: chorégraphes et maîtres de danse à Bruxelles de 1600 à 1830*, Mardaga, Liège, 1994, p.18.

63 Rudolf Rasch, 'Constantijn Huygens in Brussel op bezoek bij Leopold Wilhelm van Oostenrijk 1648–1656', *Revue belge de Musicologie / Belgisch Tijdschrift voor Muziekwetenschap*, vol.55, 2001, pp 127–46, on pp 134–5: 'Des naermiddaghs ben ick

volgens het appointement van den Eertshertogh in sijn camer gegaen, waer ick met seer beleefde vrindelickheit bejegent wierde door den Bischop van Brugge, ende nu en dan tuschen de musique door den Eertshertogh selve, die mij twee of drij-mael quam aenspreken, schynende groot vermaeck te nemen in de satisfactie die ik bethoonde te vinden in syn Musike, die uyttermaten schoon was.'

3 CHARLES AS THE ELDER BROTHER

1 Bernard Dorival, 'Les influences de l'art des Pays-Bas sur la peinture de Philippe de Champaigne', *Bulletin des Musées royaux des Beaux-Arts de Belgique*, 1970–71, pp 7–54, on pp 11–12; Anne Delvingt and Pierre-Yves Kairis, 'Charles Wautier: Status Quaestionis', in Gerlinde Gruber, Katlijne Van der Stighelen and Julien Domerque (eds), *Michaelina Wautier: Painter*, exh.cat., Kunsthistorisches Museum, Vienna, and The Royal Academy, London, 2025, pp 71–87, on p.71.

2 About possible further training, nothing is known. His youngest brother Léon registered at Leuven University in 1647. See: Delvingt and Kairis, 'Charles Wautier', p.75.

3 ibid., p.72.

4 https://balat.kikirpa.be/object/10155793 (accessed 17 March 2025).

5 See: Katlijne Van der Stighelen, 'Anna Francisca de Bruyns (1604/5–1656), Artist, Wife and Mother: A Contextual Approach to Her Forgotten Artistic Career', in Sarah Moran and Amanda Pipkin (eds), *Women and Gender in the Early Modern Low Countries 1500–1750*, Brill, Leiden, 2019, pp 192–228, on pp 211–12.

6 See: Jean Bastiaensen, 'A Revised Biography of Michaelina Wautier', in Gruber et al. (eds), *Michaelina Wautier*, pp 107–21, on p.112.

7 ibid., p.114.

8 The exact meaning is hard to determine, since it is unclear what was meant by 'buitenland' in seventeenth-century Brussels. The Dutch Republic, France and Italy were certainly considered as 'buitenland'. For a survey of women travelling to Italy, see the research project of Giovanna Ceserani: '955 Women and the Grand Tour of 18th-Century

Italy', 1 November 2024, The Clayman Institute for Gender Research, Stanford University, at https://gender.stanford.edu/news/955-women-and-grand-tour-18th-century-italy (accessed 23 April 2025).

9 See: Gruber et al. (eds), *Michaelina Wautier*, pp 16, 29, 58, 72–5, 137, 162.

10 See: Katlijne Van der Stighelen (ed.), *Michaelina Wautier 1604–1689: Glorifying a Forgotten Talent*, BAI, Antwerp, 2018, p.25.

11 In 1604, Karel van Mander wrote that Rome was the head of the schools of Pictura, but also the place where wastrels and prodigal sons squandered their patrimony. See: Dominique Vautier, *Alle wegen leiden naar Rome: Kunstenaarsreizen in Europa (16de–19de eeuw)*, exh.cat., Museum van Elsene, Brussels, 2007, p.15. There were numerous guides and travel books available, such as *Delitiae Italiae*, a Dutch translation, published in 1602, of a German travel guide. See: José van der Helm, Roos Hamelink and Geertje Wilmsen (eds), *Delitiae Italiae: Een reis door het zeventiende-eeuwse Italië*, Verloren, Hilversum, 2021, pp 9–15.

12 About the history of the Gasthuisstraat, see: Bram Vannieuwenhuyze, 'Brussel, de ontwikkeling van een middeleeuwse stedelijke ruimte', unpublished PhD diss., Ghent University, Ghent, 2008, appendix 1, entry 1.1.150; See: Bastiaensen, 'A Revised Biography of Michaelina Wautier', p.112.

13 Nothing is known about the other masters who were reprimanded, apart from Jacques Boesdonck who registered as a master in 1647. See: Rudy Jos Beerens, *Painters and Communities in Seventeenth-Century Brussels: A Social History of Art*, Leuven University Press, Leuven, 2024, p.64.

14 The reprimand reads in full: 'hadden doen calengieren . . . die aen elcken van hen hadden gelaten een relaes om hen dijenvolgende te reguleren, met expres verboth van dat sy hen nyet meer en souden vervoorderen voorts te wercken aleer de selven souden wesen poirters deser stadt ende inder supplianten ambachte behoorelyck geadmitteert'. See: Katlijne Van der Stighelen, '"Prima inter pares": Over de voorkeur van aartshertog Leopold-Wilhelm voor Michaelina Woutiers (ca.1620–na 1682)', in Hans Vlieghe and Katlijne Van der Stighelen (eds), *Sponsors of*

the Past: Flemish Art and Patronage, 1550–1700, Brepols, Turnhout, 2005, pp 91–116, on p.109; Van der Stighelen (ed.), *Michaelina Wautier*, pp 22, 38; Beerens, *Painters and Communities in Seventeenth-Century Brussels*, pp 64, 196, 213, 241.

15 The registration reads in full: '. . . de welcke betaeylt het recht vande dekens het recht vanden knaep het recht vande armbusse ende de vondelinghe desen 14 martij 1651'. See: Van der Stighelen (ed.), *Michaelina Wautier*, p.38, n.71.

16 For the source of the Crucifixion by Charles Wautier, see: Chapter 5, n.71. For the discussion of the descriptor 'N. Woutiers' in the 1659 inventory and the possible consequences for the attribution of *The Triumph of Bacchus* to Wautier, see: Gerlinde Gruber, 'Michaelina Wautier's Paintings in the Habsburg Collections', in Gruber et al. (eds), *Michaelina Wautier*, pp 123–33, on p.130.

17 Exactly the same origin was given for 'Magdalena Woutiers' in the 1659 inventory of the Archduke: 'Original von Jungfraw Magdalena Woutiers von Mons oder Berghen, Henegaw in Niderlandt' ('Original by Miss Magdalena Woutiers from Mons or Bergen, Hainaut in the Spanish Netherlands'). See: Chapter 2, n.41.

18 See: Van der Stighelen (ed.), *Michaelina Wautier*, pp 22, 271–6; Katlijne Van der Stighelen, 'Michaelina's Style: Blended Brilliance', in Gruber et al. (eds), *Michaelina Wautier*, pp 29–59, on p.29; Bastiaensen, 'A Revised Biography of Michaelina Wautier', pp 114–15.

19 See: Bastiaensen, 'A Revised Biography of Michaelina Wautier', p.109; Anne Verbrugge, 'De kunstverzameling', in M. Derez, J. Tytgat and A. Verbrugge (eds), *Arenberg in de Lage Landen: Een hoogadellijk huis in Vlaanderen en Nederland*, Leuven University Press, Leuven, 2002, pp 319–45, on p.325.

20 Jean Bastiaensen was the first to see the importance of this auction for the Wautier siblings. See: Bastiaensen, 'A Revised Biography of Michaelina Wautier', p.109; Verbrugge, 'De kunstverzameling', p.325. About the contents of the auctioned collection, little is known. Of the 520 works of art, 250 were paintings. See: Y. Lannoye, 'L'ameublement du château d'Enghien au commencement du XVIIe siècle', *Annales du Cercle archéologique d'Enghien*, vol.21, 1984, pp 325–93. Thanks to Anne Verbrugge who supplied me with the reference.

21 See: Sabine van Sprang and Lara de Merode, 'Michaelina Wautier and Artistic Brussels', in Gruber et al. (eds), *Michaelina Wautier*, pp 89–105, on pp 90–95; Gaspar de Crayer (b.1586) worked in Brussels for more than half a century (1617–64), but because his style was more closely related to that of Rubens and Van Dyck, he was not a strong influence on Charles and Michaelina Wautier.

22 For a survey of the oeuvre, see: Delvingt and Kairis, 'Charles Wautier'.

23 Oil on canvas, 59 × 79 cm, private collection, Alkmaar. The painting belonged to the Otto G. Mayer-Schöllkopf collection in Stuttgart, which was auctioned on 6 December 1926, no.104. Christie's, Paris, 14 June 2024, no.119. See: Delvingt and Kairis, 'Charles Wautier', pp 84–7, fig.65.

24 See: Van der Stighelen (ed.), *Michaelina Wautier*, p.246, fig.A (oil on canvas, 42 × 37 cm). The painting was offered for sale at the Banghaus Gallery in Hamburg in 2006 and has not been located since then.

25 Conclusion of the contribution by Delvingt and Kairis, 'Charles Wautier', p.87.

26 See: Bastiaensen, 'A Revised Biography of Michaelina Wautier', pp 114–15.

27 Van der Stighelen (ed.), *Michaelina Wautier*, pp 268–76. Since some portraits bear the signature 'Carolus Wautier delin[eavit]', this indicates that the engraving was done on the basis of a drawing and not on a painted portrait. The same applies to the allegorical portrait of Isabella van Arenberg (ibid., p.268, no.27); see: Bastiaensen, 'A Revised Biography of Michaelina Wautier', pp 113–15, fig.94.

28 Wautier's portrait of Andrea Cantelmo was used for an engraving in 1643 by the Antwerp engraver Paulus Pontius (see fig.8).

29 See: Erik Duverger, 'Nieuwe gegevens betreffende de kunsthandel van Matthys Musson en Maria Fourmenois te Antwerpen tussen 1633 en 1681', *Gentse Bijdragen tot de Kunstgeschiedenis en de Oudheidkunde*, vol.21, 1968, pp 5–250, on p.202. The portraits cost 80 rix dollars or about 200 guilders. The amount is large, but it depends of course on the number of portraits.

30 It cannot be determined with any certainty whether these were paintings executed by Charles Wautier himself. A miniature portrait has been preserved: Anonymous, *Portrait de Boguslas Radziwil*, parchment, 14 × 12 cm, Musée du Louvre, Paris, Département des Arts Graphiques, inv.no.RF 205, recto. See: https://arts-graphiques.louvre.fr/detail/oeuvres/1/111744-Portrait-de-Boguslas-Radziwil (accessed 17 March 2025); a life-size portrait of the prince cannot be linked to Charles Wautier's style. See: *Portrait of Boguslaw Radziwill*, National Museum, Palace of the Grand Dukes of Lithuania, at https://www.valdovurumai.lt/en/exhibitions/i/7545/liberator-of-the-vilnius-castles-exhibition-of-a-portrait-of-boguslaw-radziwill/ (accessed 17 March 2025).

31 See: Bastiaensen, 'A Revised Biography of Michaelina Wautier', p.116: Plantin-Moretus Archief Antwerpen, Family and Company Archive of Henri François Schilders and Sibilla Bosschaert 1657–93, Commercial Correspondence, no.175.

32 Signed 'C. Wautier / 1659'. Oil on canvas, 236 × 173 cm, Eglise Saint-Servais, Gimnée. Pierre-Yves Kairis, 'Foisonnement et diversité: les peintres du XVII siècle', in *Un double regard sur 2000 ans d'art wallon*, La Renaissance du Livre, Tournai, 2000, pp 321–41, on pp 338–9; Pierre-Yves Kairis, *Le portrait dans le Namurois au XVIIe siècle*, Société archéologique de Namur, Namur, 2002, pp 39–41.

33 See: Delvingt and Kairis, 'Charles Wautier', pp 75, 82–5, fig.61.

34 ibid., p.87; on 8 June 1685, the decision was taken to send the Antwerp painter Jan-Erasmus Quellinus a letter asking him to come to Leuven. For an unknown reason, the consultations were stopped. On 27 July 1685, the decision was taken to put the question to 'pictor Wautier of Brussels'. See: Rijksarchief Leuven, Kerkarchief Vlaams Brabant, no.1303, fols.214ᵛ, 215ʳ, 225ᵛ, 249ʳ.

35 See: Leen Kelchtermans, 'Geschilderde gevechten, gekleurde verslagen: een contextuele analyse van Peter Snayers' (1592–1667) topografische strijdtaferelen voor de Habsburgse elite tussen herinnering en verheerlijking', unpublished PhD diss., KU Leuven, Leuven, 2013, pp 414–15. My sincere thanks to Leen Kelchtermans for the reference to this document; Van der Stighelen (ed.), *Michaelina Wautier*, pp 30–32, 73. Snayers also worked on commission for Cantelmo. See: Kelchtermans, 'Geschilderde gevechten, gekleurde verslagen', pp 245, 272–7.

36 See: Van der Stighelen (ed.), *Michaelina Wautier*, p.22.

37 See: Jahel Sanzsalazar, 'La Vocacion de San Mateo: obra de Michaelina y Charles Wautier?', *Tendencias del Mercado del Arte*, vol.123, May 2019, pp 88–92; Delvingt and Kairis, 'Charles Wautier', p.86. It cannot be ruled out, however, that François Volsom is the same person as the Mons painter François Hosson, of whom only a portrait has survived. See: Van der Stighelen (ed.), *Michaelina Wautier*, p.266.

38 Katlijne Van der Stighelen and Mirjam Westen (eds), *Elck Zijn Waerom: Vrouwelijke Kunstenaars in België en Nederland, 1500–1950*, exh.cat., Koninklijk Museum voor Schone Kunsten, Antwerp, and Museum voor Moderne Kunst, Arnhem, Ludion, Ghent and Amsterdam, 1999, pp 133–7, 145–7, 144, 152–3, 164–5, 170–71, 178–80, 185–7, 190–91.

39 Klara Alen, '"Envy and Pride": Maria Faydherbe (Mechelen, 1587–after 1633), a Woman Sculptor in a Man's World', in Hannelore Magnus and Katlijne Van der Stighelen (eds), *Facts and Feelings: Retracing Emotions of Artists, 1600–1800*, Brepols, Turnhout, 2015, pp 77–99; Marjorie Trusted, 'Maria Faydherbe: A Seventeenth-Century Sculptor in Mechelen', *The Burlington Magazine*, vol.156, 2014, pp 104–6. See also: Maria Faydherbe, *Virgin and Child*, 1633, Koning Boudewijnstichting, at https://www.erfgoed-kbs.be/collectie/madonna-met-kind (accessed 9 April 2025); Maria Faydherbe, *Crucifix*, 1620–35, Museum Hof van Busleyden, Mechelen, at https://www.hofvanbusleyden.be/collection/museum-highlights/maria-faydherbe-crucifix (accessed 9 April 2025); Maria Faydherbe, *Virgin and Child*, 1600–24, Museum M, Leuven, at https://www.mleuven.be/en/collection/virgin-and-child-4 (accessed 9 April 2025).

4 WAUTIER AND HER FEMALE COLLEAGUES

1   The best survey of the early modern self-portrait in the Low Countries is still: Hans-Joachim

Raupp, *Untersuchungen zu Künstlerbildnis und Künstlerdarstellung in den Niederlanden im 17. Jahrhundert*, Olms, Hildesheim, 1984; see also: Katlijne Van der Stighelen, '"Amoris et Doloris Monumentum": Portraits and How They Were Perceived in the Baroque Age', in Katlijne Van der Stighelen, Hannelore Magnus and Bert Watteeuw (eds), *Pokerfaced: Flemish and Dutch Baroque Faces Unveiled*, Brepols, Turnhout, 2010, pp 249–73.

2   See: Katlijne Van der Stighelen, 'Michaelina Herself: From Face to Phenomenon', in Gerlinde Gruber, Katlijne Van der Stighelen and Julien Domerque (eds), *Michaelina Wautier: Painter*, exh.cat., Kunsthistorisches Museum, Vienna, and The Royal Academy, London, 2025, pp 61–9. For the context of her self-portrait as *portrait historié*, see: Chapter 1.

3   Lieke van Deinsen, 'Female Faces and Learned Likenesses: Author Portraits and the Construction of Female Authorship and Intellectual Identity', in K. Scholten, D. van Miert and K.A.E. Enenkel (eds), *Memory and Identity in the Learned Word*, Intersections, no.81, Brill, Leiden and Boston, MA, 2022, pp 81–116; Lieke van Deinsen, 'Female Faces in the Fraternity: Printed Portraits Galleries and the Construction and Circulation of Images of Learned Women in the Republic of Letters', in M. Bolufer, L. Guinot-Ferri and C. Blutrach (eds), *Gender and Cultural Mediation in the Long Eighteenth Century: Women across Borders*, Palgrave Macmillan, Cham, 2024, pp 123–49.

4   A representative example is the *Self-Portrait in a Convex Mirror* by the young Parmigianino of *c.*1523/4. Here, the convex mirror he used to paint it hangs on the wall next to him. See: Kunsthistorisches Museum, Vienna, at https://www.khm.at/en/artworks/selbstbildnis-im-konvexspiegel-1407-1 (accessed 20 November 2024). There are concealed self-portraits in representations of Saint Luke painting the Madonna, or Apelles painting Campaspe, which were made in the fifteenth century. See: Renate Trnek (ed.), *Selbstbild: Der Künstler und sein Bildnis*, exh.cat., Gemäldegalerie der Akademie der bildenden Künste Wien, Vienna, 2004; Laura Cumming, *A Face to the World: On Self-Portraits*, HarperPress, London, 2009.

5   Karolien De Clippel, *Catharina van Hemessen (1528–na 1567): Een monografische studie over een 'uytnemende en wel geschickte vrouwe in de conste der schilderyen'*, Verhandelingen van de Koninklijke Vlaamse Academie van België voor Wetenschappen en Kunsten. Nieuwe reeks, no.11, Koninklijke Vlaamse Academie van België voor Wetenschappen en Kunsten, Brussels, 2004, pp 77–81. The two original versions of this self-portrait are respectively in the Michaelisverzameling in Kaapstad and the Öffentliche Kunstsammlung in Basel. One copy is in the State Hermitage Museum, Saint Petersburg. The three portraits bear the same inscription but the addition 'ETATIS / SVAE / 20' ('at the age of 20'), possibly by another hand, only occurs on the Basel version; see also: Katrin Dyballa and Sabine Engel, 'Katharina van Hemessen (1528–nach 1565)', in Katrin Dyballa, Bodo Brinkmann and Ariane Mensger (eds), *Geniale Frauen: Künstlerinnen und ihre Weggefährten*, exh.cat., Bucerius Kunst Forum, Hamburg, and Kunstmuseum, Basel, 2024, pp 63–70.

6   A complex painting such as *Allegory of Nature as the Mother of Art* (1540–57) by Jan van Hemessen (Rijksmuseum, Amsterdam) illustrates the intellectual context in which his daughter was raised (see: https://www.rijksmuseum.nl/en/collection/object/Allegory-of-Nature-as-the-Mother-of-Art--90a4f2035dea663f1c623f7b878c4494 (accessed 6 August 2025).

7   See: Jan Papy, 'Juan Luis Vives (1492–1540) on the Education of Girls: Medieval and Spanish Sources', *Paedagogica Historica: International Journal of the History of Education*, vol.31, 1995, pp 739–65; Charles Fantazzi (ed.), *Juan Luis Vives. The Education of a Christian Woman: A Sixteenth-Century Manual*, Center for Study of History of Education, no.38, University of Chicago Press, Chicago, IL and London, 2000; Kristine Forney, '"Nymphes gayes en abry du Laurier": Music Instruction for the Bourgeois Woman Source', *Musica Disciplina*, vol.49, 1995, pp 151–87, on p.152. On female dilettantism, see: Katlijne Van der Stighelen, 'Amateur Artists: Amateur Art as a Social Skill and a Female Preserve (16th and 17th Centuries)', in Delia Gaze (ed.), *Dictionary of Women Artists*, vol.1, Taylor & Francis, London and New York, 1997, pp 66–70.

8   Jennifer Courts, 'Caterina van Hemessen in the Habsburg Court of Mary of Hungary', in Tanja L. Jones (ed.), *Women Artists in the Early Modern Courts of Europe, c.1450–1700*, Visual and Material Culture, 1300–1700, Amsterdam University Press, Amsterdam, 2021, pp 71–89, on pp 75–6.

9   ibid., p.75; E. Sutton (ed.), *Women Artists and Patrons in the Netherlands, 1500–1700*, Amsterdam University Press, Amsterdam, 2019, pp 30–32.

10 Plinius Secundus, Gaius, the Elder, *The Elder Pliny's Chapters on the History of Art*, trans. and ed. K. Jex-Blake and E. Sellers, Macmillan and Co., London, 1896, pp 170–71, rules 147–8; Sarah Vanwelden, '"Pinxere et Mulieres": Vrouwelijke schilders uit Plinius' Naturalis Historia. Reconstructie van een Nachleben in woord en beeld', unpublished Master's thesis, KU Leuven, Leuven, 2010, pp 5–6.

11 Babette Bohn, *Women Artists, Their Patrons, and Their Publics in Early Modern Bologna*, Penn State University Press, Pennsylvania, PA, 2021, pp 11–12.

12 Sarah Blake McHam, *Pliny and the Artistic Culture of the Italian Renaissance*, Yale University Press, New Haven, CT, 2013, pp 5–7, 46, 80–81.

13 Raupp, *Untersuchungen zu Künstlerbildnis*, p.304; Günther Schweikhart, 'Boccaccios De Claris Mulieribus und die Selbstdarstellung von Malerinnen im 16. Jahrhundert', in M. Winner (ed.), *Der Künstler über sich in seinem Werk. Internationales Symposium der Bibliotheca Hertziana Rom 1989*, Acta Humaniora, Weinheim, 1992, pp 113–36, on p.119. See also: Joseph Leo Koerner, *The Moment of Self-Portraiture in German Renaissance Art*, University of Chicago Press, Chicago, IL and London, 1993, pp 110–11; Catherine King, 'Looking a Sight: Sixteenth-Century Portraits of Woman Artists', *Zeitschrift für Kunstgeschichte*, vol.58, no.3, 1995, pp 381–406; Joanna Woods-Marsden, *Renaissance Self-Portraiture: The Visual Construction of Identity and Social Status of the Artist*, Yale University Press, New Haven, CT and London, 1998, pp 188, 203–4; Katlijne Van der Stighelen (ed.), *Michaelina Wautier 1604–1689: Glorifying a Forgotten Talent*, BAI, Antwerp, 2018, pp 166–8.

14 For an English translation of the complete paragraph on Marcia in Boccaccio, see: Giovanni Boccaccio, *Concerning Famous Women*, trans. Guido A. Guarino, Rutgers University Press, New Brunswick, NJ, 1963, pp 144–5; about the use of the term 'proto-feminist', see: Martha Moffitt Peacock, 'Mirrors of Skill and Renown', *Women and Self-Fashioning in Early-Modern Dutch Art Source: Mediaevistik*, vol.28, 2015, pp 325–52. This concerns 'pro-female' ideologies from the Middle Ages or the early modern era in which ideas were discussed that correspond to actually feminist convictions.

15 New York Public Library, Spencer Collection, MS 33, fol.37ᵛ. See: Miniature showing Marcia before an easel, NYPL Digital Collections, at https://digitalcollections.nypl.org/items/f71b7300-c6ce-012f-3faa-58d385a7bc34?canvasIndex=0 (accessed 24 November 2024).

16 Johannes Boccatius van Florentien, *Bescrivende van den doorluchtighen, glorioesten ende edelsten vrouwen ende van haren wercken ende gheschienissen die si gedaen hebben binnen haren leven in den ouden voorleden tiden, ende is ghenuechlick om te lesen*, Claes die Grave, Antwerp, 1525 (Paris, Bibliothèque Nationale de France, FRBNF30116723).

17 ibid., p.115.

18 De Clippel, *Catharina van Hemessen*, pp 53–4; Sutton (ed.), *Women Artists and Patrons*, pp 27–30.

19 De Clippel, *Catharina van Hemessen*, pp 53–5. On Van Beverwijck's book, see: Cornelia Niekus Moore, '"Not by Nature but by Custom": Johan van Beverwijck's *Van de wtnementheyt des vrouwelicken Geslachts*', *Sixteenth Century Journal*, vol.25, no.3, 1994, pp 633–51. For the original source, see: Johannes van Beverwijck, *Van de wtnementheyt des vrouwelicken geslachts*, 2nd edn, Dordrecht, 1643, p.199.

20 Forney, '"Nymphes gayes en abry du Laurier"', pp 170–71.

21 Cecilia Gamberini, *Sofonisba Anguissola*, Illuminating Women Artists, Lund Humphries, London, 2024, pp 25–6.

22 See: Gudrun Swoboda, *Die Wege der Bilder: Eine Geschichte der Kaiserlichen Gemäldesammlungen von 1600 bis 1800*, Kunsthistorisches Museum, Vienna, 2008, p.12. See: Bohn, *Women Artists*, p.157.

23 There are better-known versions of smaller dimensions. See: Eve Straussman-Pflanzer and

Oliver Tostmann (eds), *By Her Hand: Artemisia Gentileschi and Women Artists in Italy, 1500–1800*, exh.cat., Wadsworth Atheneum Museum of Art, Hartford, CT, and Detroit Institute of Arts, Detroit, MI, Yale University Press, New Haven, CT and London, 2021, pp 58–9; Michael W. Cole, *Sofonisba's Lesson: The Formation and Career of the First Major Woman Artist of the Renaissance*, Princeton University Press, Princeton, NJ, 2019.

24 This is a small tondo, commissioned by a Spanish Dominican, Alfonso Chacón, as a modello for an engraving, see: Bohn, *Women Artists*, pp 157–60.

25 Katlijne Van der Stighelen, '"Forced Fashioning": Aspecten van genderdifferentiatie in het zestiende-eeuwse Zuid-Nederlandse portret', in Till-Holger Borchert and Koenraad Jonckheere (eds), *Renaissanceportretten uit de Lage Landen*, exh.cat., Bozar Brussels, Brussels, 2015, pp 32–47, on p.32.

26 Woods-Marsden, *Renaissance Self-Portraiture*, pp 225–37.

27 See: Collectie Nederland: Musea, Monumenten en Archeologie, at https://data.collectienederland.nl/page/aggregation/rijkscollectie-rce/NK2399 (accessed 1 December 2024).

28 Joanna Woodall, *Antonis Mor: Art and Authority*, Waanders, Zwolle, 2016, pp 9–15.

29 About the establishment of intellectual authority via portrait engravings, see: Lieke van Deinsen, 'Visualising Female Authorship: Author Portraits and the Representation of Female Literary Authority in the Eighteenth-Century Dutch Republic', *Quaerendo: A Journal Devoted to Manuscripts and Printed Books*, vol.49, 2019, pp 283–314.

30 Katlijne Van der Stighelen, 'Anna Francisca de Bruyns (1604/5–1656), Artist, Wife and Mother: A Contextual Approach to Her Forgotten Artistic Career', in Sarah Moran and Amanda Pipkin (eds), *Women and Gender in the Early Modern Low Countries 1500–1750*, Brill, Leiden, 2019, pp 192–228, on, p.209, fig.6.10; see: Los Angeles County Museum of Art, Los Angeles, CA, at https://collections.lacma.org/node/171272 (accessed 1 December 2024).

31 Van der Stighelen, 'Anna Francisca de Bruyns', pp 215, 227–8 (see also: Chapter 5).

32 ibid., p.201, n.21.

33 ibid., pp 196–7, n.206.

34 See: Van der Stighelen (ed.), *Michaelina Wautier*, p.17.

35 ibid., p.203. On Virginia da Vezzo and her engraved portraits, see: Straussman-Pflanzer and Tostmann (eds), *By Her Hand*, pp 131–2. Esther Theiler, *Painters and Sitters in Early Seventeenth-Century Rome: Portraits of the Soul*, Irreplaceable Portraits: Studies on Portraiture from the Medieval to the Contemporary, no.2, Brepols, Turnhout, 2023, pp 25, 197–8.

36 Caroline van Eck, 'The First Dutch Feminist Tract? Anna Maria van Schurman's Discussion of Women's Aptitude for the Study of Arts and Sciences', in Mirjam de Baar, Machteld Löwensteyn, Marit Monteiro and A. Agnes Sneller (eds), *Choosing the Better Part: Anna Maria van Schurman (1607–1678)*, International Archives of the History of Ideas, no.146, Kluwer Academic, Dordrecht, Boston, MA and London, 1996, pp 43–53. We do not know much about Wautier's command of languages, but she must have seen the French edition of 1646. She put her signature on both Dutch-language and French-language notarial deeds, but French was her native language. See: Van der Stighelen (ed.), *Michaelina Wautier*, pp 34–5.

37 Van Eck, 'The First Dutch Feminist Tract?', p.44: '. . . the study of letters, that is the study of the arts and sciences'.

38 ibid., p.45.

39 Van der Stighelen, 'Anna Francisca de Bruyns', p.208: 'Dans ce changement de condition il luy fut difficile de conserver tout le temps qui luy estoit nécessaire pour l'exercice de son Art. Les soins qu'une femme est obligée de prendre de sa famille luy osterent souvent le pinceau de la main, quoy qu'à son regret.'

40 ibid., pp 193–4.

41 A representative example is Judith Leyster. See: Koos Levy-van Halm, 'Judith Leyster: leerling-gezel-meester', in James A. Welu and Pieter Biesboer, *Judith Leyster: Schilderes in een mannenwereld*, exh.cat., Frans Halsmuseum, Haarlem, Zwolle, 1993, pp 69–74.

42 Anne R. Larsen, '"My friendship with her is by no means an ordinary one": The Friendship Alliances of Christian Hebraist Anna Maria van Schurman (1607–1678)', *The Seventeenth Century*, vol.37, no.2, 2021, pp 255–80, https://doi.org/10.1080/02681 17X.2021.1899039.

43 About this network of women, see also: De Baar et al. (eds), *Choosing the Better Part*, passim.

44 See: Van Deinsen, 'Female Faces and Learned Likenesses'; Anne R. Larsen, 'Anna Maria van Schurman: Self-Portraiture, Female Scholarly Identity, and the Republic of Letters', *Renaissance Quarterly*, vol.77, 2024, pp 879–922.

45 Concerning the importance of 'scale' and the preference of women for the small scale, see: Oliver Tostmann, 'The Advantages of Painting Small: Italian Women Artists and the Matter of Scale', in Straussman-Pflanzer and Tostmann (eds), *By Her Hand*, pp 31–41.

5 WAUTIER AS A PAINTER

1 See: Katlijne Van der Stighelen, 'Ravissant of Astrant, feminien of Onvraulic?: Vrouwelijke Kunstenaars in de Zuidelijke Nederlanden tussen 1500 en 1800', in Katlijne Van der Stighelen and Mirjam Westen (eds), *Elck Zijn Waerom: Vrouwelijke Kunstenaars in België en Nederland, 1500–1950*, exh.cat., Koninklijk Museum voor Schone Kunsten, Antwerp, and Museum voor Moderne Kunst, Arnhem, Ludion, Ghent and Amsterdam, 1999, pp 28–32. Interestingly, in 1653, the Antwerp Guild of Saint Luke distinguished a separate category of girls and women. They were all 'verlichtsters' (illuminators) and 'afsetters' (sellers). While the exact meaning of these terms is difficult to define, it is clear from the context that they worked as 'illuminators', mainly colouring prints and selling them. As far as is known, they were not real artists, but rather businesswomen. For a survey of the sixteenth-century situation, see: Jan Van der Stock, 'Women Who Stood Their Ground in the Guild of St Luke at the beginning of Antwerp's "Golden Age", 1453–1552', in Lieke van Deinsen, Bert Schepers, Marjan Sterckx, Hans Vlieghe and Bert Watteeuw (eds), *Campaspe Talks Back: Women Who Made a Difference in Early Modern Art. Essays in Honour of Katlijne Van der Stighelen*, Brepols, Turnhout, 2024, pp 224–33.

2 This did not apply to 'knapen oft maerten vande schilder': male or female servants. See: Rudy Jos Beerens, *Painters and Communities in Seventeenth-Century Brussels: A Social History of Art*, Leuven University Press, Leuven, 2024, pp 217–18.

3 Charles Wautier deviated from this principle when he took in two apprentices simultaneously in 1681 (see Chapter 3).

4 Beerens, *Painters and Communities in Seventeenth-Century Brussels*, p.218.

5 These regulations may have been intended not so much for the painters, but more for other craftsmen such as the goldsmiths and the glass-blowers who were not part of the Guild of Saint Luke in Antwerp.

6 Katlijne Van der Stighelen (ed.), *Michaelina Wautier 1604–1689: Glorifying a Forgotten Talent*, BAI, Antwerp, 2018, p.90. The oeuvre of Elisabeth Seldron (c.1680–1761) is relatively extensive and she was certainly appreciated. From 1735 to 1741 she was court painter to Archduchess Maria Elisabeth. See: Frank Huygens, 'Bruno door de ogen van Elisabeth Seldron', *OKV*, vol.57, no.4, 2019, at https://www.okv.be/artikel/bruno-door-de-ogen-van-elisabeth-seldron. Nothing is known about Cattharina van Stichel.

7 Wautier did not paint any independent landscapes. In Rubens's oeuvre, all genres are represented, although he never painted independent flower still lifes.

8 In contrast to Anna Maria van Schurman, for example (see Chapter 1, n.20). For the discussion on the relation between women artists and the size of their work, see: Oliver Tostmann, 'The Advantages of Painting Small: Italian Women Artists and the Matter of Scale', in Eve Straussman-Pflanzer and Oliver Tostman (eds), *By Her Hand: Artemisia Gentileschi and Women Artists in Italy, 1500–1800*, exh.cat., Wadsworth Atheneum Museum of Art, Hartford, CT, and Detroit Institute of Arts, Detroit, MI, Yale University Press, New Haven, CT and London, 2021, pp 31–41. On the original size of the *Triumph of Bacchus*, see: Van der Stighelen (ed.), *Michaelina Wautier*, p.216; Gerlinde Gruber, 'Michaelina Wautier's Paintings in the Habsburg Collections', in Gerlinde Gruber, Katlijne Van der Stighelen and Julien Domerque (eds), *Michaelina Wautier: Painter*, exh.cat., Kunsthistorisches Museum, Vienna, and The Royal Academy, London, 2025, pp 123–33, on p.133.

9   See: Sabine van Sprang, 'Op zoek naar de caravaggist Theodoor van Loon, actief in Rome en Brussel', in Sabine van Sprang (ed.), *Theodoor van Loon*, exh.cat., Palais des Beaux-Arts (BOZAR), Brussels, and Musée national d'Histoire et d'Art (MNHA), Luxembourg, 2018–19, pp 19–34. For a reference to the letter from Puteanus to Van Loon, see pp 21–2.

10 Van der Stighelen (ed.), *Michaelina Wautier*, pp 156–61.

11 The painting is still in the church of Saint John the Baptist at the Béguinage in Brussels for which it was originally created. See: Van Sprang, 'Op zoek naar de caravaggist Theodoor van Loon'.

12 Van Sprang (ed.), *Theodoor van Loon*, pp 25, 28, 33; Sabine van Sprang and Lara de Merode, 'Michaelina Wautier and Artistic Brussels', in Gruber et al. (eds), *Michaelina Wautier*, pp 89–105, on pp 89, 91, 95–6.

13 Van Sprang (ed.), *Theodoor van Loon*, p.31.

14 Katlijne Van der Stighelen, 'Anna Francisca de Bruyns (1604/5–1656), Artist, Wife and Mother: A Contextual Approach to Her Forgotten Artistic Career', in Sarah Moran and Amanda Pipkin (eds), *Women and Gender in the Early Modern Low Countries 1500–1750*, Brill, Leiden, 2019, pp 192–228; and see Chapter 4.

15 A good example of this is the painting *Two Boys Blowing Bubbles* in the Seattle Art Museum (see fig.51), which was attributed to Jacob van Oost until 2001. See: Van der Stighelen (ed.), *Michaelina Wautier*, pp 238–41; and cf. Jean Luc Meulemeester, *Jacob van Oost de Oudere en het zeventiende-eeuwse Brugge*, Westvlaamse gidsenkring, Brugge, 1984, pp 372–3. Other paintings showing a similarity with Wautier's are, for instance, half-body representations of saints such as *Saint Peter* and *Saint John the Evangelist* (p.165), *Saint Augustine Washing the Feet of Christ* (p.172) and *Young Man Writing* (p.368).

16 Van der Stighelen (ed.), *Michaelina Wautier*, pp 159–61.

17 ibid., p.159.

18 Sabine van Sprang, 'Rubens et Bruxelles, une relation plus que courtoise', in Joost Vander Auwera and Sabine van Sprang (eds), *Rubens: A Genius at Work*, exh.cat., Royal Museums of Fine Arts of Belgium, Brussels, 2007, pp 12–17; Hans Vlieghe, 'Beschouwingen over de invloed van Theodoor van Loon', in Van Sprang (ed.), *Theodoor van Loon*, pp 97–102, on pp 100–101; Van Sprang and De Merode, 'Michaelina Wautier and Artistic Brussels', pp 89, 91, 94, 101.

19 See: Hans Vlieghe, *Gaspar de Crayer, sa vie et ses œuvres*, Monographies du Nationaal centrum voor de plastische kunsten van de 16e en 17e eeuw, no.4, 2 vols, Arcade, Brussels, 1972, pp 35, 299; Van Sprang and De Merode, 'Michaelina Wautier and Artistic Brussels', pp 89, 91. Jahel Sanzsalazar, 'The Influence of Others: The Wautiers, David Teniers and Archduke Leopold Wilhelm's Theatrum Pictorium', in Van der Stighelen (ed.), *Michaelina Wautier*, pp 67–83, on p.73, n.40, also pointed out the similarities between Wautier's *Education of the Virgin* (see fig.59) and De Crayer's *Virgin Mary Adorned by Angels in the Presence of Saint Joachim and Saint Anne*.

20 See: Van der Stighelen (ed.), *Michaelina Wautier*, p.31.

21 See: Katharina Van Cauteren, *Politiek en schilderkunst: Hendrick de Clerck (1560–1630) en de keizerlijke ambities van de aartshertogen Albrecht en Isabella*, Lanoo, Tielt, 2016.

22 Vlieghe, *Gaspar de Crayer*, pp 93–4, cat.no.A18.

23 See: Van der Stighelen (ed.), *Michaelina Wautier*, pp 230–33.

24 See: J.F.G. Cuypers van Alsinghen, *Provincie, stad, ende district van Mechelen opgeheldert in haere Kercken, Kloosters, Kapellen, Gods-huysen, Gilden, publieke Plaetsen, met de Fondatien, Patronaetschappen, ende Voorrechten, daer aen klevende*, J.B. Jorez, Brussels, 1770, vol.11, p.86: 'Achter by het portael siet men van weder zeyde over de Beucken twee Schilderyen: d'een verbeldt eenen gekruysten Christus, geschildert door N. Woutiers, ende d'ander verbeldt de Boodtschap van O.L. Vrouwe, geschildert door de Suster van den voorsz. Woutiers'.

25 See: ibid., vol.11, p.84: '. . . gegeven door Maria-Theresia Bette, des Marckgrave van Lede, gewesene Canonikersse van Bergen in Heneaguw, Weduwe van Franciscus-Carolus Coloma . . .'; Van der Stighelen (ed.), *Michaelina Wautier*, p.42.

26 See: Chapter 3, p.47.

27 See: Van der Stighelen (ed.), *Michaelina Wautier*, p.38, n.71.

28 See: Charlotte Roosen, 'Michaelina Wautier and the Influence of Antiquity', in Martina Griesser,

Gerlinde Gruber, Elke Oberthaler and Katlijne Van der Stighelen (eds), *Workshop Practice: Supplement to Michaelina Wautier, Painter*, KHM-Museumsverband, Vienna, 2025, https://doi.org/10.60477/mm49-mx04.

29　See: Kirsten Derks and Alice Limb, 'The Materials and Techniques of Wautier's *The Five Senses* in Context', in Gruber et al. (eds), *Michaelina Wautier*, pp 135–43, on pp 135–7; Kirsten Derks and Alice Limb, 'The Materials and Techniques of Wautier's *The Five Senses* (Extended Version)', in Griesser et al. (eds), *Workshop Practice*.

30　See: Kirsten Derks, Geert Van der Snickt, Stijn Legrand, Katlijne Van der Stighelen and Koen Janssens, 'The Dark Halo Technique in the Oeuvre of Michael Sweerts and Other Flemish and Dutch Baroque Painters. A 17th c. Empirical Solution to Mitigate the Optical "Simultaneous Contrast" Effect?', *Heritage Science*, vol.10, no.5, 2022, https://doi.org/10.1186/s40494-021-00634-w; Kirsten Derks, Geert Van der Snickt, Katlijne Van der Stighelen and Koen Janssens, 'Scanning Michael Sweerts', in Rieke van Leeuwen and Gert Jan van der Sman (eds), *Going South: Artistic Exchange between the Netherlands and Italy in the 17th Century*, Gerson Digital 1x, The Hague, at https://going-south.rkdstudies.nl/9-scanning-michael-sweerts/ (accessed 11 July 2025).

31　See: Lara Yeager-Crasselt, *Michael Sweerts (1618–1664): Shaping the Artist and the Academy in Rome and Brussels*, Pictura Nova, Studies in 16th- and 17th-Century Flemish Painting and Drawing, no.21, Brepols, Turnhout, 2015, pp 15–17, 121–2, 189–91. For additional information on Sweerts's biography, see: Harald Deceulaer, 'Newly Discovered Archival Documents about Michael Sweerts in Brussels in the 1650s: His House, His Social Network and His Encounter with Ghosts', *Simiolus: Journal for the History of Art*, vol.46, no.1, 2025, pp 17–41.

32　See: Van der Stighelen (ed.), *Michaelina Wautier*, p.34, fig.22.

33　The five paintings of *The Five Senses* (1650) and the two garlands (1652) are each signed and dated but are here considered as a reference to a single date.

34　See: Van der Stighelen (ed.), *Michaelina Wautier*, pp 156–61 for an extensive discussion of the portrait, an interpretation of the inscription, the biography of Cantelmo and his humanist network. There are also references to literary sources in which Cantelmo is mentioned.

35　The painting was discovered in the Séminaire diocésain in Namur by Pierre-Yves Kairis. See: Pierre-Yves Kairis, *Le portrait dans le Namurois au XVIIe siècle*, Société archéologique de Namur, Namur, 2002, pp 40–41.

36　The letter dates from 7 August 1649. See: Roberto Contini and Francesco Solinas (eds), *Artemisia 1593–1654*, exh.cat., Musée Maillol, Paris, 2012, p.237; Artemisia Gentileschi, *Lettere di Artemisia*, ed. Franceso Solinas, De Luca Editori d'Arte, Rome, 2011, p.130.

37　In this source, it says: 'J'ay acheté le portray de wautier 24 florins et la moulur 12 florins' and 'J'aij acheté le nicodème fait par M[o] Vautier 30 patacon et la moulur 9 florins'. See: Brussels, State Archives, Manuscript Collection, 1088, fols 63, 64. Van der Stighelen (ed.), *Michaelina Wautier*, pp 296–7. The low price suggests that this was a rather small painting.

38　See: Van der Stighelen (ed.), *Michaelina Wautier*, pp 200–3.

39　On the acquisition of the series and the digital catalogue, see: Jeffrey Muller (ed.), *Michaelina Wautier and The Five Senses: Innovation in 17th-Century Flemish Painting*, CNA Studies, Museum of Fine Arts, Boston, MA, December 2022, at https://d1nn9x4fgzyvn4.cloudfront.net/2022-12/mfa-cna-studies_issue1-december2022_v3.pdf (accessed 27 March 2025).

40　The fact that the signatures were not noticed on all the paintings when they were auctioned twice in Valenciennes in the late nineteenth century must be due to their different positions on the canvases. Furthermore, she used a dark colour on a dark background to sign them, the reason for which is difficult to understand. See: Florence Vandeputte, 'Van Nicolaes Maes tot Michaelina Wautier: Twee negentiende-eeuwse Franse veilingcatalogi als bron voor herkomstonderzoek', unpublished Master's thesis, KU Leuven, Leuven, 2017; see also: Derks and Limb, 'Wautier's *The Five Senses* (Extended Version)'; Kirsten Derks, 'Leaving Her Mark: Michaelina Wautier's Signing Practice', in Van Deinsen et al.

(eds), *Campaspe Talks Back*, pp 167–72.

41 See: *Catalogue d'une tres belle collection de tableaux des écoles flamande, hollandaise, francaise, allemande et italienne, la plupart du* XVII*e siecle et de dessins anciens et livres d'art dont la vente aura lieu par suite du deces de feu M. de Malherbe*, Louis Henry, Valenciennes, 17–18 October 1883, nos 86–90: 'leur facture et leur coloris dénotent un excellent disciple de Brauwer et Hals'.

42 See: https://www.rct.uk/collection/exhibitions/ treasures-from-the-royal-collection-mythology-and-regency/the-queens-gallery/the-young-card-players (accessed 30 December 2024).

43 Jeffrey Muller and Yannick Etoundi, 'How *The Five Senses* Change Our Measure of Michaelina Wautier's Work', in Muller (ed.), *Michaelina Wautier and The Five Senses*, pp 70–72.

44 Tellingly, in 2008, the portrait was sold as originating from the 'Circle of the Le Nain Brothers' (Christie's, London, 3 December 2008, lot 203; https://www. christies.com/en/lot/lot-5159407 (accessed 12 January 2025)). The connection between *The Five Senses* and Aristotle's ideas about the senses, eruditely explained in the catalogue to the CNA exhibition of 2022, does not convince me. See: Dandan Xu, 'The Five Senses and Natural Philosophy', in Muller (ed.), *Michaelina Wautier and The Five Senses*, pp 65–9.

45 For a technical study into *Garland of Flowers with Butterfly*, see: Kirsten Derks, 'Scanning Michael Sweerts and Michaelina Wautier: Uncovering the Working Methods of 17th-Century Brussels Artists by Means of MA-XRF Examination', unpublished PhD diss., 2 vols, KU Leuven, University of Antwerp, Antwerp, 2023, vol.2, pp 267–80; Kirsten Derks, Koen Janssens, Katlijne Van der Stighelen and Geert Van der Snickt, 'Michaelina Wautier's *Flower Garland with Butterfly* Investigated: Technical Studies as a Source for Scholarship on Early Modern Women', *Early Modern Low Countries*, vol.9, 2025, pp 264–76.

46 The two garlands were auctioned as companion pieces (described as 'Guirlande de roses' and 'Guirlande de différentes fleurs') in Paris on 13 June 1813, nos 227–8. Wautier is described as an 'élève de van Huysum' – a student of Jan van Huysum (1682–1749) – and it is stated: 'Les Tableaux de cette Femme habile rappellent ceux de son maître dans

certaines parties; mais ils n'en ont pas le précieux fini' ('The paintings of this skilled woman are reminiscent of those of her master in certain respects, but they lack the precious finesse'). It is obvious that this is chronologically impossible and is telling of the way the talent of women is attributed to men and is branded as inferior. The flower pieces were from the collection of the well-known lawyer-collector Marie-Antoine Didot, also known as Didot de Saint-Marc. See: Jahel Sanzsalazar, 'La mort à l'honneur: *Sénèque* et *Marsyas*, deux tableaux des Wautier retrouvés', *Bulletin de l'Institut royal du Patrimoine artistique*, vol.38, 2023, pp 36–59, n.17.

47 See, among other things: Anne T. Woollett and Ariane van Suchtelen (eds), *Rubens en Breughel: een artistieke vriendschap*, exh.cat., J. Paul Getty Museum, Los Angeles, CA and Mauritshuis, The Hague, 2006; Christine van Mulders, *Rubens. Works in Collaboration: Jan Brueghel* I *&* II, Corpus Rubenianum Ludwig Burchard, vol.XXVII, Harvey Miller, London, 2016.

48 In 1884, an anonymous art critic wrote in the journal *L'Art Moderne* that women were the greatest painters of flowers because this genre required no thought, sentiment or virtuosity: 'Il est un art dans lequel la femme excelle: c'est celui des choses qui n'exigent ni pensée profonde, ni grand sentiment, ni large virtuosité. Des fleurs, des natures mortes, des objects élégants.' See: Katlijne Van der Stighelen, 'Het stille leven van fleurige vrouwen: Twee bloemenguirlandes van Michaelina Wautier in context', in Charles Dumas, Rudi Ekkart and Carla van de Puttelaar (eds), *Connoisseurship: Essays in Honour of Fred G. Meijer*, Primavera Pers, Leiden, 2020, pp 305–15, on p.305.

49 Robert Schindler, Bernd Ebert and Anna C. Knaap (eds), *Rachel Ruysch: Nature into Art*, exh. cat., Museum of Fine Arts, Boston, MA, Alte Pinakothek, Munich, and Toledo Museum of Art, Toledo, OH, MFA Publications, Boston, MA, 2024.

50 See: Van Sprang and De Merode, 'Michaelina Wautier and Artistic Brussels', pp 104–5.

51 See: Van der Stighelen (ed.), *Michaelina Wautier*, pp 254–7; Derks et al., 'Michaelina Wautier's *Flower Garland with Butterfly*', pp 271–2. Fred Meijer writes:

'Occasionally, Seghers painted single garlands, a form that he can probably be credited with the invention'. See: Fred Meijer, *Jan Davidsz. De Heem 1606–1684*, 2 vols, Waanders Publishers, Zwolle, 2024, vol.1, p.164. An exact chronology cannot be provided because very few flower garlands by Seghers and other flower painters, such as De Heem, have been dated.

52 For more information on the use of flower pieces in interiors, based on seventeenth-century inventories of belongings in Antwerp and Brussels, see: Van der Stighelen, 'Het stille leven van fleurige vrouwen', pp 309–11.

53 My thanks go to Dr Bert Watteeuw, Director of the Rubenshuis and renowned expert in historical gardens, for the identification and interpretation of the bouquets; see also: Van der Stighelen, 'Het stille leven van fleurige vrouwen', p.308.

54 Derks, 'Scanning Michael Sweerts and Michaelina Wautier', vol.1, pp 123–4.

55 See: Roosen, 'Michaelina Wautier and the Influence of Antiquity'.

56 Katlijne Van der Stighelen, 'Michaelina's Style: Blended Brilliance', in Gruber et al. (eds), *Michaelina Wautier*, pp 29–59, on pp 29, 58; Jean Bastiaensen, 'A Revised Biography of Michaelina Wautier', in Gruber et al. (eds), *Michaelina Wautier*, pp 107–21, on p.114; Anne Delvingt and Pierre-Yves Kairis, 'Charles Wautier: Status Quaestionis', in Gruber et al. (eds), *Michaelina Wautier*, pp 71–87, on pp 72–5 (on a possible stay of Charles Wautier in Italy).

57 This research was initially conducted by Kirsten Derks. See: Derks, 'Scanning Michael Sweerts and Michaelina Wautier'. For the analysis of the *Garland*, see: Derks et al., 'Michaelina Wautier's *Flower Garland with Butterfly*'. For the technical analysis of *The Five Senses*, see: Derks and Limb, 'Wautier's *The Five Senses*'; Derks and Limb, 'Wautier's *The Five Senses* (Extended Version)'.

58 See: Jozef Mertens and Frans Aumann (eds), *Krijg en kunst: Leopold-Willem (1614–1662), Habsburger, landvoogd en kunstverzamelaar*, exh.cat., Landcommanderij Alden Biesen, Bilzen-Rijkhoven, 2003, pp 90–91; Derks et al., 'Michaelina Wautier's *Flower Garland with Butterfly*', pp 267, 271–3; Van der Stighelen (ed.), *Michaelina Wautier*, pp 136–7.

59 In Van der Stighelen (ed.), *Michaelina Wautier*, pp 11–12, this scene is interpreted as an illustration of the proverb 'Elk zijn meug' ('Everyone to his taste'), in reference to the two boys who each have their own preference. In hindsight, this is not correct, since the boys squabble about one egg. This was rightly observed by Katrijn Van Bragt: Katrijn Van Bragt and Sven van Dorst, *Studie van een jonge vrouw: Een bijzondere blik in het atelier van Michaelina Wautier*, Phoebus Focus, no.19, Phoebus Foundation, Antwerp, 2020, p.34. See also Muller and Etoundi, 'How *The Five Senses* Change Our Measure of Michaelina Wautier's Work'.

60 See: Wolfgang Stechow, 'Homo Bulla', *The Art Bulletin*, vol.20, 1938, pp 227–8.

61 A '*portrait historié*' refers to 'a portrait in the guise of a historical figure. This figure could be either mythological, biblical, historical or legendary.' See: Volker Manuth, Rudie van Leeuwen and Jos Koldeweij (eds), *Example or Alter Ego? Aspects of the Portrait Historié in Western Art from Antiquity to the Present*, Brepols, Turnhout, 2016, p.5.

62 By depicting the two girls as young saints, she even followed earlier Netherlandish examples, such as the *c.*1520 *Portrait of Margaret of Austria as Mary Magdalene* by an unknown artist. See: Wieneke Weusten, 'Mary of Burgundy or Margaret of Austria: A Search for the Identity of the Mary Magdalene from Chantilly', in Manuth et al. (eds), *Example or Alter Ego?*, pp 147–58.

63 On the subject of the early modern *portrait historié*, see: Manuth et al. (eds), *Example or Alter Ego?*, pp 147–220.

64 For a more detailed iconographical analysis of the portrait in the context of the Counter-Reformation, see: Van der Stighelen (ed.), *Michaelina Wautier*, pp 194–9.

65 The portrait was first identified by Jahel Sanzsalazar, 'Michaelina Wautier y la boda de su hermano: historia de un retrato identificado', *Tendencias del Mercado del Arte*, vol.69, January 2014, pp 90–94, who also noticed the coat of arms (possibly added later) of the Wautier family. For a detailed analysis, see: Van der Stighelen (ed.), *Michaelina Wautier*, pp 182–5.

66 For a detailed biography of Martini, his publications,

his missionary work and his influence, see: Van der Stighelen (ed.), *Michaelina Wautier*, pp 186–93. See also: Mario Cams, 'Displacing China: The Martini-Blaeu Novus Atlas Sinensis and the Late Renaissance Shift in Representations of East Asia', *Renaissance Quarterly*, vol.73, no.3, 2020, pp 953–90.

67 Golvers translated the three syllables as 'protection', 'service' and 'the land'. Martini is thus depicted as 'he who protects and serves the land'. See: Noël Golvers, 'The Newly Discovered Portrait of Martino Martini', in Luisa M. Paternicò, Claudia von Collani and Riccardo Scartezzini (eds), *Martino Martini (1614–1661), Man of Dialogue: Proceedings of the International Conference, in Trento, 15–17 October 2014*, Università degli studi di Trento, Trento, 2016, pp 9–11, on p.9. A Chinese text, written in calligraphic script in 1654 by the Chinese assistant of Martini, is considered to be the second earliest document written by a Chinese scholar in Europe. If the inscription on the portrait is by his hand (as generally assumed), this is then the second document from the same year. See: Thijs Weststeijn and Lennert Gesterkamp, 'A New Identity for Rubens's "Korean Man": Portrait of the Chinese Merchant Yppong', *Netherlandish Yearbook for History of Art*, vol.66, 2016, pp 142–69, on pp 149–50.

68 On the specific contribution of Italian Jesuits, see: Michela Catto, 'The Jesuit China Mission in an Italian Frame', *Church History and Religious Culture*, vol.104, 2024, pp 463–80.

69 See: Bastiaensen, 'A Revised Biography of Michaelina Wautier', p.113; Van Sprang and De Merode, 'Michaelina Wautier and Artistic Brussels', p.101.

70 See: Van der Stighelen (ed.), *Michaelina Wautier*, p.191.

71 Van der Stighelen (ed.), *Michaelina Wautier*, pp 42–3, 231–3. In 1770, Cuypers van Alsinghen's description of the city of Mechelen and its surroundings appeared. In his discussion of the church of the Discalced Carmelites, he wrote that he saw two paintings there, a *Crucifixion* by 'N. Wautier' and an *Annunciation* 'painted by his sister' (*Provincie, stad, ende district van Mechelen*, vol.II, p.86). See also: Gruber, 'Michaelina Wautier's Paintings', p.130.

72 Muller (ed.), *Michaelina Wautier and The Five Senses*, p.9.

73 See: Van Sprang and De Merode, 'Michaelina Wautier and Artistic Brussels', p.91.

74 A typical example is Maerten de Vos, *The Family of Saint Anne*, 1585, oil on panel, 135.3 × 170 cm, at Museum of Fine Arts, Ghent, inv.no.S-51. See: https://www.mskgent.be/en/collection/s-51 (accessed 31 August 2025).

75 See: Van der Stighelen (ed.), *Michaelina Wautier*, pp 222–4.

76 About the significance of Saint Joachim and Saint Joseph as symbols of purity and examples of the Immaculate Conception within the context of the Counter-Reformation and the personal devotion of the Archduke, see: Hannelore Magnus in Van der Stighelen (ed.), *Michaelina Wautier*, pp 204–7.

77 Adolph Berger, 'Inventar der Kunstsammlung des Erzherzogs Leopold Wilhelm von Österreich. Nach der originalhandschrift im fürstlich Schwarzenberg'schen centralarchive herausgegeben', *Jahrbuch der Kunsthistorischen Sammlungen des Allerhöchsten Kaiserhauses*, vol.1, 1883, pp LXXIX–CXCI, on p.CXXXIV, no.365: 'Ein grosses Stuckh von Öhlfarb auff Leinwath, warin desz Bacchi Triumph. In einer schwarzen Ramen, hoch 14 Span 4 Finger und 20 Span 4 Finger braidt. Original von N. Woutiers'. For a thorough analysis of the Bacchus representation within the context of the Spanish Netherlands, see: Van der Stighelen (ed.), *Michaelina Wautier*, pp 208–17; Katlijne Van der Stighelen, 'Michaelina Wautier in the Company of Bacchus: The Power of Unruly Self-Representation', in Ondřej Jakubec (ed.), *The Author, His Environment and the Work of Art: On the Possibilities of Artistic Biography Today. Proceedings of the 2nd Biennale of the Centre for Early Modern Studies, Department of Art History, Faculty of Arts*, Masaryk University, Brno, 2024, pp 75–104.

78 See: Gruber, 'Michaelina Wautier's Paintings', p.130.

79 Günther Heinz, 'Studien über Jan van den Hoecke und die Malerei der Niederländer in Wien', in *Jahrbuch der Kunsthistorischen Sammlungen in Wien*, vol.63, 1967, pp 19–164, on pp 149–52. For a survey, see: Gruber, 'Michaelina Wautier's Paintings', p.133.

80 Gustav Glück, *Rubens, Van Dyck und ihr Kreis*, A. Schroll, Vienna, 1933, p.229; see above, p.43.

81 See: Meulemeester, *Jacob van Oost*. About the drawing from examples, see: V. Sancho Lobis, 'Printed Drawing Books and the Dissemination of Ideal Male Anatomy in Northern Europe', in Karolien de Clippel, Katharina Van Cauteren and Katlijne Van der Stighelen (eds), *The Nude and the Norm in the Early Modern Low Countries*, Brepols, Turnhout, 2011, pp 51–64.

82 Today, the head is only known via a single eighteenth-century plaster copy (Real Academia de Bellas Artes de San Fernando, Madrid). See: Roosen, 'Michaelina Wautier and the Influence of Antiquity'; Van Sprang and De Merode, 'Michaelina Wautier and Artistic Brussels', pp 98, 101.

83 See: above, pp 81–5. The original text is that 'hij met grooten kost opgericht ende nu langen tijt onderhouden d'accademie van die teeckeninge naer het leven, tot die welcke veele Jongelingen daegelijcx sijn frequenterende'. See: Yeager-Crasselt, *Michael Sweerts*, pp 92–4, 121–2; and Lara Yeager-Crasselt, 'Pride and Ambition in Seventeenth-Century Brussels: The Drawing Academy of Michael Sweerts', in Hannelore Magnus and Katlijne Van der Stighelen (eds), *Facts and Feelings: Retracing Emotions of Artists, 1600–1800*, Brepols, Turnhout, 2015, pp 153–69.

84 See: Lara Yeager-Crasselt, 'Knowledge and Practice Pictured in the Artist's Studio: The "Art Lover" in the Seventeenth-Century Netherlands', *De Zeventiende Eeuw: Cultuur in de Nederlanden in interdisciplinair perspectief*, vol.32, no.2, 2016, pp 110–26.

85 See: Babette Bohn, 'Designing Women: Drawings by Women Artists in Early Modern Italy', in Andaleeb Badiee Banta and Alexa Greist (eds), *Making Her Mark: A History of Women Artists in Europe, 1400–1800*, exh.cat., Baltimore Museum of Art, Goose Lane Editions, Baltimore, MD, 2023, pp 43–57, on pp 52–3. I don't understand why the author rejects this possibility.

86 See: Van der Stighelen (ed.), *Michaelina Wautier*, p.213; Van der Stighelen, 'Michaelina Wautier in the Company of Bacchus'.

87 See: Frédérique Verrier, *Le miroir des Amazones: Amazones, viragos et guerrières dans la littérature italienne des XVe et XVIe siècles*, L'Harmattan, Paris, 2003; Joan Dejean, 'Violent Women and Violence against Women: Representing the "Strong" Woman in Early Modern France', *Signs*, vol.29, 2003, pp 117–47, on pp 121–9.

88 See: https://www.clarkart.edu/artpiece/detail/Bacchante (accessed 11 August 2025).

EPILOGUE

1 On the history of the painting, see: Gerlinde Gruber, 'Michaelina Wautier's Paintings in the Habsburg Collections', in Gerlinde Gruber, Katlijne Van der Stighelen and Julien Domerque (eds), *Michaelina Wautier: Painter*, exh.cat., Kunsthistorisches Museum, Vienna, and The Royal Academy, London, 2025, pp 123–33, on pp 130–33.

2 See: *Michaelina Wautier: Baroque's Leading Lady*, 1 June–2 September 2018, CODART, at https://www.codart.nl/guide/agenda/michaelina-wautier/ (accessed 1 September 2025).

3 See: 'M Leuven Acquires Rare Masterpiece by Michaelina Wautier', 6 'June 2023, at https://mleuven.prezly.com/m-leuven-acquires-rare-masterpiece-by-michaelina-wautier (accessed 4 March 2025).

4 See: Gruber et al. (eds), *Michaelina Wautier*.

Bibliography

[A.D.], 'Le Mémorial d'une famille montoise 1587–1716', *Bulletin du bibliophile et du bibliothécaire*, 1866, pp 295–6.

Alen, Klara, '"Envy and Pride": Maria Faydherbe (Mechelen, 1587–after 1633), a Woman Sculptor in a Man's World', in Magnus and Van der Stighelen (eds), *Facts and Feelings*, pp 77–99.

Arschot, Comte d', and Joseph Cuvelier, 'La Clientele d'un Maître a danser a Bruxelles, au XVIIe siecle: Adam-Pierre de la Grené', *Revue belge de philologie et d'histoire*, 15, December 1924, pp 3–15.

Avancini, Nicolas, *Le prince dévôt et guerrier ou les vertus héroiques de Leopold Guillaume Archiduc d'Autriche*, 1667, trans. H. Bex, Hachett BnF, Paris, 2017.

Barker, Sheila, *Artemisia Gentileschi*, Illuminating Women Artists, Lund Humphries, London, 2022.

Bastiaensen, Jean, '"Finding Clara": Establishing the Biographical Details of Clara Peeters (ca.1587–after 1636)', *Boletin del Museo del Prado*, vol.34, 2016, pp 17–31.

—, 'A Revised Biography of Michaelina Wautier', in Gruber et al. (eds), *Michaelina Wautier*, pp 107–21.

Beerens, Rudy Jos, *Painters and Communities in Seventeenth-Century Brussels: A Social History of Art*, Leuven University Press, Leuven, 2024.

Berger, Adolf, 'Inventar der Kunstsammlung des Erzherzogs Leopold Wilhelm von Österreich. Nach der originalhandschrift im fürstlich Schwarzenberg'schen centralarchive herausgegeben', *Jahrbuch der Kunsthistorischen Sammlungen des Allerhöchsten Kaiserhauses*, vol.1, 1883, pp LXXIX–CXCI.

Birnfeld, Nicole, 'Ein Leben für die Kunst? – Anmerkungen zu Pictura-Darstellungen nördlich der Alpen', in Simone Roggendorf and Sigrid Ruby (eds), *(En)gendered: Frühneuzeitlicher Kunstdiskurs und weibliche Porträtkultur nördlich der Alpen*, Jonas Verlag, Marburg, 2004, pp 111–22.

Blake McHam, Sarah, *Pliny and the Artistic Culture of the Italian Renaissance*, Yale University Press, New Haven, CT, 2013.

Boccaccio, Giovanni, *Concerning Famous Women*, trans. Guido A. Guarino, Rutgers University Press, New Brunswick, NJ, 1963.

Boccatius van Florentien, Johannes, *Bescrivende van den doorluchtighen, glorioesten ende edelsten vrouwen ende van haren wercken ende gheschienissen die si gedaen hebben binnen haren leven in den ouden voorleden tiden, ende is ghenuechlick om te lesen*, Claes die Grave, Antwerp, 1525.

Bohn, Babette, *Women Artists, Their Patrons, and Their Publics in Early Modern Bologna*, Penn State University Press, Pennsylvania, PA, 2021.

—, 'Designing Women: Drawings by Women Artists in Early Modern Italy', in Andaleeb Badiee Banta and Alexa Greist (eds), *Making Her Mark: A History of Women Artists in Europe, 1400–1800*, exh.cat., Baltimore Museum of Art, Goose Lane Editions, Baltimore, MD, 2023, pp 43–57.

Cams, Mario, 'Displacing China: The Martini-Blaeu Novus Atlas Sinensis and the Late Renaissance Shift in Representations of East Asia', *Renaissance Quarterly*, vol.73, no.3, 2020, pp 953–90.

Catto, Michela, 'The Jesuit China Mission in an Italian Frame', *Church History and Religious Culture*, vol.104, 2024, pp 463–80.

Cauchies, Jean-Marie, Virginien Horge, Corentin Rousman and Sophie Simon, *Histoire de la ville de Mons: Politique, militaire, aménagement du territoire*, Racine, Brussels, 2024.

Christiansen, Keith, and Judith W. Mann, *Orazio and Artemisia Gentileschi*, exh.cat., The Metropolitan Museum, New York, 2001.

Cole, Michael W., *Sofonisba's Lesson: The Formation and Career of the First Major Woman Artist of the Renaissance*, Princeton University Press, Princeton, NJ, 2019.

Contini, Roberto, and Francesco Solinas (eds), *Artemisia 1593–1654*, exh.cat., Musée Maillol, Paris, 2012.

Courts, Jennifer, 'Caterina van Hemessen in the Habsburg Court of Mary of Hungary', in Tanja L. Jones (ed.), *Women Artists in the Early Modern Courts of Europe, c.1450–1700*, Visual and Material Culture, 1300–1700, Amsterdam University Press, Amsterdam, 2021, pp 71–89.

Cumming, Laura, *A Face to the World: On Self-Portraits*, HarperPress, London, 2009.

Cuypers van Alsinghen, J.F.G., *Provincie, stad, ende district van Mechelen opgeheldert in haere Kercken, Kloosters, Kapellen, Gods-huysen, Gilden, publieke Plaetsen, met de Fondatien, Patronaetschappen, ende Voorrechten, daer aen klevende*, J.B. Jorez, Brussels, 1770.

De Baar, Mirjam, 'Now as for the Faint Rumours of Fame Attached to my Name . . . The Eukleria as Autobiography', in De Baar et al. (eds) *Choosing the Better Part*, pp 87–102.

De Baar, Mirjam, Machteld Löwensteyn, Marit Monteiro and A. Agnes Sneller (eds), *Choosing the Better Part: Anna Maria van Schurman (1607–1678)*, International Archives of the History of Ideas, no.146, Kluwer Academic, Dordrecht, Boston, MA and London, 1996.

Deceulaer, Harald, 'Newly Discovered Archival Documents about Michael Sweerts in Brussels in the 1650s: His House, His Social Network and His Encounter with Ghosts', *Simiolus: Journal for the History of Art*, vol.46, no.1, 2025, pp 17–41.

De Clippel, Karolien, *Catharina van Hemessen (1528–na 1567): Een monografische studie over een 'uytnemende en wel geschickte vrouwe in de conste der schilderyen'*, Verhandelingen van de Koninklijke Vlaamse Academie van België voor Wetenschappen en Kunsten. Nieuwe reeks, no.11, Koninklijke Vlaamse Academie van België voor Wetenschappen en Kunsten, Brussels, 2004.

Dejean, Joan, 'Violent Women and Violence against Women: Representing the "Strong" Woman in Early Modern France', *Signs*, vol.29, 2003, pp 117–47.

De Laet, Veerle, *Brussel binnenskamers: Kunst-en luxebezit in het spanningsveld tussen hof en stad, 1600–1735*, Studies Stadsgeschiedenis, Amsterdam University Press, Amsterdam, 2011.

—, 'At Home in Seventeenth-Century Brussels: Patterns of Art and Luxury in Private Households', in Van der Stighelen et al. (eds), *Embracing Brussels*, pp 11–19.

Del Torre Scheuch, Francesca, and Gerlinde Gruber, 'L'abondance & la diversité: The Gallery of Archduke Leopold Wilhelm', in Van der Stighelen (ed.), *Michaelina Wautier*, pp 53–65.

Delvingt, Anne, and Pierre-Yves Kairis, 'Charles Wautier: Status Quaestionis', in Gruber et al. (eds), *Michaelina Wautier*, pp 71–87.

Denucé, Jan, *Ná Peter Pauwel Rubens: Documenten uit den kunsthandel te Antwerpen in de xviie eeuw*, De Sikkel, Antwerp, 1949.

Derks, Kirsten, 'Scanning Michael Sweerts and Michaelina Wautier: Uncovering the Working Methods of 17th-Century Brussels Artists by Means of MA-XRF Examination', unpublished PhD diss., 2 vols, KU Leuven, University of Antwerp, Antwerp, 2023.

—, 'Leaving Her Mark: Michaelina Wautier's Signing Practice', in Van Deinsen et al. (eds), *Campaspe Talks Back*, pp 167–72.

Derks, Kirsten, and Alice Limb, 'The Materials and Techniques of Wautier's *The Five Senses* in Context', in Gruber et al. (eds), *Michaelina Wautier*, pp 135–43.

—, 'The Materials and Techniques of Wautier's *The Five Senses* (Extended Version)', in Griesser et al. (eds),

Workshop Practice.

Derks, Kirsten, Koen Janssens, Katlijne Van der Stighelen and Geert Van der Snickt, 'Michaelina Wautier's *Flower Garland with Butterfly* Investigated: Technical Studies as a Source for Scholarship on Early Modern Women', *Early Modern Low Countries*, vol.9, 2025, pp 264–76.

Derks, Kirsten, Geert Van der Snickt, Katlijne Van der Stighelen and Koen Janssens, 'Scanning Michael Sweerts', in Rieke van Leeuwen and Gert Jan van der Sman (eds), *Going South: Artistic Exchange between the Netherlands and Italy in the 17th Century*, Gerson Digital IX, The Hague, at https://going-south.rkdstudies.nl/9-scanning-michael-sweerts/ (accessed 11 July 2025).

Derks, Kirsten, Geert Van der Snickt, Stijn Legrand, Katlijne Van der Stighelen and Koen Janssens, 'The Dark Halo Technique in the Oeuvre of Michael Sweerts and Other Flemish and Dutch Baroque Painters. A 17th c. Empirical Solution to Mitigate the Optical "Simultaneous Contrast" Effect?', *Heritage Science*, vol.10, no.5, 2022, https://doi.org/10.1186/s40494-021-00634-w.

De Vriendt, F., 'Le père Charles Malapert S.J. (1581–1630), un savant montois au temps de l'apogée des Jesuites', in J. Lory, A. Minette and J. Walravens (eds), *Les Jesuites à Mons: Liber memorialis*, Association Royale des anciens élèves du Collège Saint-Stanislas, Mons, 1999, pp 107–35.

De Vroede, Maurits, *'Kwezels' en 'zusters': De geestelijke dochters in de Zuidelijke Nederlanden*, AWLSK, Brussels, 1994.

Dorival, Bernard, 'Les influences de l'art des Pays-Bas sur la peinture de Philippe de Champaigne', *Bulletin des Musées royaux des Beaux-Arts de Belgique*, 1970–71, pp 7–54.

Du Rieu, Florent, *Les tableaux parlans du peintre namurois*, P. Gérard, Namur, 1658.

Duverger, Erik, 'Nieuwe gegevens betreffende de kunsthandel van Matthys Musson en Maria Fourmenois te Antwerpen tussen 1633 en 1681', *Gentse Bijdragen tot de Kunstgeschiedenis en de Oudheidkunde*, vol.21, 1968, pp 5–250.

Dyballa, Katrin, and Sabine Engel, 'Katharina van Hemessen (1528–nach 1565)', in Dyballa et al. (eds), *Geniale Frauen*, pp 63–70.

—, 'Michaelina Wautier (1604–1689)', in Dyballa et al. (eds), *Geniale Frauen*, pp 98–105.

Dyballa, Katrin, Bodo Brinkmann and Ariane Mensger (eds), *Geniale Frauen: Künstlerinnen und ihre Weggefährten*, exh.cat., Bucerius Kunst Forum, Hamburg, and Kunstmuseum, Basel, 2024.

Eaker, Adam, *Gesina ter Borch*, Illuminating Women Artists, Lund Humphries, London, 2024.

Fantazzi, Charles (ed.), *Juan Luis Vives. The Education of a Christian Woman: A Sixteenth-Century Manual*, Center for Study of History of Education, no.38, University of Chicago Press, Chicago, IL and London, 2000.

Forney, Kristine, '"Nymphes gayes en abry du Laurier": Music Instruction for the Bourgeois Woman Source', *Musica Disciplina*, vol.49, 1995, pp 151–87.

Gamberini, Cecilia, *Sofonisba Anguissola*, Illuminating Women Artists, Lund Humphries, London, 2024.

Garas, Klara, 'Die Entstehung der Galerie des Erzherzogs Leopold Wilhelm', *Jahrbuch der Kunsthistorischen Sammlungen in Wien*, vol.27, no.63, new series, 1967, pp 39–80.

Gentileschi, Artemisia, *Lettere di Artemisia*, ed. Franceso Solinas, De Luca Editori d'Arte, Rome, 2011.

Glück, Gustav, 'Aus Rubens' Zeit und Schule: Bemerkungen zu einigen Gemälden der Kaiserlichen Galerie in Wien', *Jahrbuch der Kunsthistorischen Sammlungen des Allerhöchsten Kaiserhauses*, vol.24, 1903, pp 1–48.

—, *Rubens, Van Dyck und ihr Kreis*, A. Schroll, Vienna, 1933.

Golvers, Noël, 'The Newly Discovered Portrait of Martino Martini', in Luisa M. Paternicò, Claudia von Collani and Riccardo Scartezzini (eds), *Martino Martini (1614–1661), Man of Dialogue: Proceedings of the International Conference, in Trento, 15–17 October 2014*, Università degli studi di Trento, Trento, 2016, pp 9–11.

Gregory, Philippa, *Normal Women: 900 Years of Making History*, William Collins, London and Dublin, 2023.

Griesser, Martina, Gerlinde Gruber, Elke Oberthaler and Katlijne Van der Stighelen (eds), *Workshop Practice: Supplement to Michaelina Wautier, Painter*, KHM-Museumsverband, Vienna, 2025, https://doi.org/10.60477/mm49-mx04.

Gruber, Gerlinde, 'Michaelina Wautier's Paintings in the Habsburg Collections', in Gruber et al. (eds), *Michaelina Wautier*, pp 123–33.

Gruber, Gerlinde, and Julien Domerque, 'The Challenges of Reconstruction', in Gruber et al. (eds), *Michaelina Wautier*, pp 11–16.

Gruber, Gerlinde, Katlijne Van der Stighelen and Julien Domerque (eds), *Michaelina Wautier: Painter*, exh.cat., Kunsthistorisches Museum, Vienna, and The Royal Academy, London, 2025.

Haupt, Herbert, 'Kultur und kulturgeschichtliche Nachricht vom Wiener Hofe: Erzherzog Leopold Wilhelm in den Jahren 1646–1654', *Mitteilungen des Österreichischen Staats Archivs*, vol.33, 1980, pp 346–55.

Heinz, Günther, 'Studien über Jan van den Hoecke und die Malerei der Niederländer in Wien', in *Jahrbuch der Kunsthistorischen Sammlungen in Wien*, vol.63, 1967, pp 19–164.

Henne, Alexandre, and Alphonse Wauters, *Histoire de la ville de Bruxelles*, 5 vols, Librairie Encyclopédique de Perichon, Brussels, 1845.

Honnoré, Laurent, René Plisnier, Caroline Pousseur and Pierre Tilly (eds), *1000 Personnalités de Mons & de la Région: Dictionnaire Biographique*, Avant-Propos, Waterloo, 2015.

Hyman, Aaron M., *Rubens in Repeat: The Logic of the Copy in Colonial Latin America*, Getty Publications, Los Angeles, CA, 2021.

James, Carolyn, 'Margherita Cantelmo and the Worth of Women in Renaissance Italy', in Karen Green and Constant J. Mews (eds), *Virtue Ethics for Women, 1250–1500*, Springer, Dordrecht, New York, 2011, pp 145–58.

James, S.E., 'The Horenbout Family Workshop at the Tudor Court, 1522–1541: Collaboration, Patronage and Production', *Cogent Arts & Humanities*, vol.8, no.1, 2021, pp 3–5, 21–2, https://doi.org/10.1080/23311983.2021.1915933.

Kairis, Pierre-Yves, 'Foisonnement et diversité: les peintres du XVII siècle', in *Un double regard sur 2000 ans d'art wallon*, La Renaissance du Livre, Tournai, 2000, pp 321–41.

—, *Le portrait dans le Namurois au XVIIe siècle*, Société archéologique de Namur, Namur, 2002.

Kelchtermans, Leen, 'Geschilderde gevechten, gekleurde verslagen: een contextuele analyse van Peter Snayers' (1592–1667) topografische strijdtaferelen voor de Habsburgse elite tussen herinnering en verheerlijking', unpublished PhD diss., KU Leuven, Leuven, 2013.

—, 'Portret van een zeventiende-eeuwse schildersvrouw: Anna Schut, huisvrouw en weduwe van Peter Snayers', *Oud Holland*, vol.126, 2013, pp 178–97.

King, Catherine, 'Looking a Sight: Sixteenth-Century Portraits of Woman Artists', *Zeitschrift für Kunstgeschichte*, vol.58, no.3, 1995, pp 381–406.

Klinge, Margret, 'David Teniers d. J. – Theatrum Pictorium', in Mertens and Aumann (eds), *Krijg en kunst*, pp 101–8.

Koerner, Joseph Leo, *The Moment of Self-Portraiture in German Renaissance Art*, University of Chicago Press, Chicago, IL and London, 1993.

Krempel, León, *Family Affairs: Broers en zusters in de kunst. Frères et soeurs dans l'art*, exh.cat., Bozar, Brussels, 2006.

Lannoye, Y., 'L'ameublement du château d'Enghien au commencement du XVIIe siècle', *Annales du Cercle archéologique d'Enghien*, vol.21, 1984, pp 325–93.

Lanoye, Diederik, 'Het verblijf van Koningin Christina van Zweden in de Nederlanden (1654–1655)', in Mertens and Aumann (eds), *Krijg en kunst*, pp 53–64.

Larsen, Anne R., '"My friendship with her is by no means an ordinary one": The Friendship Alliances of Christian Hebraist Anna Maria van Schurman (1607–1678)', *The Seventeenth Century*, vol.37, no.2, 2021, pp 255–80, at https://doi.org/10.1080/026811 7X.2021.1899039.

—, 'Anna Maria van Schurman: Self-Portraiture, Female Scholarly Identity, and the Republic of Letters', *Renaissance Quarterly*, vol.77, 2024, pp 879–922.

Leemans, Annemie, 'Tra storia e legenda. Indigani sul network artístico tra Sofonisba Anguissola, Giulio Clovio e Levina Teerlinc', *INTRECCI d'arte*, vol.3, 2014, pp 35–55, https://doi.org/10.6092/issn.2240-7251/4580.

Levy-van Halm, Koos, 'Judith Leyster: leerling-gezel-meester', in Welu and Biesboer, *Judith Leyster*, pp 69–74.

Louant, Armand (ed.), *Le Livre de ballades de Jehan et Charles Bocquet, bourgeois de Mons au XVIe siecle*, Palais des Académies, Brussels 1954.

Magnus, Hannelore, and Katlijne Van der Stighelen (eds), *Facts and Feelings: Retracing Emotions of Artists, 1600–1800*, Brepols, Turnhout, 2015.

Manuth, Volker, Rudie van Leeuwen and Jos Koldeweij (eds), *Example or Alter Ego? Aspects of the Portrait Historié in Western Art from Antiquity to the Present*, Brepols, Turnhout, 2016.

Meijer, Fred, *Jan Davidsz. De Heem 1606–1684*, 2 vols, Waanders Publishers, Zwolle, 2024.

Mertens, Jozef, and Frans Aumann (eds), *Krijg en kunst: Leopold-Willem (1614–1662), Habsburger, landvoogd en kunstverzamelaar*, exh.cat., Landcommanderij Alden Biesen, Bilzen-Rijkhoven, 2003.

Meulemeester, Jean Luc, *Jacob van Oost de Oudere en het zeventiende-eeuwse Brugge*, Westvlaamse gidsenkring, Brugge, 1984.

Moffitt Peacock, Martha, 'Mirrors of Skill and Renown', *Women and Self-Fashioning in Early-Modern Dutch Art Source: Mediaevistik*, vol.28, 2015, pp 325–52.

Moore, Cornelia Niekus, '"Not by Nature but by Custom": Johan van Beverwijck's *Van de wtnementheyt des vrouwelicken Geslachts*', *Sixteenth Century Journal*, vol.25, no.3, 1994, pp 633–51.

Moran, Sarah, 'Resurrecting the "Spiritual Daughters": The Houtappel Chapel and Women's Patronage of Jesuit Building Programs in the Spanish Netherlands', in Moran and Pipkin (eds), in *Women and Gender in the Early Modern Low Countries*, pp 266–322.

Moran, Sarah, and Amanda Pipkin (eds), *Women and Gender in the Early Modern Low Countries 1500–1750*, Brill, Leiden, 2019.

Muller, Jeffrey (ed.), *Michaelina Wautier and The Five Senses: Innovation in 17th-Century Flemish Painting*, CNA Studies, Museum of Fine Arts, Boston, MA, December 2022, at https://d1nn9x4fgzyvn4.cloudfront.net/2022-12/mfa-cna-studies_issue1-december2022_v3.pdf (accessed 27 March 2025).

Muller, Jeffrey, and Yannick Etoundi, 'How *The Five Senses* Change Our Measure of Michaelina Wautier's Work', in Muller (ed.), *Michaelina Wautier and The Five Senses*, pp 70–72.

Papy, Jan, 'Juan Luis Vives (1492–1540) on the Education of Girls: Medieval and Spanish Sources', *Paedagogica Historica: International Journal of the History of Education*, vol.31, 1995, pp 739–65.

Platteschorre-Weurman, C.J., 'De peignoir', *Kostuum: Jaarboek van de Nederlandse Vereniging voor Kostuum*, 2008, pp 17–29.

Plinius Secundus, Gaius, the Elder, *The Elder Pliny's Chapters on the History of Art*, trans. and ed. K. Jex-Blake and E. Sellers, Macmillan and Co., London, 1896.

Porteman, Karel, 'Het Spaanse Spook', *Spiegel der Letteren*, vol.47, 2005, pp 206–10.

Proot, Goran, 'Leopold Willem en het Jezuïetentoneel in de "Provincia Flandro-Belgica"', in Mertens and Aumann (eds), *Krijg en kunst*, pp 65–70.

Pültau, Dirk, 'De affirmatieve vrouw in de kunst: Over Gynaika en "Inside the Visible"', *De witte raaf*, vol.63, 1996.

Raeymaekers, Dries, 'Review of José Eloy Hortal Muñoz, Pierre-François Pirlet and África Espíldora García (eds), '*El ceremonial en la Corte de Bruselas del siglo XVII: Los manuscritos de Francisco Alonso Lozano*', *Early Modern Low Countries*, vol.3, no.2, 2019, pp 306–7, https://doi.org/10.18352/emlc.121.

Rasch, Rudolf, 'Constantijn Huygens in Brussel op bezoek bij Leopold Wilhelm van Oostenrijk 1648–1656', *Revue belge de Musicologie / Belgisch Tijdschrift voor Muziekwetenschap*, vol.55, 2001, pp 127–46.

Raupp, Hans-Joachim, *Untersuchungen zu Künstlerbildnis und Künstlerdarstellung in den Niederlanden im 17. Jahrhundert*, Olms, Hildesheim, 1984.

Reinhard, Wolfgang, *Lebensformen Europas: Eine historische Kulturanthologie*, Beck, Munich, 2004.

Roosen, Charlotte, 'Michaelina Wautier and the Influence of Antiquity', in Griesser et al. (eds), *Workshop Practice*.

Ruiz Goméz, Leticia (ed.), *A Tale of Two Women Painters: Sofonisba Anguissola and Lavinia Fontana*, exh.cat., Museo Nacional del Prado, Madrid, 2019.

Sancho Lobis, V., 'Printed Drawing Books and the Dissemination of Ideal Male Anatomy in Northern Europe', in Karolien de Clippel, Katharina Van Cauteren and Katlijne Van der Stighelen (eds), *The Nude and the Norm in the Early Modern Low Countries*, Brepols, Turnhout, 2011, pp 51–64.

Sanzsalazar, Jahel, 'Michaelina Wautier y la boda de su hermano: historia de un retrato identificado',

Tendencias del Mercado del Arte, vol.69, January 2014, pp 90–94.

—, 'The Influence of Others: The Wautiers, David Teniers and Archduke Leopold Wilhelm's Theatrum Pictorium', in Van der Stighelen (ed.), *Michaelina Wautier*, pp 67–83.

—, 'Michaelina Wautier y la incomparable Anna Maria van Schurman: feminismo, arte y erudición en los Países Bajos en el siglo XVII', *Tendencias del Mercado del Arte*, vol.113, May 2018, pp 86–91.

—, 'La Vocacion de San Mateo: obra de Michaelina y Charles Wautier?', *Tendencias del Mercado del Arte*, vol.123, May 2019, pp 88–92.

—, 'La mort à l'honneur: *Sénèque* et *Marsyas*, deux tableaux des Wautier retrouvés', *Bulletin de l'Institut royal du Patrimoine artistique*, vol.38, 2023, pp 36–59.

Schad, Martha, *Die Frauen des Hauses Fugger von der Lilie (15.–17. Jahrhundert): Augsburg-Ortenburg-Trient*, Mohr, Tübingen, 1989.

Schindler, Robert, Bernd Ebert and Anna C. Knaap (eds), *Rachel Ruysch: Nature into Art*, exh.cat., Museum of Fine Arts, Boston, MA, Alte Pinakothek, Munich, and Toledo Museum of Art, Toledo, OH, MFA Publications, Boston, MA, 2024.

Schreiber, Renate, *'Ein Galeria nach meinem Humor': Erzherzog Leopold Wilhelm*, Schriftenreihe des Kunsthistorischen Museums, no.8, Kunsthistorisches Museum Vienna, 2004.

Schweikhart, Günther, 'Boccaccios De Claris Mulieribus und die Selbstdarstellung von Malerinnen im 16. Jahrhundert', in M. Winner (ed.), *Der Künstler über sich in seinem Werk. Internationales Symposium der Bibliotheca Hertziana Rom 1989*, Acta Humaniora, Weinheim, 1992, pp 113–36.

Stechow, Wolfgang, 'Homo Bulla', *The Art Bulletin*, vol.20, 1938, pp 227–8.

Straussman-Pflanzer, Eve, and Oliver Tostmann (eds), *By Her Hand: Artemisia Gentileschi and Women Artists in Italy, 1500–1800*, exh.cat., Wadsworth Atheneum Museum of Art, Hartford, CT, and Detroit Institute of Arts, Detroit, MI, Yale University Press, New Haven, CT and London, 2021.

Strumwasser, Gina, *Politically Incorrect: Women Artists and Female Imagery in Early Modern Europe*, Cognella, San Diego, CA, 2012.

Stryckers, Piet, 'Music and Music Production in Seventeenth-Century Brussels', in Van der Stighelen et al. (eds), *Embracing Brussels*, pp 59–79.

Sutton, E. (ed.), *Women Artists and Patrons in the Netherlands, 1500–1700*, Amsterdam University Press, Amsterdam, 2019.

Swoboda, Gudrun, *Die Wege der Bilder: Eine Geschichte der Kaiserlichen Gemäldesammlungen von 1600 bis 1800*, Kunsthistorisches Museum, Vienna, 2008.

Theiler, Esther, *Painters and Sitters in Early Seventeenth-Century Rome: Portraits of the Soul*, Irreplaceable Portraits: Studies on Portraiture from the Medieval to the Contemporary, no.2, Brepols, Turnhout, 2023.

Thieffry, Sandrine, 'L'Archiduc Leopold-Guillaume a Bruxelles (1647–1656): le bon usage du mecenat musical et temps de guerre', *Revue belge de Musicologie / Belgisch Tijdschrift voor Muziekwetenschap*, vol.56, 2002, pp 159–75.

Tittler, Robert, 'The "Feminine Dynamic" in Tudor Art: A Reassessment', *British Art Journal*, vol.17, no.1, 2016, pp 123–30.

Tostmann, Oliver, 'The Advantages of Painting Small: Italian Women Artists and the Matter of Scale', in Straussman-Pflanzer and Tostmann (eds), *By Her Hand*, pp 31–41.

Trnek, Renate (ed.), *Selbstbild: Der Künstler und sein Bildnis*, exh.cat., Gemäldegalerie der Akademie der bildenden Künste Wien, Vienna, 2004.

Trusted, Marjorie, 'Maria Faydherbe: A Seventeenth-Century Sculptor in Mechelen', *The Burlington Magazine*, vol.156, 2014, pp 104–6.

Van Aelbrouck, Jean-Philippe, *Dictionnaire des danseurs: chorégraphes et maitres de danse à Bruxelles de 1600 à 1830*, Mardaga, Liège, 1994.

Van Belle, Jean-Louis, and Pierre-Jean Niebes (eds), *Vivre à Mons aux XVIIe et XVIIIe siècles: Le témoignage des chroniques*, Collection Témoins d'Histoire, no.8, Éditions Safran, Brussels, 2021.

Van Beverwijck, Johannes, *Van de wtnementheyt des vrouwelicken geslachts*, 2nd edn, Dordrecht, 1643.

Van Bragt, Katrijn, and Sven van Dorst, *Studie van een jonge vrouw: Een bijzondere blik in het atelier van Michaelina Wautier*, Phoebus Focus, no.19, Phoebus Foundation, Antwerp, 2020.

Van Cauteren, Katharina *Politiek en schilderkunst: Hendrick de Clerck (1560–1630) en de keizerlijke ambities van de aartshertogen Albrecht en Isabella, Lanoo, Tielt, 2016.

Van Deinsen, Lieke, 'Visualising Female Authorship: Author Portraits and the Representation of Female Literary Authority in the Eighteenth-Century Dutch Republic', *Quaerendo: A Journal Devoted to Manuscripts and Printed Books*, vol.49, 2019, pp 283–314.

—, 'Female Faces and Learned Likenesses: Author Portraits and the Construction of Female Authorship and Intellectual Identity', in K. Scholten, D. van Miert and K.A.E. Enenkel (eds), *Memory and Identity in the Learned Word*, Intersections, no.81, Brill, Leiden and Boston, MA, 2022, pp 81–116.

—, 'Female Faces in the Fraternity: Printed Portraits Galleries and the Construction and Circulation of Images of Learned Women in the Republic of Letters', in M. Bolufer, L. Guinot-Ferri and C. Blutrach (eds), *Gender and Cultural Mediation in the Long Eighteenth Century: Women across Borders*, Palgrave Macmillan, Cham, 2024, pp 123–49.

Van Deinsen, Lieke, Bert Schepers, Marjan Sterckx, Hans Vlieghe and Bert Watteeuw (eds), *Campaspe Talks Back: Women Who Made a Difference in Early Modern Art. Essays in Honour of Katlijne Van der Stighelen*, Brepols, Turnhout, 2024.

Vandeputte, Florence, 'Van Nicolaes Maes tot Michaelina Wautier: Twee negentiende-eeuwse Franse veilingcatalogi als bron voor herkomstonderzoek', unpublished Master's thesis, KU Leuven, Leuven, 2017.

Van der Helm, José, Roos Hamelink and Geertje Wilmsen (eds), *Delitiae Italiae: Een reis door het zeventiende-eeuwse Italië*, Verloren, Hilversum, 2021.

Van der Stighelen, Katlijne, '"Une robustesse extraordinaire chez une femme": de schilderijen van Michaelina Woutiers', in Leen Huet and Wim Neetens (eds), *An Unexpected Journey: Vrouw en kunst – Woman and Art*, Gynaika, Antwerp, 1996, pp 286–94.

—, 'Amateur Artists: Amateur Art as a Social Skill and a Female Preserve (16th and 17th Centuries)', in Delia Gaze (ed.), *Dictionary of Women Artists*, vol.1, Taylor & Francis, London and New York, 1997, pp 66–70.

—, 'Ravissant of Astrant, feminien of Onvraulic?: Vrouwelijke Kunstenaars in de Zuidelijke Nederlanden tussen 1500 en 1800', in Van der Stighelen and Westen (eds), *Elck Zijn Waerom*, pp 28–32.

—, '"Prima inter pares": Over de voorkeur van aartshertog Leopold-Wilhelm voor Michaelina Woutiers (ca.1620–na 1682)', in Vlieghe and Van der Stighelen (eds), *Sponsors of the Past*, pp 91–116.

—, '"Amoris et Doloris Monumentum": Portraits and How They Were Perceived in the Baroque Age', in Katlijne Van der Stighelen, Hannelore Magnus and Bert Watteeuw (eds), *Pokerfaced: Flemish and Dutch Baroque Faces Unveiled*, Brepols, Turnhout, 2010, pp 249–73.

—, '"Forced Fashioning": Aspecten van genderdifferentiatie in het zestiende-eeuwse Zuid-Nederlandse portret', in Till-Holger Borchert and Koenraad Jonckheere (eds), *Renaissanceportretten uit de Lage Landen*, exh.cat., Bozar Brussels, Brussels, 2015, pp 32–47.

— (ed.), *Michaelina Wautier 1604–1689: Glorifying a Forgotten Talent*, BAI, Antwerp, 2018.

—, 'Anna Francisca de Bruyns (1604/5–1656), Artist, Wife and Mother: A Contextual Approach to Her Forgotten Artistic Career', in Moran and Pipkin (eds), *Women and Gender in the Early Modern Low Countries*, pp 192–228.

—, 'Het stille leven van fleurige vrouwen: Twee bloemenguirlandes van Michaelina Wautier in context', in Charles Dumas, Rudi Ekkart and Carla van de Puttelaar (eds), *Connoisseurship: Essays in Honour of Fred G. Meijer*, Primavera Pers, Leiden, 2020, pp 305–15.

—, 'Het sleuteltje van het "sackhorologie" van Michaelina Wautier (1614–1689): Een detail van een detail', *Verslagen en Mededelingen van de Koninklijke Academie voor Nederlandse Taal en Letteren*, vol.134, 2024, pp 65–72.

—, 'Michaelina Wautier in the Company of Bacchus: The Power of Unruly Self-Representation', in Ondřej Jakubec (ed.), *The Author, His Environment and the Work of Art: On the Possibilities of Artistic Biography Today. Proceedings of the 2nd Biennale of the Centre for Early Modern Studies, Department of Art History, Faculty of Arts*, Masaryk University, Brno, 2024, pp 75–104.

—, 'Michaelina Herself: From Face to Phenomenon', in

Gruber et al. (eds), *Michaelina Wautier*, pp 61–9.

—, 'Michaelina's Style: Blended Brilliance', in Gruber et al. (eds), *Michaelina Wautier*, pp 29–59.

Van der Stighelen, Katlijne, and Mirjam Westen (eds), *Elck Zijn Waerom: Vrouwelijke Kunstenaars in België en Nederland, 1500–1950*, exh.cat., Koninklijk Museum voor Schone Kunsten, Antwerp, and Museum voor Moderne Kunst, Arnhem, Ludion, Ghent and Amsterdam, 1999.

Van der Stighelen, Katlijne, Leen Kelchtermans and Koenraad Brosens (eds), *Embracing Brussels: Art and Culture in the Court City, 1600–1800*, Brepols, Turnhout, 2013.

Van der Stock, Jan, 'Women Who Stood Their Ground in the Guild of St Luke at the beginning of Antwerp's "Golden Age", 1453–1552', in Van Deinsen et al. (eds), *Campaspe Talks Back*, pp 224–33.

Van Eck, Caroline, 'The First Dutch Feminist Tract? Anna Maria van Schurman's Discussion of Women's Aptitude for the Study of Arts and Sciences', in De Baar et al. (eds), *Choosing the Better Part*, pp 43–53.

Van Elck, Martine, '"Blessed art thou, Reader, if you are not of that sex": Public Femininity in the Seventeenth Century', in Van der Stighelen (ed.), *Michaelina Wautier*, pp 121–33.

Van Mulders, Christine, *Rubens. Works in Collaboration: Jan Brueghel I & II*, Corpus Rubenianum Ludwig Burchard, vol.xxvii, Harvey Miller, London, 2016.

Vannieuwenhuyze, Bram, 'Brussel, de ontwikkeling van een middeleeuwse stedelijke ruimte', unpublished PhD diss., Ghent University, Ghent, 2008.

Van Schurman, Anna Maria, *Eucleria, of uitkiezing van Het Beste Deel*, facsimile edn, intro. S. van der Linde, De Tille, Leeuwarden, 1978.

Van Sprang, Sabine, 'Rubens et Bruxelles, une relation plus que courtoise', in Joost Vander Auwera and Sabine van Sprang (eds), *Rubens: A Genius at Work*, exh.cat., Royal Museums of Fine Arts of Belgium, Brussels, 2007, pp 12–17.

—, 'Op zoek naar de caravaggist Theodoor van Loon, actief in Rome en Brussel', in Van Sprang (ed), *Theodoor van Loon*, pp 19–34.

— (ed.), *Theodoor van Loon*, exh.cat., Palais des Beaux-Arts (BOZAR), Brussels, and Musée national d'Histoire et d'Art (MNHA), Luxembourg, 2018–19.

Van Sprang, Sabine, and Lara de Merode, 'Michaelina Wautier and Artistic Brussels', in Gruber et al. (eds), *Michaelina Wautier*, pp 89–105.

Vanwelden, Sarah, '"Pinxere et Mulieres": Vrouwelijke schilders uit Plinius' Naturalis Historia. Reconstructie van een Nachleben in woord en beeld', unpublished Master's thesis, KU Leuven, Leuven, 2010.

Vautier, Dominique, *Alle wegen leiden naar Rome: Kunstenaarsreizen in Europa (16de–19de eeuw)*, exh.cat., Museum van Elsene, Brussels, 2007.

Verbrugge, Anne, 'De kunstverzameling', in M. Derez, J. Tytgat and A. Verbrugge (eds), *Arenberg in de Lage Landen: Een hoogadellijk huis in Vlaanderen en Nederland*, Leuven University Press, Leuven, 2002, pp 319–45.

Vergara, Alejandro (ed.), *The Art of Clara Peeters*, exh.cat., Museum Snijders and Rockoxhuis, Antwerp, and Museo Nacional del Prado, Madrid, 2016.

Vergara Sharp, Alejandro, *Clara Peeters*, Illuminating Women Artists, Lund Humphries, London, 2025.

Verrier, Frédérique, *Le miroir des Amazones: Amazones, viragos et guerrières dans la littérature italienne des xve et xvie siècles*, L'Harmattan, Paris, 2003.

Vlieghe, Hans, *Gaspar de Crayer, sa vie et ses œuvres*, Monographies du Nationaal centrum voor de plastische kunsten van de 16e en 17e eeuw, no.4, 2 vols, Arcade, Brussels, 1972.

—, 'The Decorations for Archduke Leopold William's State Entry into Antwerp', *Journal of the Warburg and Courtauld Institutes*, vol.39, 1976, pp 190–98.

—, *Rubens. Portraits of Identified Sitters Painted in Antwerp*, Corpus Rubenianum Ludwig Burchard, vol.xix.2, Harvey Miller, London, 1987.

—, '"Frayicheyt ende kunst daer syne inclinatie toe stryckt": beschouwingen over het mecenaat van aartshertog Leopold-Wilhelm tijdens zijn landvoogdij over de Zuidelijke Nederlanden (1647–1656)', in Vlieghe and Van der Stighelen (eds), *Sponsors of the Past*, pp 61–90.

—, 'Beschouwingen over de invloed van Theodoor van Loon', in Van Sprang (ed.), *Theodoor van Loon*, pp 97–102.

Vlieghe, Hans, and Katlijne Van der Stighelen (eds), *Sponsors of the Past: Flemish Art and Patronage, 1550–1700*, Brepols, Turnhout, 2005.

Welu, James A., and Pieter Biesboer, *Judith Leyster: Schilderes in een mannenwereld*, exh.cat., Frans Halsmuseum, Haarlem, Zwolle, 1993.

Weststeijn, Thijs, and Lennert Gesterkamp, 'A New Identity for Rubens's "Korean Man": Portrait of the Chinese Merchant Yppong', *Netherlandish Yearbook for History of Art*, vol.66, 2016, pp 142–69.

Weusten, Wieneke, 'Mary of Burgundy or Margaret of Austria: A Search for the Identity of the Mary Magdalene from Chantilly', in Manuth et al. (eds), *Example or Alter Ego?*, pp 147–58.

Woodall, Joanna, *Antonis Mor: Art and Authority*, Waanders, Zwolle, 2016.

Woods-Marsden, Joanna, *Renaissance Self-Portraiture: The Visual Construction of Identity and Social Status of the Artist*, Yale University Press, New Haven, CT and London, 1998.

Woolf, Virginia, *A Room of One's Own*, ed. David Bradshaw and Stuart N. Clark, Wiley-Blackwell, Oxford, 2015.

Woollett, Anne T., and Ariane van Suchtelen (eds), *Rubens en Breughel: een artistieke vriendschap*, exh.cat., J. Paul Getty Museum, Los Angeles, CA and Mauritshuis, The Hague, 2006.

Xu, Dandan, 'The Five Senses and Natural Philosophy', in Muller (ed.), *Michaelina Wautier and The Five Senses*, pp 65–9.

Yeager-Crasselt, Lara, *Michael Sweerts (1618–1664): Shaping the Artist and the Academy in Rome and Brussels*, Pictura Nova, Studies in 16th- and 17th-Century Flemish Painting and Drawing, no.21, Brepols, Turnhout, 2015.

—, 'Pride and Ambition in Seventeenth-Century Brussels: The Drawing Academy of Michael Sweerts', in Magnus and Van der Stighelen (eds), *Facts and Feelings*, pp 153–69.

—, 'Knowledge and Practice Pictured in the Artist's Studio: The "Art Lover" in the Seventeenth-Century Netherlands', *De Zeventiende Eeuw: Cultuur in de Nederlanden in interdisciplinair perspectief*, vol.32, no.2, 2016, pp 110–26.

—, *Portrait of a Gentleman: Michael Sweerts (1618–1664) and the Elegance of Brussels Portraiture*, Phoebus Focus, no.21, Hannibal Books, Veurne, 2021.

Image Credits

Art Collection 3 / Alamy Stock Photo: fig.23
ARTGEN / Alamy Stock Photo: fig.66
ARTGEN: fig.34
Collectie Het Noordbrabants Museum, 's-Hertogenbosch, loan of a private collection (photo Peter Cox): fig.49
David Rumsey Map Collection, David Rumsey Map Center, Stanford Libraries: fig.7
Gabinetto Fotografico delle Gallerie degli Uffizi: fig.65
© KHM-Museumsverband: figs 15, 16, 17, 18, 19, 63
© KIK-IRPA, Brussels: figs 31, 33, 54
© Kirsten Derks: fig.50
The Klesch Collection: figs 55, 58
The Kremer Collection: fig.47
M Leuven Collection, source: artinflanders.be, photo: Cedric Verhelst: fig.61
Marly-Le-Roi, Musée du Domaine Royal de Marly (photo: David Bordes): fig.34
Museum of Fine Arts, Boston: figs 39–43
© Nationalmuseum: fig.44
© National Portrait Gallery, London: fig.21
piemags / Alamy Stock Photo: fig.5

© The Phoebus Foundation: figs 25, 38, 62
© Photographic Archive Museo Nacional del Prado: figs 12, 13
Private Collection, by courtesy of the Hoogsteder Museum Foundation, The Hague: fig.59
Rijksmuseum, Amsterdam: fig.46
Royal Museums of Fine Arts of Belgium, Brussels (Photo d'art Speltdoorn & Fils): fig.36
© Royal Collection Enterprises Limited 2025 | Royal Collection Trust: figs 4, 30, 45
Royal Museum of Fine Arts Antwerp: figs 54, 55, 56
Seattle Art Museum, Seattle, gift of Mr Floyd Naramore: fig.51
© The Trustees of the British Museum: fig.25

Index